THE GURU AND THE WARRIOR

THE **GURU** & THE **WARRIOR**

Discovering True Power

JAMES GRAY ROBINSON, ESQ.

The Guru and The Warrior

© 2026 by James Gray Robinson, Esq.

All rights reserved. No portion of this publication may be reproduced, stored in a retrieval system, or transmitted by any means—electronic, mechanical, photocopying, recording, or any other—except for brief quotations in printed reviews, without the prior written permission of the publisher.

Library of Congress Control Number: 2025920811

ISBN: 978-1-964686-90-5 (paperback)   978-1-964686-91-2 (ebook)

Although this publication is designed to provide accurate information about the subject matter, the publisher and the author assume no responsibility for any errors, inaccuracies, omissions, or inconsistencies herein. This publication is intended as a resource, however, it is not intended as a replacement for direct and personalized professional services.

Cover and Interior Design: Emma Elzinga

Printed in the United States of America

First Edition

3 West Garden Street, Ste. 718
Pensacola, FL 32502
www.indigoriverpublishing.com

Ordering Information:

Quantity sales: Special discounts are available on quantity purchases by corporations, associations, and others. For details, contact the publisher at the address above.

Orders by US trade bookstores and wholesalers: Please contact the publisher at the address above.

With Indigo River Publishing, you can always expect great books, strong voices, and meaningful messages. Most importantly, you'll always find . . . *words worth reading*.

Contents

Forward VII

Preface IX

Introduction XIII

1   The Story of the Brain 1
2   Never Ruin a Good Story with the Facts. 11
3   The Brain's Trauma Response. 25
4   Early Trauma. 33
5   Watch This! 41
6   Lasting Trauma. 49
7   Shame Enough for All 53
8   The Legacy of Shame 57
9   How Do You Spell Pneumonia?. 63
10 Trauma and Teenagers. 67
11 The Vacations from Hell 71
12 Adverse Childhood Experiences 85
13 Duty, Honor, Country 89
14 Negative Thinking and the Brain 95
15 What Doesn't Kill Us Makes Us Stronger 99
16 The Brain on Eggshells. 103
17 A Battle of Willpower 109
18 The Curse of Cortisol. 113
19 Civil Rights 115
20 Nightmares and Sleepwalking 119
21 Lead Balloons Don't Fly. 121
22 Near-Death Experiences 131
23 Alternate Realities 133
24 Scapegoating. 139
25 Don't Change Dicks in the Middle of a Screw—Vote for Nixon in '72. . . 143
26 Functional Neurological Disorder. 147
27 On the Outside Looking In. 149

28	The Brain and Alcohol	155
29	Summer Camp Comes to an End	161
30	Impostor Syndrome	167
31	A Funny Thing Happened on the Way to Law School	171
32	Obsessive-Compulsive Personality Disorder	175
33	Shit Hits the Fan	179
34	Adrenaline Junkies	185
35	Independence Day	189
36	Effect of Injury on the Mind	195
37	That's Going to Leave a Mark	197
38	Halley's Comet	205
39	Praise Jesus	209
40	The Blue Light Special	215
41	Self-Sabotage	219
42	The Definition of Insanity	223
43	Perfectionism	227
44	Strike Two	231
45	Dysfunction: The Gift That Keeps on Giving	241
46	The End of the Beginning	247
47	Emotional Maturity	255
48	Elvis Has Left the Building	259
49	The Search for Enlightenment	269
50	High Magic	273
51	Freedom from Our Mind	277
52	The Leprechauns	281
53	The Illusion of Desire	291
54	The Greatest Lesson	295
55	Healing Myself	305
56	Goodbye, Dad	309
57	All Perception Is Projection	313
58	Redemption	319
59	Activate the Guru	321

Epilogue 325

Forward

I've had the privilege of meeting many brilliant minds, and Sir James Gray Robinson, Esq. stands apart for a remarkable reason—he lays his truth bare. While so many exhaust themselves maintaining an illusion of perfection, Gray courageously shares the parts of his journey that others might keep hidden. He does so with a singular purpose: to help others sidestep the painful lessons he had to learn firsthand. He, like so many people, tried his best to "play by the rules" of society, doing what was expected of him. Ignoring his truths and letting his trauma lead to many decisions eventually pushed his body and mind into a total breakdown and an abrupt exit from a successful law career. Most people I know would either curl up in a ball for a few years or continue to try to force their round parts into square holes, exemplifying the faulty thinking that the same choices could create different outcomes. Gray chose to use the painful experience to embark on a new life path, one of profound healing and teaching. I was honored when he first asked me to collaborate on a powerful project, and I relish the opportunity to introduce him to new audiences who can benefit greatly from the magical medicine he shares. If you like a story packed with plot twists, in addition to great learning, you've come to the right place.

My work has also always focused upon accessing parts of the mind that people often overlook, to their detriment. I believe in a spiritual world, in divinity and miracles, yet I am equally committed to practical strategies. It's rare to find someone who blends these elements as seamlessly as Gray has in this book. From the onset, it is established that he is destined to be a seeker and expand beyond the confines of what was originally expected of him. Like so many, he tried to "follow the rules," only to realize that many of those rules were deeply flawed and counterproductive. He could have chosen to remain on a more standard path, but when his body literally shut down, he chose to use the painful experience as an opportunity to change direction. It wasn't easy, and it wasn't linear, but through his trials and life experiences, he went into the abyss and came out carrying the keys to freedom. Freedom from unhappy relationships, depression, addiction, an unhealthy body, and the restraints that your mind can build more securely than any cage.

This book is for everyone looking to expand their perception, their choices, and their motivations. If you've been looking for a guide to help you sustainably change your mindset and, therefore, your life, you've stumbled upon gold. *The Guru and the Warrior* is relevant and applicable to everyone, as our brains are wired in ways that can be intentionally and powerfully harnessed once they are understood. Gray makes neuroscience and the fundamental processes of the brain easily accessible, showing the reader how they can make changes accordingly. This, along with the backdrop of his incredible life story, makes this book a must-read for everyone. If you're committed to learning how to attract what you truly want in your life, by trading in some of the power of your Warrior, your life will be forever changed. As Gray likes to say, "Hack your brain so that your Guru can reign."

—Dr. Joe Vitale, star of *The Secret*, author of *Zero Limits*

Preface

Until 2004, I had been a successful third-generation trial attorney making hundreds of thousands of dollars a year. After twenty-seven years of practicing law, I had a nervous breakdown, a burnout, and I walked away from my lifetime career.

At the time, I was going through my second divorce and defending a lawsuit that was embarrassing and expensive. No one knew the shame, guilt, stress, and anxiety I was experiencing, especially since I appeared so successful. Despite my professional success, my life felt like it was doomed to failure. Everything I touched turned to ashes, and I felt like I was all alone.

I had been practicing law for twenty-seven years to please my parents and meet the expectations of my family tradition. My success was a tribute to my mental discipline; I got no joy from doing it. The money was a powerful incentive not to quit, but even that could not quiet the call of my soul. Eventually, my ego crashed and burned, and I had a nervous breakdown.

Quitting my law practice was the final failure. I just couldn't take the pressure anymore. I had reached the point where the money was not worth the pain.

In 2004, the mental and emotional health industry was just beginning to understand the way the brain processes information. Burnout was perceived as weakness or a lack of willpower. That only added to my shame and guilt.

I went on a journey to find out what happened to me and how to fight back and overcome the negative thoughts, emotions, and behaviors that were ruining my life. Therapy wasn't working, so I shifted to studying with world-famous doctors, healers, gurus, trainers, coaches, and scientists to discover how to change my life from one of pain and misery to one of pleasure and success. I am honored to be certified in over thirty healing therapies, the success of which I have witnessed with my own eyes on five continents.

I tried talk therapy for my stress and anxiety, but it did not seem to help my negative emotions and thoughts. I believed I had been doing everything right, but I still burned out. What was wrong with me? I was depressed and full of self-judgment, but my therapist said he would be concerned if I wasn't depressed. I was overweight and couldn't sleep, and he prescribed medication. I didn't want medication; I wanted my brain to start working.

This is the story of my journey back to mental and emotional health. I wanted to go in depth into the science of trauma and burnout because I needed to understand the "why," to understand why all the conventional medical wisdom wasn't working. Thankfully, Dr. Stephen Porges and others started making groundbreaking discoveries about our nervous systems and the brain, which explain why people burn out. It saved my life.

This is a story of a million-mile journey, from my head to my heart. It is a story of the discovery of the importance of spirituality in everyone's life. It is a story of awakening the mind-heart-body-soul connection that can bring great joy and achievement into even the most damaged life. It is a journey I hope you will take with me, discovering the ways that you can easily understand your brain and finally take control of your life.

Due to the ways of the world, I have had to change my name and the names of many of the cast of characters in my life. The facts are all true (or based on true events). In any event, never ruin a good story with the facts.

Introduction

L**ong, long ago, the Guru** and the Warrior lived together, peaceably. Their goals were the same: to keep the humans they served safe and happy. Most of the time, they worked together, even side by side. Occasionally, the Guru would take the lead in solving a human problem—a loss of a loved one or an argument between tribesmen—while the Warrior was at ease, always watchful but also confident in the balancing act they had always managed so well. Other times, the Warrior burst to the forefront. When a dinosaur loomed outside the cave, it knew just what to do to chase it away. Meanwhile, the Guru was more than content to keep those in the cave singing and humming and going about their time with faith in the Warrior's powers of protection.

The balance began to tip during the human period of industrialization, when it became more and more difficult to work in tandem, as they always had. In many cases, humans removed environmental threats (different from the ones we have created today) and replaced them with psychological threats. Many people moved to cities, and culturally we lauded the concept of "rugged individualism." Humans needed to compete for resources and opportunities. Despite these changes, the Guru and the Warrior had always trusted each other's powers and believed that the balance between them was the key to the humans' happiness. And they would do all that they could to maintain it.

But the divide continued...

The Warrior began taking over more and more frequently, often with poor results. When they were alone together, the Guru tried to reason with the Warrior, reminding It that It could handle many of the issues that the Warrior immediately leapt into. But the Warrior only became more and more vigilant, seeing danger and the need for protection almost everywhere. The Guru tried to insert itself here and there, when It knew It could help.

But often the Warrior already had the humans in such a frenzy that the Guru's voice was lost in the fray. Until eventually the Guru became accustomed to sitting in the background, mournfully rubbing Its hands together, as It watched the Warrior fighting perceived enemies from all angles.

The Guru sighed, and humans around the world shifted uncomfortably in their skins. How could balance be restored? How could It get the Warrior to calm down long enough to teach the humans what the Guru knows?

These two powerful characters, who live inside of every single one of us, will follow us through this book. You may call them what you wish, but the scientific functions they each serve are irrefutable. They'll accompany us on this journey of investigating the intersections between science and our lives. If you're reading this, you're one of the seekers of knowledge, one who wants to connect your own dots and take control of your life.

What I have created for you within the pages of this book is a blend of science, truth, amalgamation, and personification. These elements are often kept separate, but if you can open your mind to explore their intersecting paths with me, it can truly show you how to begin to create sustainable balance and resilience in your life. If I could do it, with the scientific support of the Guru and the Warrior, you can do it too.

I am not the first to personify these two aspects of our psyche. Religion divides good from evil, angels from devils. Religious texts try to explain this divide by allegory, such as eating the fruit of the forbidden tree of knowledge. The stories of Gilgamesh, Quetzalcóatl, and the Mahabharata attempt to explain something that neurobiologists are just now starting to understand: how the brain affects how we see the world.

This book is for the Guru and the Warrior in all of us. The world is currently presenting us with a constant onslaught of information, leading our Warriors to feel they must be first responders to every emergency, every calamity. Humans in earlier times only heard about and experienced events that occurred near enough to matter. Today, we have all the world news at our fingertips, and many of our media outlets strategically show us upsetting images and stories that leave us feeling disempowered, since what can we truly do to help? This is in addition to our individual lives and struggles, our past, and our demanding present culture. Our Warriors are stretched beyond imagination, beyond anything they were originally designed to do, trying to fight battles within, battles nearby, and battles across the world.

We cannot continue in this way. Because you are reading this, I know you know that change must start within. Regardless of what is going on in the rest of the world, the only way to show up at our best is to successfully navigate the lows and enjoy the incredible highs (and create more of them!). The easiest means by which to do this is to understand and regulate what I call our Guru and our Warrior.

The good news is that it can be done! Begin with this book as your guide and start to traverse the paths of your own personal history and how the Guru and the Warrior have played roles in your life. But you're not going to stay there! You're going to go back, following the trail, and when you can see what tripped you up, what causes your triggers today that started a long time ago, you'll return to your present self armed with new and invaluable awareness. And the understanding of how to scientifically hack your brain so that your Guru can reign.

We are all capable of creating change on our own, but of course coaches and guides can be of great help too. It's amazing to me sometimes how readily someone will hire a personal trainer for their body, but not for their mind. Before I leave this earth, it is my life's passion to help you train your mind by sharing the knowledge and wisdom I have painstakingly gathered over my seven decades and worldwide travels.

Freedom and the life you want are always within your reach. So let's uncover what is in the way and convince your Guru to come out and stay. Speaking of the Guru, there are two significant characters whom you will meet throughout this book. They are the secret passengers who ride within all of us. As we traverse this path together, between truth, poetic license, and science, they will be our invisible yet ever-present guides. My hope (and theirs too) is that by the end of this book, you will become familiar with them in yourself and know how to balance the two. Their story begins next . . .

CHAPTER ONE

The Story of the Brain

This is my story. Before you can understand my story or your story, we must understand the narrator of these stories: the brain. This is because our "story" is just the brain's way of making sense of our experiences, beliefs, thoughts, emotions, and perceptions. Just like my story may or may not be based on reality, your story is the same because it may be based on emotionally tainted memories, half-remembered facts, and distortions of the mind.

Our stories are driven largely by our behavior, which is based primarily on our beliefs and our automatic response to stimuli. In trying to make sense of our behavior, the consequences of our behavior, and our increasingly complex environment, our brains resort to stories. To simplify and rationalize our experiences, culture, and programming in the context of our family, tribes, countries, and the world, we summarize it all into a narrative that makes sense to us. We put a pretty bow around it and create an identity that defines who we are.

I write my story because it is my version of what happened over the last seventy-one years. You may recognize and remember, in your own way, the events that I catalog from my story, which began in 1953.

You may even recognize some of your story in my story, and I hope that some of the science I learned along the way helps explain why that happened and empowers you.

Many people know very little about the history and evolution of the human brain. The brain has evolved over millions of years, beginning with primitive brains that held just a few cells to regulate the other cells in a multi-cell organism. As our bodies changed and became more complex, so did the human brain.

Neurobiologists initially believed that the human brain was made of three distinct parts, from oldest to newest: (1) brain stem (fight or flight), (2) limbic system (emotions), and (3) cortex (reasoning). It is now believed that these three parts are not independent, but interconnected.

We are now beginning to understand the role of neuroplasticity in our neurobiology. In the past, we believed that neural pathways were set and didn't change. Now we understand that neuroplasticity allows new neural pathways to form as we learn new information and desire different results. Changing our thinking patterns physically changes our brains.

Our thoughts determine our neural pathways, and our neural pathways determine our thoughts, emotions, and behavior. As we learn new information or release negative thoughts, emotions, and behavior, our neural pathways change. You really can teach an old dog new tricks—or, precisely, we can change how an old dog thinks.

The most recent neurological research has focused on our nervous systems.[1] Experts believe these nervous systems regulate how information is interpreted by the rest of the brain. Our nervous systems operate on a pre-thought basis and influence our behavior depending on how we perceive our environment. Our thoughts, emotions, and beliefs can alter how we perceive the environment, and our environment

---

1   Cara M. Altimus et al., "The Next 50 Years of Neuroscience," *Journal of Neuroscience* 40, no. 1 (January 2, 2020): 101–6, https://doi.org/10.1523/jneurosci.0744-19.2019.

can alter our thoughts, emotions, and beliefs.

The most important functions of our brain are to analyze our environment for safety or threat, predict our most optimal future, and plan how to accomplish that future. We rely on memory, motivation, and cognitive beliefs to succeed or fail at the accomplishments we desire.

Modern research has found that trauma can negatively impact our reasoning and perception skills.[2] The pain and suffering from physical, emotional, or mental abuse can damage our hippocampus and amygdala so that we experience maladaptive stress responses and chronic stress, depression, and anxiety.

For people who experience chronic stress, anxiety, or depression, the path to mental and emotional health can be fraught with barriers and stumbling blocks. It is critical for people struggling with negative thoughts, emotions, and beliefs to identify the trauma that caused those symptoms and heal them.

As we chronicle my story, it is helpful to notice the traumatic events in my life. I have healed through all of them, but the first step is to be aware of trauma in our lives. We can't change what we don't know. This has taken years of introspection and contemplation. To change stumbling blocks into stepping stones, we must fearlessly accept our past and understand how it limits our present and damages our future.

The first thing we must recognize is that the brain shapes our reality by way of forming biases, beliefs, and opinions. The brain is a highly complex and complicated organ that processes billions of neural signals through billions of cells at any given moment. How this works gives us glimpses into why we think, believe, and act as we do. Due to advances in imaging technology, we have been able to identify which parts of the brain control different functions of our body.

For example, parts of the frontal cortex handle decision-making, problem-solving, and planning. Other areas of the brain handle sight,

---

2   Center for Substance Abuse Treatment, "Understanding the Impact of Trauma," Trauma-Informed Care in Behavioral Health Services - NCBI Bookshelf, 2014, https://www.ncbi.nlm.nih.gov/books/NBK207191/.

smell, touch, and auditory input, while the limbic system handles memory and emotions. These various regions must work together to perform complex tasks such as eating, learning, analysis, and motor skills.

The first order of business for the brain is to receive and interpret sensory data. Our brain is continuously processing signals sent through our eyes, ears, nose, mouth, and skin. In addition to the traditional five senses, scientists now recognize other kinds of sensations, including pain, pressure, temperature, joint position, and movement.

Specialized sensory neurons respond to sensory input from the environment and convert those signals into electrochemical messages to the areas of the brain tasked with analyzing and acting on the input. Subsequently, multiple types of sensory input are integrated, thus allowing the mass of information to be interpreted into an appropriate (motor) response.

It is important to understand that millions of processes occur between the reception of sensory stimuli and conscious thought. That is why we are so vulnerable to misinterpretation of data. These signals are interpreted several times before this data reaches conscious thought. This information is analyzed by the autonomic nervous system and our subconscious mind—which includes bias, judgment, and emotional responses—before it reaches our conscious minds. How and what we think is subjectively determined by these filters.

With all this sensory input and analysis, the brain has evolved shortcuts to be more effective. These are called biases, which act as adaptive processes that allow us to use prior knowledge and experiences to inform our decisions and actions in the present. In other words, our brain makes judgments and conclusions based on data and experiences from the past. It is a function of our survival mechanisms, because predators forced us to make quick decisions.

When these biases are negative, they can lead to poor decision-making and behavior. This is especially true when it comes to adverse childhood experiences (ACEs) and trauma. Our brain forms beliefs and judgments about painful experiences and heavily weights avoidance strategies to keep us safe. However, if the pain is coming from experiences that are misunderstood or taken out of context, we may end up preventing healthy growth and achievement. Biases are both the result and the cause of bad decision-making.

There are two major kinds of bias: explicit and implicit. Explicit bias is conscious bias that we are aware of. Prejudice, discrimination, and quotas are all examples of explicit bias. Then there is subconscious bias, biases which we are not aware of, but culturally we assume are true. We learn these biases from our family, our friends, or authority figures. These are based on what we assume means safety: people who think the same as we do, people who look the same as we do, and people who act the same as we do.

There are hundreds of different types of biases we carry in our subconscious mind, but these can be condensed into six overall types:

- Safety: We tend to prioritize the avoidance of pain over seeking pleasure.
- Similarity: We tend to feel more comfortable around people we perceive as being, acting, or looking like us over people who are different.
- Effectiveness: We tend to jump to conclusions to minimize cognitive effort.
- Familiarity: We tend to believe that our perceptions are truer than someone else's perceptions, especially if they are different.
- Proximity: We tend to value things that we perceive are closer than those far away.
- Confirmation: We only see what we expect to see. We take in only the examples that align with our preexisting notions and stereotypes. We ignore and discard the counterexamples that would challenge these worldviews.

Our brain relies on shortcuts all the time. Our brain uses what it has learned from the environment to make assumptions about how to feel, whom to trust, what to say, and how to act or react. If what we have learned about our environment is distorted or misunderstood due to age or pain, we can't always trust our brain to make correct assumptions. When our thought patterns are erroneous, our perceptions can be erroneous as well.

It is believed that human beings unconsciously perceive anyone different as a threat because our brain has an evolutionary requirement to do so. The capacity to discern "us" from "them" is fundamental to our survival. However, it can lead to problems in our ability to form relationships and grow. These decisions are made in milliseconds without our conscious thought or analysis. Thus, we avoid people and institutions that we don't like without knowing why.

Basically, we have two ways of thinking: "fast" and "slow." "Fast" thinking involves intuition and impressions and is automatic and efficient. However, it is hurried and prone to mistakes. It is centered in the limbic system, particularly the amygdala, which operates without conscious thought.[3]

This instinctive thought process focuses on patterns, which is a key survival skill. In doing so, however, we can jump to conclusions of causality based upon even the sketchiest of information. We try to interpret scant input by creating a narrative that is highly unreliable.

"Slow" thinking is deliberate and systematic and is centered in the cerebral cortex. It takes much longer to process and considers a much broader range of experience, memory, and beliefs. It is more thorough, testing complexities, concepts, and subtle nuances.

In healthy individuals, these patterns work in tandem, giving us a wide range of choices of response and reaction. However, since unconscious bias is much faster than the slower thinking process, it can sabotage our analysis of the situation. In other words, our unconscious

---

[3] "Daniel Kahneman Explains the Machinery of Thought," Farnam Street, November 10, 2019, https://fs.blog/daniel-kahneman-the-two-systems/.

bias can cause our intellect to malfunction.

When the amygdala is activated, the tendency is to generalize more, which increases the likelihood of accidental connections. There is a tendency to err on the safe side, shrinking from opportunities. People become more likely to react defensively to stimuli. This means that our ability to understand, make decisions, remember, memorize, plan, inhibit impulses, solve problems, and communicate is impaired. We struggle to see the big picture, and ultimately, our overall productivity drops.

The good news is that our brains can rewire through neuroplasticity, and we can unlearn these implicit biases. It takes a good deal of self-analysis and contemplation to uncover these unconscious biases, usually with a trained guide. When implicit bias is coupled with trauma, a perfect storm of impulsivity and unconscious behavior is unleashed, creating negative thinking, beliefs, and behavior.

So let us dive into the deep end and put my evolution into perspective. The context of any self-growth is to learn from our experiences. Unaware people repeat their mistakes, aware people learn from their mistakes, and wise people learn from the mistakes of others. I hope you learn from my experiences and use your new knowledge to achieve your life's desires.

The oldest part of the brain on the evolutionary scale is the brainstem, which includes the medulla. The brainstem was one of the first organized brain structures, evolving from the original neural networks that controlled multicellular organisms. This part of the modern brain is what is known as the reptilian brain and is millions of years old. It houses the autonomic nervous system, which controls the automatic functions of the body, such as breathing, digestion, heart rate, and enzyme and hormone production.

The next part of the brain that evolved was the limbic brain, which consists of the amygdala, the hippocampus, and the thalamus. This part of the brain handles emotion, judgment, memory, and production of various brain chemicals, such as melatonin, serotonin, and endorphins.

The latest addition to our brain is the neocortex, or frontal cortex, which handles intellectual and executive function, language, communication, connection, rational thought, and civilization-building skills.

When we are stimulated through the five senses, this information is delivered first to the reptilian brain and then distributed through the limbic brain and neocortex for processing. The most important function of the reptilian brain is to classify the information as either safety or danger. It is important to remember that all of this takes place before the conscious parts of the brain receive the information.

As indicated, the reptilian brain houses the autonomic nervous system. This system is divided into two parts: the sympathetic nervous system and the parasympathetic nervous system. The sympathetic nervous system is activated when the stimulus is perceived as a threat, while the parasympathetic nervous system is activated when the stimulus is perceived as safe.

I refer to the sympathetic nervous system as the Warrior, and the parasympathetic nervous system as the Guru. This is because when the Warrior is activated, the brain and body react in fight or flight, while if the Guru is activated, the brain and body react as relax and digest. There is a sliding scale because both the Warrior and the Guru are always ready to engage, and both can activate at the same time. However, certain bodily functions will occur depending on which one is fully engaged.

This does not have anything to do with the conscious mind. We can't stop the Warrior or the Guru from activating. However, we can regulate one or the other with our conscious mind if we are aware of what is happening.

For example, people get upset by the behavior of others when their autonomic nervous system interprets it as threatening. Loud noises, inappropriate language, or injury can activate the Warrior, as can threats, challenges, risky behavior (either inside or outside the body), and pain. My experience is that many people today regularly activate their Warrior nervous system and rarely turn it off.

When the Warrior is activated, It signals the limbic system to go into defensive mode, depending on the severity of the threat. We experience negative emotions such as anger, fear, rage, guilt, and remorse. The brain signals the body to produce adrenaline and cortisol. This signals the conscious brain to fight or flee. If the danger is severe, we can freeze, faint, or lose consciousness. This is why some people will pass out if "scared to death."

The reasoning parts of the brain can shut down, as does the digestive tract, while the heart rate and blood pressure increase. This is because the Warrior marshals all the body's resources for defense. Any energy not needed for fight or flight is diverted to the muscles. This is all due to evolution and survival of the fittest. However, it was only intended to be used temporarily, until the danger passed.

Conversely, when we feel safe and the Guru is activated, the brain and the body produce melatonin, serotonin, endorphins, and oxytocin. All these chemicals make us feel pleasant and relaxed. Our higher brain functions of reasoning and imagination come online, and we can love, be compassionate, converse, create, and cooperate. All of this is impossible when the Warrior is activated.

What we perceive depends on whether the Warrior or the Guru is activated. If an individual is not paying attention, they may not even know which one is running the show. The problem is that people who live with the Warrior for any length of time have a far more negative perception of their environment, because they are focusing on danger everywhere.

The ego originally evolved to assess and strategize fear and danger. People who stay in their Warrior mode can experience high levels of stress and toxicity in their bodies, because those are the natural results of Warrior mode. It is the cause of many emotional issues and can ultimately lead to full breakdowns.

When we are operating with the Guru, life is fun, multidimensional, and safe.

Conversely, when we are stuck with the Warrior, life is hard and dangerous. All of this is completely under the conscious spectrum of thought. This is what is meant by "We create our own reality."

We inherit the Warrior and the Guru when we are born. They dictate much of our behavior throughout our lives, especially if we are not aware of their presence. As we will see through the events of my life and the application of neuroscience to them, numerous things affect our behaviors, beliefs, and happiness. If we are aware of these influences, we can better understand what is happening and why it is happening, and we can create a better life for ourselves.

CHAPTER TWO

Never Ruin a Good Story with the Facts

My name is James Gray Johnson. I was born in 1953 in Charlotte, North Carolina. At that time, birthing was quite different from the low lighting, easy chair, and midwife birthing procedure more popular today. Newborns are now gently encouraged to begin breathing while they are lying on their mother's chest. The two heartbeats can continue to be shared while the infant gets over the ordeal of birth. Due to many lessons learned from the traumatic effects on newborns by harsh environments, bright lighting, and lack of physical contact with the mother, birthing now aims to be as low stress and soothing as possible.[4]

The theory is that the more the outside environment simulates the womb, the more it reduces the initial stress of leaving the womb. Some mothers go so far as to give birth underwater in amniotic fluid-like water. Compare this to the doctor's old customary whack on the ass as the infant was held upside down by the ankles to force breathing,

---

4   Ashley Weber and Tondi M. Harrison, "Reducing Toxic Stress in the Neonatal Intensive Care Unit to Improve Infant Outcomes," *Nursing Outlook* 67, no. 2 (November 22, 2018): 169–89, https://doi.org/10.1016/j.outlook.2018.11.002.

followed by the cutting of the umbilical cord—yikes! As an adult, I cannot imagine a more barbaric welcome into a hostile world. My baby Warrior came out screaming.

The year 1953 brought big changes to modern American life. The Shah of Iran was restored to power. The Korean War ended after three years and one month. The average cost of a new house was $9,550, and gas cost twenty-nine cents per gallon. The first color television sets appeared in affluent homes. TV Guide published its first issue, and the 1950s housewife's life was changed by her new automatic washing machine. The first polio vaccine was developed, and the dictator Joseph Stalin died. Marilyn Monroe pushed boundaries on the movie screen with *Gentlemen Prefer Blondes*.

After years of healing work, my memories began to extend back to even this dramatic beginning of my life. I remember the birthing room as a harshly lit stark chamber with fluorescent lights, surgical gowns, stainless steel, and instruments resembling crowbars. The room was cold and smelled harshly of metal and disinfectant. The only thing I knew when labor began was that I was a twin, as I had felt another presence with me as I grew, and I got banged around a lot. My twin was the first out, followed by me—kicking and pushing as hard as I could. Her name was Katherine Louise Johnson, who would be Kitty to me when we were little and, as she later explained it, then grew up to be a "Kat."

Prenatal care was nonexistent at that time, and smoking and drinking to excess were common practices. My mother was no exception. The daughter of one of the wealthiest entrepreneurs in the world, she enjoyed a lavish social lifestyle. The discomfort and inconvenience of pregnancy were easily medicated with nicotine and alcohol. Knowledge of the aftereffects of fetal alcohol syndrome was not even on the horizon yet, and it would be decades before I would understand its ramifications in my life. Her forms of self-medication hid the tell-tale signs of anything unusual from my mother. Especially the presence of two bodies in her womb.

According to my mother, I was a total surprise to all in the room. She reportedly told one of the nurses to go outside and tell my father to go buy one more of everything in the nursery at home. The tip-off came when the obstetrician exclaimed, "Damn, there is another one. He's not supposed to be here."

Those were the first words I heard on this planet. After being pulled out by forceps, I gasped my first breath as I was gruffly whacked on the ass, despite my tiny size. My twin and I were both covered in bruises. God only knows what went on during our first eight months of life in the womb, but it certainly foretold our relationship from then on. My twin said many times that she was first out because ladies always come first. We would be ultra-competitive for the rest of our lives.

Due to the unexpected early delivery, fetal alcohol syndrome, and low birth weight (three pounds, ten ounces), we were promptly placed in separate metal boxes called incubators. Tubes were unceremoniously inserted at top and bottom to help us survive the initial overwhelming ordeal of life. Being overwhelmed would be a common theme for me through my early years. My first impression was that the world was a very strange place with glass and metal walls and no one there to hold me.

Viewed through my tiny, unfocused vision, my surroundings inspired complete terror. I was in the metal box for six weeks, and during that time I never experienced human touch, not even the beating heart of my mother. It took me six weeks to grow enough to live in ordinary temperatures without the chance of pneumonia setting in. Doctors didn't know that would happen, just that it might.

I had my first contact with humans when I was six weeks old. As I had lain there isolated in the metal box, I had developed a desperate need for human contact, a condition that would follow me all my life. I felt alone, terrified, and abandoned. Those emotions would also take center stage in my psyche for years to come. My Guru tried Its best to soothe me, but my Warrior had already seen how dangerous and lonely life could be, and It developed at a pace that my Guru could not match. The only problem with coming out of the box was the circumcision that followed. Being six weeks old, it was much more painful than it could have been at two days old, when it is normally performed. My Warrior screamed in agony, barely able to understand why this brutal practice was customary. Pain became familiar to me from the start.

The only thing that brought light to my isolated existence was the angels that kept me company, or at least I perceived them as angels. The beings seemed very real at the time, even though they were not seen by any of the nurses. When I would point to the angels, the nurses thought I was convulsing.

These beings kept me calm and peaceful by touching me ethereally. I would laugh whenever they did. The nurses thought I was what they called "touched," as in crazy. If their definition included seeing other worlds, they were right, as I would be touched by angels all my life. I have always been aware of these beings around me and was quite surprised when I discovered that many people don't see them or know that they are perpetually by our side.

It seemed conflicting that I knew that these beings were always around me, and yet I felt so alone in the world. This was one of the lessons I had come to this life to learn—that nothing is as it seems, and no two people experience anything in the same way. My twin never saw these beings and scoffed when I would talk about them. Eventually, I would conform.

I was named after my maternal grandfather, James Gray Seagram, one of the wealthiest men from one of the wealthiest families in the world. My grandfather was a successful entrepreneur who owned dozens of businesses employing over one hundred thousand people. His annual income was in the millions, which translates to hundreds of millions a year now.

"Mr. Gray," as my grandfather was called, died when I was quite young, and I have no memory of him. Naming a child after an ultra-successful relative can be either a blessing or a curse. For me, it was both. To set the stage of this story, my father was named Richard

"Dick" Johnson. He went to West Point during World War II, graduating in 1943. When he completed his tour of duty, he retired from his commission to become a lawyer. In 1955, he was elected to the North Carolina Supreme Court, a position he would hold until his death in 2017.

It was during a summer social that he first met my mother, Delores Louise Seagram. My father had been invited up to the Seagram summer compound in the Allegheny Mountains of northwest North Carolina to meet my mother.

When my father found out who the lovely lady with a drink in her hand was, and who her father was, he told everyone who would listen that it was love at first sight. As a soldier who was unfamiliar with great luxuries, he was highly motivated to conquer her love. The intoxicating combination of magnolia blossoms, money, and bourbon could be an overwhelming love potion.

My father had grown up in the Great Depression before the war, and financial security was the topmost priority in his life. It was more important than anything. It was more important than kindness, more important even than love.

He set his military mind on acquiring my mother as his wife, and that, as they say, was that. My father told me many times that I could make more money in ten minutes at the altar than a lifetime of hard work. It was not the best introduction to relationships, to be sure.

He convinced Mr. Gray that he was an excellent choice as a suitor. Mr. Gray immediately agreed, because my mother was continually falling in love with members of the staff and men below their status. He had just put his foot down and forbade her from marrying her true love, a local realtor.

Mr. Gray was impressed with my father's ambition and military background. It was just the sort of discipline that he thought my mother needed. My mother reluctantly agreed, and they were married in a lavish ceremony in the Lutheran Church of the Redeemer. Mr. Gray was instrumental in funding the building of the new cathedral built in

1952, and Dick and Delores's wedding was one of the first weddings in the church. Thousands attended.

The newlyweds began their lives together in the thriving yet quaint Southern city of Charlotte, North Carolina. My father yearned to be accepted into its close-knit elite society, but he found that cracking the invisible bubble around that golden life was more difficult than imagined. The upper crust of the city's Southern society was renowned for being cliquish, and outsiders were treated like interlopers. My father's tunnel vision about being accepted drove him to be one of the most successful attorneys and businessmen in North Carolina. Later, Mr. Gray used all his political connections to help my father get elected to the Supreme Court.

I never knew my maternal grandparents. I grew up with almost godlike accounts of their existence, and being my grandfather's namesake came with great responsibility. Mr. Gray was one of the most successful businessmen in Charlotte. The fact that I was his namesake created a surreal social barrier around both me and my twin from the start.

My maternal grandparents lived with a score of maids, chauffeurs, groundskeepers, and staff in a mansion in the middle of Charlotte. My parents lived in a house on the same huge block, approximately five acres right in the center of the city, not far from the Belk compound in South Park.

My twin sister and I were not allowed to socialize with people in lower socioeconomic classes and therefore lived an exclusive and sheltered childhood. We were photographed often by the local newspaper and displayed on the social pages, usually wearing adult clothes that were unusual for four-year-olds. Photos of us in my father's law office, by the country club swimming pool with inflatable rubber swans, at the family mountain resort, and in our home regularly hit the local newspaper society column. I was quite oblivious to the notoriety, but it was clear that our lives held many expectations.

My maternal grandmother was a bit of a mystery. A devout Catholic, Daisy Barclay Frieze was from another well-to-do family whose roots reached deep into the culture of North Carolina. Mr. Gray chose her based on her family connections and wealth. This was an old-fashioned arranged marriage between two of the wealthiest families in the city. My family tree was filled with branches stuffed with fortunes, but none made from love.

Having been born into these families, I was constantly reminded that I had a lot to live up to. The pressure to succeed was ladled on from an early age, and my Warrior took umbrage from the start. Unfortunately for me, my father had a military approach to everything. His Warrior seemed to run his life, which for him was a series of targets and goals to be captured or acquired with proper military planning and maneuvering. So, when he had to go purchase "one more of everything" after my unexpected arrival into the world, it deviated from his military plan, a surprise he found most vexing.

God forbid one should disrupt a proper military operation by being born. That was worse than dying. Dying could be planned for; it was expected in a military operation. An unexpected birth was a divine event that had no place in proper military planning.

My father was my biggest teacher, and the person I feared the most. From him, I inherited my birthright of stubbornness, impatience, obsessive-compulsiveness, competitiveness, and a generally pervasive self-image of inadequacy. Yet at times he also drilled generosity, philanthropy, and discipline into my impressionable mind. His mixed messages had me chasing my proverbial tail as soon as I was old enough to try to please him. There were many a day in the early years that I wished I could climb back into my metal box, even though it was the first place that my Warrior learned to scream and my Guru to cower.

The first sign that I had a significant streak of rebelliousness buried shallowly under my conscious behavior manifested when I was three years old. My parents always compared my later predicaments with this initial act of defiance. Soon I would step fully into my role of troublemaker, but at that point I was just a creative, albeit risk-taking, toddler. After that day, my father would commonly remark, "I knew you were going to be a handful when I came home and discovered we were having potluck for six months."

The event had both comic and Machiavellian aspects, both of which were to become recurrent themes in my story. In our home, my parents had built a pantry for canned and dry foods. It was floor-to-ceiling shelves of canned okra, peas, corn, meats, prepared pasta, soup, exotic appetizers, and fruit—food which could not properly be identified without a proper label. Some of these foods had been purchased on trips abroad, which my parents took from time to time to get away; some were gifts from family or friends trying to impress.

I thought it would be a grand idea to take all the labels off the cans and bins. When I felt the paper tearing away from the can, it shifted the air inside me; my senses all ignited. Years later, I would go down many rabbit holes looking for these visceral feelings, these jagged edges exposed. It felt like I was truly accomplishing something, one of my first big statements to the world. I thought it would be a wonderful gift to have all those shiny aluminum and tin cans gleaming in row after row of identical anonymous design.

One question that always lay in the back of my mind like a sleeping dog that couldn't be moved was why a three-year-old had enough unsupervised time to accomplish such a feat of daring without being discovered. A three-year-old climbing up shelves ten feet tall, unsupervised, gives a window into the amount of attention I was lacking in our massive home. In addition to removing the labels, I also thought it would be fun to rearrange everything so that there would be more variety on each shelf. After all, the peas didn't really need to be all in the same place. Boring!

In any event, my early act of inspiration and creativity was not well received. It was my first memorable experience with punishment. Especially punishment that far exceeded the crime. My afternoon of thinking outside the box resulted in my parents not knowing what kind of food we would be eating for months to come. My father couldn't handle the uncertainty and decided to go buy more food so he would know what he was opening for supper.

This triggered two of my father's control issues: wasting money and unplanned surprises. Not to mention that my mother was horrified that I was climbing around like a monkey on the highest shelves without someone to catch me if I fell. As a result, I experienced my first corporal punishment. It may have only been three or four blows, but it planted a seed of mortality and fear. The world was no longer a safe place, and my parents could no longer be trusted. My Warrior was fully awakened.

When human babies are brought forth on the planet, their mother is usually the first person they see. This person feeds them from her breasts, holds them close, keeps them clean and warm, bathes and clothes them. This activates the Guru and engrains feelings of safety in the baby. From those feelings of safety evolve our understanding of love.

I didn't experience that initial bonding. My rigid metal box, where hands appeared through holes in the wall to clean and feed me, was not a place where my Guru could thrive. I never knew the breast, only the bottle, never felt the soft touch or heard the sweet lullabies that only a mother can provide. Hence my Guru was unfamiliar to me from the start.

In my life, the frequent punishment I got would irreparably separate me from both parents: my father, who angrily doled out the punishment, and my mother, who didn't protect me. It created in me a need to manipulate my parents so that I would not get punished again, which I managed to do quite successfully over the next few years, with some spectacular exceptions.

Disappointingly, Kitty and I never bonded like many twins. Perhaps it was the fact that we were separated at birth and immediately placed in separate metal boxes. But the bruises covering both of our newborn bodies were some evidence that our division preceded our birth. I once talked to a psychic who said that we had been ancient enemies in prior lifetimes and had chosen to be born as twins to get over our long-held hatred. The deep purple bruises marking us both seemed to corroborate the tale.

My personal theory was that I was a bit faster than my twin, and she had dawdled on the way out of the womb, so I was just trying to help her along. This help was in the form of a few kicks. Instead of allowing us to develop as two separate beings, my parents insisted that we be raised as a unit. We were dressed in matching clothes until nature took over and I got much larger than Kitty. The fashion industry at the time called my size "husky," while Kitty stayed impeccably thin. We both were relieved when we didn't have to wear coordinating outfits any longer.

As I grew up, my father practiced a military style of parenting, filled with gaslighting and competition. This kept the troops manageable and under control. In this case the troops were young children, but his tactics remained unmodified. He instilled a latent competitiveness between me and my sisters (I would get more sisters later), which was fully reminiscent of a foxhole mentality. It was every man for himself. It was always me against my sisters.

Living with sisters constantly felt hazardous. They ratted on me a lot. They ganged up on me and constantly accused me of aggressiveness, although I was mostly just a young boy with a lot of energy to get out. It was a traumatic existence spent walking on eggshells, as even the most benign behavior was reported to my parents for appropriate action. Usually, it was an action I would not like, and one that would bring my Warrior to a boil.

My father was quite big; he enjoyed eating. While giving lip service to exercise and looking fit, the truth was he had had enough of exercise in the military and vowed never to do anything that required sweat again. He gorged on three huge meals a day, starting with cereal and milk, eggs, bacon, toast, doughnuts, grits, or oatmeal for breakfast.

For lunch, he would have a three-course meal involving gravy- and butter-covered anything. Supper would inevitably include a four- or five-course meal with cocktails and dessert.

Although I loved it and sought refuge in it, even food wasn't safe for me. My parents grew up in the Great Depression, and in the back of their minds all food that was prepared had to be eaten, because one day there might not be any food to eat. The belief at the time was that the more you fed a child, the healthier that child would be. That worked for my sisters, but not for me.

I often incurred the wrath of my parents by not finishing off the gargantuan meals I was served. Not only was I served a large portion of guilt with uneaten food, but I was often slapped or shaken if I said I couldn't finish it. Food was a sign of luxury and abundance for my father, who told me that he grew up without much food during the Depression. He regularly swore that he would force it down my throat if necessary, and I supposedly would like it.

One evening, my parents gave me the usual order, "Finish the food on your plate."

I protested, "But I'm full and can't finish it."

My father's temples began visibly throbbing, an indication I would come to recognize as a rapid spike in his blood pressure. Trying very hard to keep his temper in check, my father barked, "I worked very hard to put food on this table, and I will not hear of you saying no. Finish the food or I will have to send it to China so that it won't be wasted."

Showing early signs of resistance, I said, "Go ahead and send it; they need it more than I do."

The following silence and steely look in my father's eyes foretold another spanking in my immediate future. My Warrior began kicking the table legs, which added to my punishment. My Guru, who loved comfort food, shrank in fear. This began my lifelong love-hate relationship with food.

The only other significant memory I had of my earliest years was my encounter with a horse, which would come full circle in my later years. My parents traveled a great deal, leaving me and my sisters with sitters or nannies. One woman who was frequently asked to keep the children was Mrs. O'Neill. She had a son who owned a farm, and that day she thought it would be a great idea to take us to visit it.

When I got there, I was happily overwhelmed by all the animals. There were geese to avoid, chickens to chase, dogs to pet, cows to milk, and, out in a pasture, the most magnificent white stallion I could possibly imagine. I wanted to get closer, but Mrs. O'Neill warned me not to go into the pasture. This presented me with an early dilemma: whether to obey or get what I wanted. My Guru was oddly whispering loudly for me to go, so I followed my instincts and crawled through the fence to get to the horse.

Horses, being flight animals, will normally back away when approached, especially independent stallions. However, for some reason, the stallion watched me approaching with my eager arms outstretched and did not run. Perhaps something that small wasn't threatening. Perhaps my Guru was talking to it in ways I couldn't hear. In any event, when I reached the stallion, I held my arms up to touch its thick mane. The stallion bowed his head, letting me stroke his muzzle. I was in total joy. I sat down between the horse's front hooves and watched as the horse grazed. My Warrior napped peacefully, and my Guru sang a little tune, one that I heard so rarely, one that was the sweetest sound to my small ears.

The next thing I knew, Mrs. O'Neill's son was walking as fast as he dared towards us without spooking the stallion. What I didn't know was that the stallion was extremely aggressive and usually attacked whoever came into the pasture. The horse spun and bolted, leaving me wondering what in the world had happened, as my body ached where it had been touching the warmth of the horse. All I knew was my friend had left me, and my Guru had disappeared too. I started crying, and Mrs. O'Neill's son picked me up and ran out of the pasture.

The son thought I had been injured by the horse, but I was only upset that my friend had been scared off, and that feeling, that elusive peaceful feeling was again gone. When we got back to the group of people headed by Mrs. O'Neill, I got my first scolding from her. I tried to tell them that I was alright and nothing bad had happened. I also wanted to tell them that they should have left me alone with the horse. I kept it to myself, but inside my love of horses bloomed madly, along with my preference for horses over most people.

CHAPTER THREE

The Brain's Trauma Response

As my story has already shown, many things can affect the autonomic nervous system and our behavior. The Warrior and the Guru are autonomic nervous system responses to our environment. This normal brain activity can be grossly damaged if a child is exposed to abuse and trauma at an early age. Simply put, the child can get stuck in Warrior mode, incapable of enjoying the Guru brain state.

When a child is traumatized, the brain neurons associated with the Warrior connect more strongly with each other while isolating from other neuroreceptors. My experience was that anytime I remembered a traumatizing event, it seemed like I was instantly transported back to that event, and I experienced all the emotions, thoughts, and shock as if it were happening again. It felt like a loop I could not escape. Hence, the Warrior never turned off.

This is due to the production of adrenaline and cortisol, which rush to the brain and imprint the memory of the trauma into the amygdala in the limbic system, which controls our emotions.[5] The

---

5   Harvard Health, "Understanding the Stress Response," April 3, 2024, https://www.health.harvard.edu/staying-healthy/understanding-the-stress-response.

memory is embedded in the emotional brain, separate from the frontal cortex that controls rational thought and reasoning. As a result, stimuli that would ordinarily be interpreted as non-threatening may trigger a strong emotional response. The brain loses the ability to differentiate between what is threatening and what is safe.

These neural networks fixate on the past and resist change, even though new information is being experienced in the present. When the Warrior is activated, we feel unsafe and lack self-worth. This may continue even when our circumstances have radically changed for the better.

If the trauma has resulted in post-traumatic stress disorder (PTSD), this rigidity in the traumatized neural networks causes us to perceive our environment inaccurately, and we can overreact or underreact. When traumatic memories are incorporated into these rigid neural systems, we associate with the traumatic memory and can't perceive any change in circumstances.

In other words, we flash back into the memory and feeling of the traumatic moment in inappropriate times and circumstances, and can't downregulate our emotions and feelings into a more appropriate emotional state. We compound the problem by attempting to bury the feelings or avoid feeling negative emotional states. We try to "white knuckle it" and work through the hurt and pain.

We try to compartmentalize the negative emotions and beliefs, so we don't have to deal with them. We can even deny the feelings or memories and pretend they never happened. We focus on distractions, such as drugs, sex, food, exercise, or work. When we overdo the distractions, we become unhealthy or burn out. Even burnout is better than the uncomfortable process of dealing with our buried past.

Eventually, this avoidance strategy becomes "normal." Neuroplasticity is good news and bad news, because new neural connections can be established over time. If the new connections are negative, it becomes harder and harder to "change our minds." If the new connections are positive, even if it takes years to change our habitual thinking, it will change.

Many people attribute the age of agriculture as the genesis of civilization. With the ability to grow and store foodstuffs, large populations could form and focus on things other than finding food and avoiding predators. However, it was the development of our limbic brain and frontal cortex millions of years ago that gave us these abilities to communicate, connect, socialize, analyze, and plan. This made it possible to have civilization.

With these new aspects of our brain, we were able to develop language, abstract thinking, mathematics, art, music, religion, medicine, and philosophy. We are unique in the animal kingdom in our ability to think and reason in such complex ways. We can connect dots that the rest of nature doesn't even see, except on some instinctive genetic level.

The Guru, the parasympathetic nervous system, allows the rest of the brain to rest and relax and engage in such esoteric pursuits as socialization, art, and communication. Many mental health professionals believe this is our natural state of being. We are hardwired to be happy, and yet the Warrior aspect of our nervous system seems to hijack our existence uninvited, resisting all effort to shut it off.

To be blunt, the need for our Warrior sympathetic nervous system has been replaced by our ability to connect and communicate. The Warrior has become an outdated defense strategy and often overwhelms us when we mistake events as being threatening. We have failed to regulate the Warrior as we should, and this has had tragic consequences for our social and emotional development.

Evidence suggests that children with ACEs grow up with stunted judgment and stress disorders.[6] When the trauma is parental abuse, children can develop attachment disorders, which occur when a child fails to bond with any authority figures. This is a common cause of

---

6   Erica M. Webster, "The Impact of Adverse Childhood Experiences on Health and Development in Young Children," *Global Pediatric Health* 9 (January 1, 2022), https://doi.org/10.1177/2333794x221078708.

addiction because the child seeks pleasure in anything that can give them a substitute for safe authority figures.

With abuse, the functions of the autonomic nervous system are skewed towards fear and stress. The ego developed as the brain's survival mechanism. It constantly scans the environment for danger and operates out of fear. When the Guru is activated, there is no need for a danger radar, and the ego subsides. We feel good, calm, and relaxed.

With the Guru, we can seek out relationships and connect to like-minded people. We form tribes, guilds, businesses, social clubs, or other social classes. With the Warrior, it is everyone for themselves. The Warrior is always looking for problems, while the Guru is looking for solutions.

A complicating factor is society's mistaken emphasis on physical prowess and neglect of emotional and mental maturity. Focusing on strength instead of maturity has caused great problems for the psyche of huge numbers of children, adolescents, and young adults. One only needs to observe the antisocial behavior of highly paid athletes to understand this point.

The Guru is predicated on social interaction and connection. The only time we need to be in Warrior mode is when we are faced with a physical threat. The Warrior is antithetical to society, and people who are stuck in the Warrior mode due to emotional or physical trauma exhibit antisocial behavior.

It is fascinating to observe society's obsession with gladiator sports, whether individual or team. We are like the ancient Romans, who distracted the masses with blood sports and carnage in the Colosseum. We love football, rugby, basketball, high-speed motor cars, wrestling, boxing, and other risky sports. The more blood, the better. No one would watch NASCAR without the possibility of a multicar pileup, nor would they bet on boxing if they weren't waiting anxiously to see their chosen athletes knock someone unconscious.

The paradox of all paradoxes is society's fascination with the antisocial Warrior. As a culture, we are addicted to adrenaline and cortisol.

Imagine a world where the Guru is in control, and we seek connection, cooperation, maturity, and support.

If we empowered our Guru as much as we worship the Warrior, the landscape of our world would be a very different place.

Neuroscience has recently discovered that we not only have a conscious and a subconscious, but also a "nonconscious" aspect. Stimuli are filtered first through the nonconscious, activating either the Warrior or the Guru autonomic nervous system before reaching conscious awareness in the frontal cortex. We don't precisely know the distinction between the subconscious and the nonconscious, other than that the nonconscious is the initial receptor of information. After processing and internalizing, the information is then stored in the subconscious.

Our nonconscious/subconscious minds occupy 90–99 percent of our brain function. We are simply unaware of this activity because it is occurring in areas of the brain that do not have cognitive function. The brain stem, limbic system, and sensory parts of the brain are not conscious. It can take anywhere from 0.3 to 0.5 seconds for our brain to become conscious of information received by the nonconscious.[7] Information goes through various "filters" of processing in the brain before we have a thought about it. In other words, there is detection before awareness.

When we detect information from our senses, this stimulus is converted into electrochemical signals. These signals are then organized according to relevance by an "attention filter" that directs the signals to the appropriate cognitive process. For information to be analyzed, it first must be stored as short-term, working, or long-term memory. When this process is disrupted, we have a hard time functioning and behaving in the world.

The primary function of these brain processes that occur after we

---

7   Hans Liljenström, "Consciousness, Decision Making, and Volition: Freedom Beyond Chance and Necessity," *Theory in Biosciences* 141, no. 2 (May 28, 2021): 125–40, https://doi.org/10.1007/s12064-021-00346-6.

detect anything is to determine whether we are safe or under threat. If it appears safe, we automatically go into a social engagement system (Guru). If it appears dangerous, we automatically go into a surveillance and vigilance system (Warrior). When the nonconscious mind is damaged due to trauma, PTSD, stress, or mental disorders, the ability to recognize safety or danger is compromised.

Disruption of these functions can compromise the ability of our limbic system (hippocampus, amygdala, and thalamus) to make decisions, respond with appropriate emotions, accurately remember events, and make conscious what is subconscious. We react for no reason, we act inappropriately, or we experience delusions that affect our behavior.

Continuing trauma, stress, and anxiety will make life difficult to understand and navigate. Negative thoughts and emotions will take control and make functioning difficult. We isolate, seeking safety from perceived problems, which compounds our dysfunction. One need only look at the detrimental effects of the pandemic quarantine on our society.

Trauma incurred during childhood developmental years tends to damage normal emotional growth. Negative emotions can be ingrained into neuroplasticity so that events that would not be troublesome to healthy individuals can be catastrophic for wounded children. This is sometimes described as the "wounded inner child" or the "inner critic." A traumatized child can develop a negative inner conversation that further blocks healthy emotional growth.[8]

Trauma can take many forms: physical, emotional, mental, and spiritual. It results in negative beliefs about the self, negative emotional loops, fear of the future, and obsession with the past. Traumatized children can feel abandoned, rejected, guilty, ashamed, angry, afraid, and unsafe, all of which trigger the Warrior into action.

---

8   Sarah Peterson, "Effects of Complex Trauma," The National Child Traumatic Stress Network, June 11, 2018, https://www.nctsn.org/what-is-child-trauma/trauma-types/complex-trauma/effects.

Common symptoms, all of which I experienced, include:

- Feelings of self-pity
- Insecurity and constant need for validation
- Shyness
- Low self-worth
- Lack of boundaries
- Victimhood
- Attraction to abusers
- Shame/blame
- Fear of isolation
- Fear of rejection/abandonment
- Codependency
- Manipulative tendencies
- Attraction to emotionally unavailable people
- Fear of being hurt
- Lack of trust
- Selfishness
- Feelings of unsafety
- Poor decision-making
- Emotional repression
- Difficulty saying no
- Disempowerment in relation to authority figures
- Difficulty making friends

To heal this dysfunction, we need to understand how this process works to eliminate the causes of the dysfunction. In other words, we must learn how to support the Guru and downregulate the Warrior.

CHAPTER FOUR

Early Trauma

The year 1959 greatly expanded the world's view of itself, although my sixth year wasn't pleasant for me or my parents. The Soviets launched their first space rocket. Castro and Che Guevara overthrew Cuba, and the Communists established a foothold just miles from the US coast. Charles de Gaulle took office as president of France. Buddy Holly, Ritchie Valens, and others unexpectedly perished on "The Day the Music Died." The first successful test of a Titan intercontinental rocket was conducted. The Barbie doll debuted at the American International Toy Fair in New York City. Hawaii became recognized as the fiftieth state. Xerox introduced the first plain paper copiers. *The Twilight Zone* scared television audiences, and *Ben-Hur* became a box office smash.

Kitty and I suffered a total of twenty-seven earaches over that winter, more than our parents had time for or patience to deal with. Modern medicine would have put in ear tubes to help the ear canal drain and avoid infection. However, the medical thinking of the time dictated that the tonsils be removed, so at six years old, we went to the hospital named for my great uncle to have our tonsils removed.

For me, it was both a frightening and painful experience. Luckily, one of the hospital's policies for tonsillectomy patients was to give them ice cream to help with the pain and to make the children more compliant. As I was a bit larger than most children my age, I did not get to eat a lot of ice cream at home. At the hospital, I got to eat ice cream until my throat froze. I was in heaven.

My twin Kitty, on the other hand, loved the experience. She thought the doctors with their white coats were glorious and godlike, and the nurses who jumped at the doctors' command were the perfect servants. She was really, really, really impressed. Our divergent experiences probably dictated the different paths that we would eventually pursue. She would later become a revered doctor herself, while I became addicted to ice cream.

I later wondered which was better, to be a doctor or to eat a lot of ice cream. Many aspects of ice cream were more appealing. Doctors were always telling me what to do or what not to do, and were generally disagreeable. A lovely bowl of blueberry ice cream was always easy to get along with. My Guru and my Warrior also both loved ice cream, and it was generally next to impossible to find anything in my life that they agreed upon.

That summer, my family started vacationing in the Appalachian Mountains at the resort founded by Mr. Gray. With a spring-fed fifty-acre lake, stables, a golf course, tennis courts, and huge mansions dotting the ridge of the Appalachian Mountains, the wealthy families of North Carolina had created a summer retreat where they could hide from the Southern summer heat.

My mother loved this resort, and she had spent every summer of her youth at her father's ten-bedroom mansion overlooking the flat farmlands of the Piedmont. My father preferred the coast, but part of the price of marrying money is that you vacation where the money is. However, on these vacations, there always seemed to be a burr under my father's proverbial saddle. A big one.

I had to be especially careful when we were at the mountain palace, not to upset my father and his omnipresent Warrior. I loved to ride horses, and even though I was overweight, I was quite good at it. An early ability to get horses to cooperate was beginning to grow, and it was that summer when the seed of love for horses, planted at Mrs. O'Neill's family farm, began to fully bloom.

I would spend every spare moment at the stables. As I was just six years old, the hired help tried to shoo me away, but I was happy just sitting on the steps of the tack room watching the horses. I loved everything about it, including how much I could hear my Guru's song when I was near the horses. The closer I was to them, the more I could feel my Guru and hear the soulful tune. When the time for my ride finally arrived, I would jump up and run over to my assigned horse's stall and wait, every muscle in my body tense and excited to ride. My assigned horse was a dapple-gray thoroughbred that was old and bombproof. The stable owner could not afford the liability of putting the rich lawyer's kid on a skittish horse.

Even though I tried and tried to get the horse to gather up something more than a trot in the ring, it was far too old for such heroics. I wanted my father to see me ride so he would be proud of me for something. I kept begging him to come see, but he always had a round of golf with clients or businessmen from the flatlands. One day, though, he told me that he would play in the morning and be through in time to pick me up at the stables.

I was overjoyed, my Guru delighted at the chance. Finally, I was going to be able to show my father that I was good at something, at least in his eyes. Every time I came around the riding ring, I would glance at the big clock over the tack room that kept track of how long I had to ride. I was so concerned that my father would get there too late and miss me doing something I loved.

With five minutes to spare, my father arrived, and I couldn't wait to show off. I kicked the horse as hard as I could to get it to trot up to the fence where my father was standing. Unfortunately, the horse had been ridden hard that morning and had suffered quite enough of my heavy-handed tugging at the reins and attempts to maneuver. When I least expected it, the horse bucked.

The buck was not enough to toss me clear, but I lost my stirrups, and the horse took that as a cue to head back to the stall at a full gallop. I went upside down over the back of the horse in a backwards somersault, worthy of Hollywood's best stuntman. The one chance of my short life to impress my father ended with me landing on my arm and dislocating my elbow.

I was in shock. My Warrior was howling. Not only had my attempt to impress my father failed miserably, but I was also in excruciating pain. Being six years old, I did the only thing I knew to do, which was to start screaming in unison with my Warrior. My father was instantly overwhelmed with too much happening at once. Already in a bad mood because, as usual, he had not played well in his round of golf, he couldn't handle his son getting in a bad riding accident and screaming his head off—and a runaway horse.

My father also started screaming, at me, at the stable master, at God, and the four corners of the universe that he was going to sue their asses, and their grandchildren would starve to death after he was through with them. His Warrior was formidable to all. A quick trip to the resort infirmary revealed that I would have to wear a sling for a few weeks but wouldn't have any permanent injury.

After seeing me get seriously injured, my parents had a natural tendency to first go into shock in fear, and when that wore off, they wanted to punish me. Thus, I experienced not only the embarrassment of failing miserably in front of my father and the pain of a dislocated elbow, but the doubly painful spanking I got later for upsetting my father. My Warrior was infuriated. I was becoming more and more confused about whether my parents loved me or not.

A few weeks later, however, my sixth year came to an end with a fateful game of hide-and-seek at the Seagram compound. By that time, I had two younger sisters, a set of twins named Michelle Lisette

Johnson and Evelyn Crossley Johnson. Being the only son continued to be both a blessing and a curse.

A few neighborhood kids were in the hide-and-seek game as well, so there was a group of us playing. When trying to find a place to hide, I thought the chauffeur's quarters would be a perfect hiding place. Hiding in either the closet or under the bed did not require the athletic ability of climbing into the hayloft of their stables or up one of the apple trees in the orchard below the house.

As I walked towards the bed, I saw something I had never seen before. On the night table, there was a shiny, brand-new silver dollar. I didn't even know it was money. I had no need for money and did not know what it was for. I picked it up and put it in my pocket, planning to give it a better examination later. I had no idea there was anything wrong with what I did. The game wore on, and I finally came out from under the bed because I was getting bored.

I left the room and ran into our chauffeur. He was a black man named George Washington. George was known to drink when he was off duty. When he saw me come out of his quarters, George had bloodshot eyes and was not friendly. That was his only private domain, and he was understandably very possessive of his privacy.

He looked down at me and frowned, asking me what I was doing in his room. I shrugged and replied that I was hiding from my friends in a game of hide-and-seek and was hiding under his bed. George demanded to know if I had taken anything from his room. I was genuinely scared at that point, and forgetting the coin in my pocket, I said that I would never take anything from George. I escaped his suspicious glare and ran into the house to find my friends.

A bit later, my friends and I were playing on the lawn when my father exploded out of the front door of our house with George close behind. "James Gray Johnson!" he yelled, grabbing my healthy arm and dragging me into the house. I had never seen him so angry. Frozen with fear, I knew this one was going to hurt. My father was shaking with fury, jaws clenched through his thin lips.

He stood in front of me with his finger shaking. "James Gray, George says you took a silver dollar from his room. God help you if you did!"

I could not answer; I was frozen in place by the look in my father's eyes, the anger of his words, and the finger poking in my face. "I, I, I . . ." I stammered.

George said, "Mr. Johnson, you need to check his pockets!"

My father looked at George with the blood draining from his face. He had clearly expected me to deny taking the coin. It didn't take long for the truth to come out and my fate to be sealed. My father took George aside, pulling a twenty-dollar bill from his wallet, and put his arm around George to apologize.

While handing George the bill, he said, "I apologize for my son, and he will be sorry he ever went into your room. It will never happen again." Turning to me, my father simply said, "I will deal with you after supper."

Supper was a tense affair. My mother was crying into her bourbon, and my father wouldn't look at me. My sisters knew I was going to catch hell for the afternoon's misadventure. I almost threw up several times during the meal, having no stomach for food, knowing that I was about to be beaten. However, I also knew that I had to eat everything on my plate, or my punishment would be doubled. My Guru was already shrinking inside me to make room for my Warrior, who was expanding in size every second, preparing for an onslaught of pain.

With all the tugging and pulling during the brief but intense interrogation, my arm was throbbing and pulsing with little bolts of lightning running from my elbow to my wrist. Finally, I was called up to my parents' bedroom where my father was sitting on the end of the bed with his biggest, thickest belt in his massive hand. The room was dimly lit by one antique Chantilly lace lamp that my mother cherished and my father despised.

He simply said, "Drop your pants. I don't want to do this, because it is going to hurt me more than it is going to hurt you."

I couldn't help but take a small jab, which I soon paid for: "I doubt that."

My mother was nowhere to be seen. This caused my Warrior to go into overdrive, knowing It was the only one who could protect me.

Twenty minutes later, I was pulling my pants back up, wondering if I was bleeding anywhere. It certainly felt like it. Although there were only six blows, each one striped a line not only on my skin but grooved deeply into my soul. At that point, I became convinced that no one loved me and that my life would be one of suffering until the end of time. Afterwards, my father sent me to my room to "think about what I had done." I thought of it while my body throbbed and my Warrior roared, and I thought of that beating throughout the rest of my life.

I would be confused for a very long time about the notion of physical punishment and love. It didn't seem right for someone to claim that they loved me and then beat me with a demon-like passion. It just didn't add up for me. When I learned that stealing was bad and that what I had done was stealing, I understood that I shouldn't have done it. What I never understood was why my father never let me explain what happened, or where my mother disappeared to. She always vanished when punishment was about to be delivered, letting me know that she would never protect me.

The year was not quite over. During the Christmas holidays, my sisters and I played cowboy hide-and-seek in the downstairs playroom in our house. Before my mother started insisting that they act like ladies, they were quite the tomboys. They had no trouble roughhousing and playing games. It was tremendous fun; two of us would hide while the other two would try to find us. The object was to be the first to shoot our cap pistols at each other. The victim would be declared dead, and the game would continue until there was only one team left.

Unfortunately for my younger sister Lisette, we were on opposite sides and chasing after one another. We met each other under the staircase, she clumsily ran towards me, and her eye accidentally collided directly with the end of my gun. Time seemed to stand still, and then she started screaming. Clutching her face and wailing, she ran upstairs to the kitchen where my parents were eating breakfast before my father went to court.

Bedlam immediately broke loose. My parents thought I had punctured her eyeball, and they were freaking out. The bad news for me was that my father was in no mood for distractions of any kind, let alone this intensity, and decided to take it out on me. Once again, I was punished with his belt, but this time there was no conversation. He just came downstairs, grabbed me by the neck, and took me into the maid's bedroom. I don't remember how many times he whipped me; even my Warrior was in shock from the magnitude of my father's strength and fury. My Warrior instinctively knew that he was no match for my father's long-trained Warrior, but it didn't stop his resentment from starting to build a mighty fortress. I was sent to my room to "think about it."

After a trip to the emergency room, Lisette was told her injury wasn't permanent. She wore an eyepatch for cosmetic reasons and got to be a pirate for a few days. She finally did admit to my parents that it was an accident, and I hadn't meant to hurt her. What truly wounded me was that neither of my parents ever apologized for the beating my father gave me. Somehow, they assumed I would know it was a justified mistake.

My sister's bruises healed in a few days. The scars that the belt left on me didn't heal until sixty years later. My Guru still flinches a tiny bit when I think of it. In those days, the prevailing parenting belief was "spare the rod, spoil the child." I believe that if my father had any knowledge of how trauma damages the brain, he would not have sent me to my room "to think about it." The permanent damage comes from not supporting the child after the punishment. Banishing me to my room to think of how I deserved to be hurt only reinforced my identity development from the abuse. My brain ingrained the negative self-image into my neural pathways. My Warrior took it the hardest, as It hadn't been able to protect me. Its silent wrath grew leaps and bounds that day and would see through that lens for decades to come.

CHAPTER FIVE

Watch This!

My childhood was one injury after another. Today, I believe it was caused by the incredible imbalance between my Guru and my Warrior, but as a child, I simply thought that I was awkward and clumsy. The first major injury occurred when I was six years old. For most of my childhood, my parents thought it would be better to give Kitty and me a joint gift for our birthday and Christmas. I personally hated having to share every gift I received over the course of my childhood. To my way of thinking, having to share my gifts was as bad as not getting any at all.

For our sixth birthday, my twin and I had been given a Mickey Mouse projector set that would project slides of Disney characters on the wall while reading along with the book that came with it. Unfortunately, when we opened the present, we discovered that there were no batteries included. Nettie, our maid, and George Washington were quickly dispatched to the local drugstore. In the meantime, I was sent outside to play. I decided to go swing on the swing set we had been given the year before.

It was a large swing set, the envy of the neighborhood. It had six swings, a slide, a monkey bar, and a seesaw. Made with three-inch steel pipe and concreted into the ground, it made me feel invincible. My mother was in the process of planting daffodils and had been doing some landscaping with a rather sharp triangular hoe to dig through the red clay dirt around the house.

I had established myself as a daredevil, and I loved to see how far I could jump at the end of a swing's arc. Every time, I meticulously drew a line on the ground to record my prodigious leaps. When I really got going, I could launch myself fifteen feet or more in the air. My imaginary Olympic judges were in awe whenever I stuck a landing. If my sisters weren't watching, I would go so far as to bow to an imaginary audience and revel in the thunderous applause whenever I managed to beat my old record.

When George and Nettie pulled up in the driveway, I was very excited. So much so that I didn't see that my mother had put the hoe down on the ground to pick up a box of daffodils. She placed the hoe down point up, because she was a good twenty feet from the swings, and no one was nearby. She did not anticipate my attempt at a new world record.

When I launched myself from the swing, I knew I was going to set a new Olympic record in my personal competition. The trajectory was perfect. In the air, I could tell that it was much longer than any jump I had attempted before. I landed with precision that couldn't have been repeated, with my bare right foot directly onto the upward-pointing hoe. The hoe pierced the bottom of my foot and went straight through, the point coming out the other side. As my weight came down on the hoe, the handle pivoted up and caught me right between my eyes, knocking me unconscious. Far from the most fun birthday I ever had, it certainly was one of the most dramatic.

While I was unconscious, I remember having the strangest dream. I was in a large hall, filled with light, and there were a lot of people around me. "People" isn't the right word; they weren't flesh and blood.

They were more like ethereal bodies, filled with the most wonderful white light. The hall reminded me of a Greek temple and felt vaguely familiar. Inside it, I felt safe, content, and connected to the most wonderful energy I had ever experienced.

I was approached by a tall being I thought was an angel. "Welcome home." It spoke in a tone that sounded like it could effortlessly put anything that had ever been broken back together. Its voice lulled me as much as its words confused me. "*This is the first level of existence above the physical plane. There are many more, but this is the level where all souls exist at a higher consciousness.*"

I said, "I don't understand, where am I?"

The Angel replied, "*This is a dimension that is above the physical world. Most people recognize it as the place they go when they dream. You may see some things or people that seem familiar, just like in a dream. You perceive this dimension through your unique beliefs, thoughts, emotions, and experiences. It is different for everyone. Many people mistake this dimension for heaven, but you must go through this space to get to the dimension we call heaven.*"

I thought about this for a while and asked, "Who lives here?"

The Angel nodded and said, "*Good question. You must understand that the term 'life' only applies to the physical plane. You are perceiving beings in this dimension because you believe in that concept. You believe that there are angels. That is why you see me. If you had different beliefs, you would see me differently.*

In fact, you don't see me, because in this dimension you don't have eyes. You are experiencing me only through your (un)consciousness. You could 'see' me in the physical plane if you knew where and how to look."

"Will I experience this when I die?"

The Angel said, "*You will experience this dimension every time you let go of your body, whether you are unconscious, dreaming, or dead.*"

"So, am I dreaming?" I asked.

"Not exactly," said the Angel. "*Let's say that your awareness exists on many levels. The physical world is one dimension. This dimension* is another, which you experience when the logical mind shuts down, like now, when you are unconscious. Many more dimensions exist, depending on the level of your consciousness and what you learned on the physical plane."

"Will I remember this?" I asked.

The Angel said, "*Probably not. Memory is a function of your logical mind, and you are not thinking with your logical mind. You can access this dimension when you meditate. But you won't find out about meditation for another ten or fifteen years.*"

That seemed terribly far off to me. "Will I meet you on the physical plane?"

The Angel smiled and said, "*If you pay attention, yes.*"

Abruptly, I woke up and was whisked to the emergency room, blanketed, and strapped to a gurney. My foot was x-rayed and stitched, with a liberal application of anesthetic. I was issued a set of crutches and discharged with the admonition, "Be careful." My forehead also got a couple of stitches, during which my Warrior never left my side.

When I told the doctors about my dream, they just smiled and nodded. I asked them what it meant, and they tried to assure me it was just a dream. I was not so sure. It seemed real to me. When I got home, my father had arrived home from work. He looked at me and made his "spitting watermelon seeds" face, a mix of disgust and frustration with which I was all too familiar, and one my Warrior detested.

I knew my father was disappointed, if not disgusted with me, which made my injuries hurt even more. Dick felt like he was the brunt of a huge cosmic joke, having a son who was so accident-prone. He looked at me and only said, "You keep that up and you'll never get into West Point." That totally confused me. I didn't want to go to West Point. My father had other ideas.

To make matters worse, the family had made plans to go to the fair that was in town. My father announced that due to my unfortunate injury, the family trip to the fair would have to be canceled. The whole family was greatly disappointed with this turn of events. I loved the fair and begged my father to take us. I promised that I would not be a burden or hold them up. To show my father that I could keep up, I started hobbling through the house as fast as I could on my crutches.

When I got to the kitchen, my crutches slipped out from under me, and I crashed headlong into one of the hardwood chairs. The top of the chair caught me in the side, and I felt something crack, knocking the wind out of me. As I lay there trying to get my breath, my father ran up and started pounding me on the back to get me to breathe. This caused my ribs to torque and exacerbated the cracked ribs. I had to go straight back to the hospital. My Guru could barely believe how quickly it all happened, and my Warrior roared in pain and defeat, having failed to protect me yet again.

I was thoroughly miserable by the time I returned home. Being so young, the doctors felt that all I had to do was strap my torso as tightly as possible, and the ribs would heal on their own. Wearing the corset they gave me was extremely painful and restricted my breathing. I wheezed constantly, and with each wheeze came a sharp pain. Every step on the crutches was agonizing. I only wanted to go to bed, heal quickly, and never go back to the hospital again.

The next time I went to the hospital was even more dramatic. It was just a few months after my Olympic moment on the swing and the subsequent broken ribs. We had a poplar tree in the backyard with lots of branches for climbing. I was a natural-born climber, despite my size, and I loved seeing how high up in the tree I could get. This often caused problems because I would get stuck, unable to get myself down.

On this occasion, my twin had set a new high mark on the tree, going higher than either one of us had gone before. With a haughty air, she climbed back down and said to me: "You'll never get higher than that, the branches won't hold your weight."

She couldn't have done more to fuel my competitive fire, and of course my Warrior was always up for a challenge. I began to climb. Higher and higher I went until I got to my twin's mark. I looked around, and I had to admit that the branches that high were quite thin. But the thought of being bested by my twin was unacceptable to me.

I wrapped my arms around the tree's flimsy upper trunk and inched my way up. There was a branch about two feet above my hand, and if I could just touch that branch, I would set a new high mark. As I reached up, a strong breeze blew in, and the top of the tree started to sway. It wasn't much, but it was enough.

I grabbed at whatever I could, but I dropped to the ground, breaking branches as I fell. When I hit, the bones in my right ankle shattered. The pain shot up my leg and out through the top of my head, unable to be contained. Even though I had already experienced severe pain in my life, it couldn't compare to the sensation of my ankle being driven up into my shin bones. My Warrior howled like a wounded wildebeest. At first, I couldn't breathe, and I went into immediate shock. My mother came running out of the house to find me grimacing in pain with tears coming down my face, even though I was trying my best not to cry.

Trips to the emergency room had become routine. I knew what to expect: lying on the gurney, getting tucked into the familiar blanket, and being strapped down. The pain in my ankle was severe, and I couldn't talk much. I wanted to scream, but my Warrior was doing enough of that inside me. The X-rays showed that I had fractured two bones in my ankle but didn't need surgery.

The surgeons felt that I was young enough that the bones would pretty much heal if put in a cast, but I had to keep them immobile. That meant six weeks of immobility and boredom for me, but it also gave me a lot of time to read. My parents lectured me on being careless and taking unnecessary risks. Despite their admonitions, which felt hollow to me, as they would hurt me too, I would continue to be a regular visitor to the emergency room.

I started having dreams about the angels I had met when I was unconscious on my sixth birthday.

"You do realize that only angels can fly," mocked the Angel kindly.

I frowned. "I wasn't trying to fly."

The Angel asked, *"Then what were you doing?"*

"I was trying to be better than my sister."

The Angel laughed. *"Comparing yourself to others is a sure way to endure suffering."*

I said, "That is all I know, being compared to my sisters. And coming up short."

The Angel sighed. *"I know, and it will be a long time before you stop comparing yourself to others. That is one of the problems with humans, they all are trained to believe they must be better than their counterparts."*

"What about grades and school and athletics and first place and all of that?"

The Angel said, *"Eventually you will learn that all of that is an illusion, and you are best not trying to be better than anyone. Just be the best you can be."*

That sounded like rhetoric to me. "When will I learn that?"

The Angel smiled, *"Maybe never. But pain has a way of changing people's minds."* And then he vanished, leaving me with my numbing pain.

Perhaps the most traumatic event during my sixth year had nothing to do with physical pain. That year, my parents decided to clear some acreage beside the house and hired a company to cut down and clear away the dozens of pine trees that grew on that side of our home.

My mother instructed me that morning to stay inside while they were cutting trees. Excited by all the machinery and activity, I sat in the house, enviously watching the crew taking everything down. When the trees had all been felled, the crew started sawing up the trees for removal. I thought that it would be okay to go outside and see what they were doing.

I headed out and was sitting on one of the trees lying on the ground, watching the men chainsaw tree after tree into manageable lengths. It was fascinating to me; I would always love the power of a chainsaw. It wasn't long, though, before I heard my mother screaming at the top of her lungs for me to "get my ass inside."

Having never heard my mother use that kind of language before, I sensed something must be very wrong. I didn't think it had anything to do with me, as I had waited until the trees had been cut down as instructed. I ran at top speed to the house to find out what was happening.

When I entered the house, I found my mother in a total meltdown rage. She grabbed me and put me across her knee and started lashing me with a wide leather belt. With each blow, she would scream. "I [whack] TOLD [whack] YOU [whack] NOT [whack] TO [whack] GO [whack] OUTSIDE!" Both my Guru and my Warrior could barely believe what was happening. Usually, my mother failed us by allowing my father to beat me, but now she had become the bully herself. In that instant, I was totally alienated from my parents. I no longer felt safe with either one. My Warrior was ready to tear her to pieces.

I tried to tell her, between my tears and her repeated blows, that I had waited until all the trees had been cut like she had told me to. What I didn't know was that my mother had just come back from the beauty parlor, where she would usually drink at least a bottle of wine while she had her hair done. In that state, she was unable to understand what I was saying and thought I was being disrespectful.

After my beating, she finally started to calm down. She said, "I am sorry, but I had to teach you to obey me. You are never, ever allowed to go outside until I say so! GO TO YOUR ROOM!" I went up the stairs and wondered how in God's name I had been born into this family. My Warrior and I both schemed ways to escape.

It was that evening, while I was hiding in my room reading another science fiction novel, that I decided that I was really an heir to a royal family on a far-off planet, and I had been kidnapped and sold to this insane family. It was the only thing that made sense. The traumatic realization that my mother was no longer safe to trust at all and was as dangerous as my father was devastating. I vowed never to let down my guard and never be hurt again. I would be a warrior for the rest of my life!

CHAPTER SIX

Lasting Trauma

As you can see, my early life was repeatedly traumatic. No one ever commented on the number of injuries, verbal and physical discipline, and abuse I endured. If anything, I was told I had a normal childhood and that I was lucky to be born into such a successful and respected family. Unbeknownst to me, the seeds of future events were being sown.

I discovered that trauma can cause PTSD, which can go undiagnosed for years. I also suffered from depression, substance abuse, dissociation, and health problems, which were likely trauma-related. Traumatic stress can lead to long-term changes to the limbic system, the hippocampus, the amygdala, and the prefrontal cortex.[9] It leads to increased cortisol and norepinephrine responses to subsequent stressors. It reduces the size of the hippocampus (memory and neuroplasticity) and increases the functioning of the amygdala (threat detection and emotional regulation).

---

9   J. Douglas Bremner, "Traumatic Stress: Effects on the Brain," *Dialogues in Clinical Neuroscience* 8, no. 4 (December 31, 2006): 445–61, https://doi.org/10.31887/dcns.2006.8.4/jbremner.

I learned that PTSD caused many of my mental health problems, including intrusive thoughts and overthinking, nightmares and sleepwalking, memory and concentration disruptions, and panic attacks.

Fortunately, the brain's neuroplasticity allows it to recover from trauma. We can rewire and retrain the brain to reverse the effects of trauma. Left untreated, however, the effects of unhealed trauma can be devastating. My untreated trauma led to symptoms including:

- Negative assumptions about what others thought of me
- Reluctance to be transparent with others
- Difficulty compromising
- Inflexibility
- People-pleasing
- Suppressed emotions
- Difficulty in recognizing, regulating, or expressing emotions
- Anxiety, worry, and depression
- Nightmares
- Chronic pain
- Digestion disorders
- Panic attacks
- Inability to form relationships
- Low self-esteem
- Insecurity
- Depression
- Exhaustion
- Insomnia
- Unpredictable and irrational emotions
- Disorientation and overwhelm

- Short attention span
- Isolation
- Tension
- Brain fog
- Headaches
- Obesity

Anything that reminds us of past trauma can trigger a stress response, including:

- Smells
- Sounds
- Places
- Objects
- People
- People's characteristics or traits
- Situations
- Emotions

Probably the most debilitating aspect of trauma is that it keeps us focused on the past. We become obsessed with the past and find it difficult to get over the memories of the trauma. Anything that even remotely reminds us of past trauma captures us back in the moment of pain.

Trauma distorts the ego, which was originally a survival technique. A healthy ego is integral to the individuation of each person and makes us who we are. It is primarily involved in self-interest, hunting and gathering, winning, mating, and rivalry for supremacy, all of which are necessary in competitive societies.

Even the untraumatized ego function can be destructive:

- The ego separates us from society ("I" versus "we").
- The ego is insatiable.
- The ego is averse to the unknown.
- The ego hates lack of control.
- The ego craves attention.
- The ego must win and take credit.
- The ego enjoys the suffering of others.
- The ego loves the spotlight.
- The ego resists letting go.
- The ego hates being ignored.
- The ego is desire and always wants more.
- The ego clings to the past and fears the future.
- The ego cannot forgive.

The traumatized ego, on the other hand, metastasizes these traits into all-consuming flaws. Narcissism, codependency, attachment disorders, and other personality disorders can result from a damaged ego. This interferes with a healthy self-image and interpersonal relationships. Left untreated, the damaged ego can make life a living hell of guilt and shame.

CHAPTER SEVEN

Shame Enough for All

In 1963, the United States experienced dramatic change. John F. Kennedy was assassinated, and Lyndon Johnson became president, which resulted in a major expansion of the conflict in Vietnam. AT&T introduced the first push-button telephone. The US cut off all relations with Cuba. *Lawrence of Arabia* won the Oscar for best movie, and Tito was named president for life in Yugoslavia. Tab was the first diet drink sold by Coca-Cola. Zip codes were instituted by the US Postal Service. The first instant replay was used during the Army-Navy football game.

By the time I turned ten, I was still a "husky" boy. In 1963, the term husky was a kinder version of obese. There was a special husky boys' section in the local clothing store, and I was already starting to feel uncomfortable watching my sisters go to the normal-sized clothing racks while I had to go to the husky section.

I wasn't terribly self-conscious about my size yet, but all of that was going to change soon. My biggest complaint was that the choices of clothing in the husky section were limited, while brighter patterns and colors were abundant in the "normal" section. This was 1963, after all. Dark grays and blues felt drab and colorless, and I was starting to appreciate more hippie-style clothes. Unfortunately, I could only get those clothes about halfway up my thighs before volume conquered style.

There was a bright spot that year to my clothing dilemmas. The local clothing store held an annual fashion show, and that year it was going to be held at Graylyn, the French Renaissance castle built by my granduncle Bowman Barclay in the 1920s. They moved into the huge residence in 1932. The house had been brought over from France and was 46,000 square feet with sixty rooms.

With our family connections to Bowman Barclay and to cement our family's business, the clothing store invited my twin and me to be models in the fashion show. I had clothes specially tailored for me, and I thought I looked rather dashing in the sports coat and pants, gaily colored and of the best fabrics. My Guru swooned at the sight of me in them, and I was feeling good.

We paraded through the house, runway style, where the guests were seated. We were the delight of the show, and the patrons laughed and applauded as we passed by. I was in heaven. I relished the attention and the feel of being dashing. My Guru loved the dynamic colors and this newfound feeling. At one point, I opened my jacket to show the bright paisley lining to the crowd. They went wild, and my Guru and I both basked in the attention.

The clothing store let us keep the clothes we modeled, and I was overjoyed. Finally, I would have some brightly colored clothes I could wear! I couldn't bear to take them off and lose that feeling. When I got home, I proudly wore my new clothes to the dinner table. My father took one look at me and started yelling.

"Take those awful clothes off, right now!" he roared.

I was mortified and stammered, "But Dad, I love them. Can't I wear them for a little while longer?"

My father slammed his hand down on the table as his face turned explosively red. "Absolutely not! No son of mine is going to wear girly clothes. Take them off immediately. I am going to burn them!"

I started shaking with disappointment and fear. Even my Warrior hadn't seen this coming, but It was now standing on the table, meeting my father's eyes with steel in Its own. I couldn't understand why my father was so upset. I was even more distraught over not being able to wear the clothes anymore. Rather than getting hit, I slowly got up from the table and went upstairs to change my clothes. I was in shock from being yelled at for simply wearing something I liked. I couldn't get my mind around it. I slowly changed clothes and went back downstairs. In a bit of silent rebellion, I took off my shirt and returned wearing only shorts.

When I got downstairs, my father looked at me, his eyes still seething with disgust. What I didn't know, and would not find out for years, was that my father had just heard a rumor that his brother had come out of the closet and announced that he was gay. My father was so infuriated about it that seeing what he thought could be an indication that his only son was gay caused his blood pressure to approach heart attack levels.

My father was extremely sensitive about his position in society and would not allow his wife or children to do anything that could jeopardize that standing. He always felt a bit ostracized by Charlotte society because he visualized himself as a Horatio Alger type and was constantly petrified that something would happen to alienate him from elite social circles. He was also extremely intolerant and was going to nip any sign of such behavior in me "in the bud."

When he saw me without a shirt, emphasizing my rolls of fat, my father blew another gasket. He was trying to teach me how to dress in a proper masculine fashion, and not wearing a shirt to the dinner table flew in the face of those efforts. What he said next would destroy my confidence and self-esteem for years: "Well, why don't you wear a bra with those tits?"

I had no idea how to respond to that. Even my Warrior was speechless, even though It was ready for retaliation. I looked at my mother, but she quickly looked away. I stared down at my plate and didn't say a word, willing myself not to cry. My father then laughed and tried to turn it into a joke, and my sisters joined in the laughter. It felt like they were laughing at me, and I made every effort to sink in my chair through the imported mahogany floor below me. Plunging into self-loathing, I soon turned the dagger my Warrior carried as defense and drove it into my own heart. At that moment, my Warrior shut off any feelings for my sisters. They were clearly part of the enemy camp.

I could only shake my head and wonder how parents could be so cruel and disconnected from the effect their words had on their children. It would be more than a decade before I regained any confidence and pride. That night, I had one of my mystical dreams.

"So how are you feeling?" asked the Angel.

"Like shit," I said.

"You certainly chose a dramatic classroom to grow up in," said the Angel.

"What do you mean?" I asked, thoroughly confused.

"We all choose how we are going to grow up and what we learn while we are growing up. Don't let your father's problems get you down," the Angel said.

"I don't understand what you are getting at."

"That's okay," said the Angel. *"One day you will."*

I couldn't hide my bitterness. "That is not at all helpful."

"One day you will understand that when people say mean things, it isn't about you, it is about them," said the Angel. *"One day, you will appreciate all the lessons you are learning about how not to be. The only way that we can appreciate the light is when we experience darkness."*

I stared at the Angel, and my Warrior helped me to form the words. "That is the most ridiculous thing I have ever heard."

The Angel looked at me for a while and then smiled. He said, *"Just keep breathing."*

CHAPTER EIGHT

The Legacy of Shame

As I grew up feeling ashamed, I could not know what was happening to my brain, personality, or feelings of depression. When faced with shame, the brain reacts as if faced with physical danger, activating the Warrior and the fight/flight/freeze response. Children who feel shame want to disappear. They will shrink and slouch, and their expressions become blank. The Warrior interferes with our ability to think clearly and makes us feel that we are powerless because there is something wrong with us.

As infants, we learn how to interact with our parents and other caregivers based upon how our needs are met. These experiences are stored in our memory, in our limbic system, and color our interpretation of life. When we do not bond with our caregivers because we don't feel safe, the result is Attachment Deficit Disorder.[10]

Attachment disorders are psychiatric illnesses that impact children who do not bond with authority figures. This can cause reluctance to form personal relationships, or the opposite, a lack of discretion about

---

10   Karl Heinz Brisch, *Treating Attachment Disorders: From Theory to Therapy* (Guilford Publications, 2014).

who the child relates to. When abuse, trauma, or neglect create attachment disorders, children can exhibit:

- Withdrawal, fear, sadness, or irritability
- Not seeking comfort or showing no response when comfort is given
- Failure to smile
- Not engaging in social interaction

Adults who were abused by their parents can also exhibit these traits and have trouble forming close relationships. This results from a child not having a consistent emotional connection with their parents. Adults can have anxiety about their relationships and be uncomfortable with intimate relationships. They may prioritize independence in their relationship because their parents were not aware of their needs.

Adults can also fear rejection and abandonment, causing low self-worth and esteem issues in relationships. They don't feel worthy and are reluctant to express their needs because their partners may reject them. They also may exhibit conflicting behaviors, craving intimacy yet pushing people away. Their relationships are chaotic and unpredictable.

In many cases, people with attachment disorders seek out substance abuse to feel better and get high. Their relationship with the substance of choice replaces the nonexistent relationship of their youth. Even more difficult is that the consequences of substance abuse fit with their perception that they deserve to suffer. A child who is the victim of toxic shaming has a dilemma. They can experience the arousal of the Warrior and the Guru at the same time. The result is that they sit and spin their tires, unable to move forward in their understanding of other relationships they encounter later in life. This is because the toxic shame experienced in childhood impacts the limbic system (hippocampus).

In childhood, our limbic system internalizes via memory how we should respond to situations where we feel uncomfortable or uncertain.

If we are mistreated, our limbic system internalizes negative messages about ourselves and what we can expect from others.

The effect is that when we encounter uncomfortable situations later in life that remind us in any way of what we encountered in childhood, we feel shame. This triggered response then sends us spiraling into a complicated dance of arousal and fear that adversely affects how we form new relationships with others. We also focus on what can go wrong with the relationship, rather than what could be right.

Prolonged shame can result in permanently flawed autonomic nervous system responses and inappropriate imbalance between the Warrior and the Guru. This creates a heightened sense of vulnerability to others. When shame causes us to believe that there is something wrong with us, we have no power. We think everything is our fault.

Children's lives are marked by chronic anxiety, exhaustion, depression, and a losing struggle to achieve perfection, because shame generates the formation of low self-esteem, anxiety, irrational guilt, perfectionism, and addiction. Depression, eating disorders such as bulimia and anorexia nervosa, PTSD, and complex PTSD are only a few of the mental health issues related to toxic shame.

The messages we internalize in childhood during a highly traumatic event cause feelings of helplessness and victimization. We see life and other human beings as potential threats to our well-being, and our limbic systems are constantly on the alert in a hyper-aroused state, looking for danger. We isolate ourselves in anxiety and shame.

The damage to our self-esteem limits our ability to seek out and enjoy satisfying relationships. We are afraid to trust because it opens us up to hurt and pain. We are terrified. We may be consumed with self-hate and rage, and feel alienated from the people around us.

We can become codependent on others. We feel we must care for others because taking care of ourselves is wrong. If we do find a relationship, we must maintain that relationship at all costs because we will never find anyone else. We can't instill boundaries because we think to ourselves, "No one else will ever want me." The isolation, fear, or codependency leaves us trapped in a quagmire of pain that we need help to escape.

A Word from Kitty

I never know how to act when my father attacks my brother. He's my twin. We share a closeness that may lie way under the surface, yet it is there. And when he is hurt, a small ache throbs in the center of my heart. But we're all afraid of our father, so my brother not only suffers those wretched embarrassments and violent punishments from my father, but he also experiences every female in his life watching it all in silence.

I've watched my brother's body expand, while I stay slim. Of course I know that, as a girl, I must stay as small and pretty as I can, and he probably doesn't feel that, but I also suspect that it is another way that he hides.

He's often hiding. But truthfully, I think everyone in this family is always hiding something. Father hides in work, my mother in all her pills and "elixirs," my brother in reckless pursuits, and my little sisters will surely figure out their ways of hiding soon enough. The words unspoken in our house behave like ghosts, haunting each of us with different lures.

When our father told my brother to wear a bra, my Warrior screamed so loudly I almost fell out of my chair. "Do something!" It cried over and over. "What kind of sister are you? Help him! Defend him!" The cries were so overwhelming that I had to grit my teeth as tightly as I could so that I wouldn't scream myself. The power of unspoken words is mighty.

But I've never been able to stand up to our father. I guess I take after my mother in that way, because she doesn't do it either. I wonder if her Warrior is screaming as deafeningly as mine. I wonder if my Warrior would stop if I did take a stand.

Our last trip to the hospital gave me a glimpse of some way that I can be of service, of some way that I can help others in ways I cannot help my own brother. Some of the doctors, and many of the nurses, were so kind that I could literally feel their Gurus convincing mine to come out of its hiding place.

That hospital stay showed me a glimpse of who I can be, if I can quiet my Warrior's screams and create a life where my Guru can thrive.

For now . . . continuing with our unspoken family tradition (so very much unspoken!), I'll keep it a secret. I watch my father already grooming my brother for West Point, and although many things are hard about being a girl, in this case I feel lucky. The only expectation for me is that I "marry well." And have babies. And do as I'm told. So I'll stay quiet as I'm supposed to and plan my future on my own. I dare not even write about it in my diary for fear that someone will somehow discover it and try to block my path.

I shall keep it between me and my Guru.

And for all the ways that I'm failing my brother, someday my work will make it right. Someday our Gurus can sit together, and I can tell him: "I'm sorry."

Someday. Till then, I'll block out my Warrior's cries however I can and learn to find the places where I can hear my Guru.

Wish me luck.

CHAPTER NINE

How Do You Spell Pneumonia?

By 1965, the world was swiftly changing. The sit-ins by black students at the Greensboro Woolworth's in 1960 had begun the civil rights movement. John F. Kennedy's brief, brilliant career had come and tragically gone. Civil unrest swept much of the country, with rioting in Watts and DC. Malcolm X had been assassinated. The war in Vietnam was escalating, the race into space was in full swing, and the march to Selma led to the passage of the Voting Rights Act. Most of this escaped me in my insulated, silk-lined prison of affluence. At the end of 1965, I would once again end up in a hospital—for a much longer stay.

In December 1965, both Kitty and I came down with the flu. The pediatrician had come over to give us antibiotic shots. He had a clever way of giving his shots. He would tell his patient that he would give the injection on the count of three, and then give it when he said "two." The purpose was to make sure the patient was not clenching their muscles when the needle went in, because that just made it worse. It didn't foster a great deal of trust in doctors, however.

Having suffered countless injections, I knew that I needed to be relaxed, but knowing his trick well, I involuntarily clenched at "two." When the doctor pulled the trigger and inserted the needle, it hurt ten times more than it had to, but that seemed to be my lot in life. I couldn't know it yet, but I was becoming addicted to the pain, addicted to my Warrior responses. The regret titled "If only I had relaxed" would play out repeatedly in my life.

Three days later, Kitty started feeling better, but I was getting worse. I was having a hard time breathing, and I slept most of the day. I started dreaming of that hall with the light people again, and I was running a fever of 103°F+. After a week had passed, I was taken to the hospital for diagnosis. A battery of tests determined that I had double bronchial pneumonia, which was potentially fatal. I stayed in the hospital for observation for four days and was then sent home with a basket full of medication. The doctors indicated that if the fever didn't break within a few days, I would have to come back.

I continued to sleep more than eighteen hours a day. My fever wasn't coming down, and I had to have my lungs cleared every few hours. This consisted of me lying on my stomach with my head below my waist while someone whacked me on the back repeatedly. This broke the congestion in my lungs, which I would then have to cough out. Both my Guru and my Warrior stayed right by my side, hating every second of it.

It was very painful and exhausting, and I felt like I was going to die. I spent Christmas in bed, not even going downstairs to see what Santa had brought. At that point, I couldn't care less. After a week, the fever was still 103°F+ and not coming down. So back to the hospital I went.

I started to dream of the angels again. "Well, this sucks," I thought.

The Angel responded, *"You are too depressed. This is God's way of slowing you down and making you rest. You are thinking way too many negative thoughts about yourself."*

I thought for a minute. "Well, you'd be depressed too if you had to live with my family."

"Probably not," said the Angel. *"It all has to do with your attitude, how you think about things. You could recognize how lucky you are to have such a rich family. You live in a beautiful home, you have plenty to eat, and you have an allowance. Life is pretty good for you."*

I contemplated that for a few minutes. "I just get so tired of hearing my parents say what a sacrifice they are making for us. My father is always talking about how hard he works, and my mother is always talking about all the things she does for us. Why don't they just have fun? If money means being miserable all the time, what good is it?"

The Angel responded, *"That is what I am talking to you about. You need to act like you're happy and having fun. Find something to focus on that pleases you. Just because you aren't getting your way doesn't mean you can't be happy. That is what is meant by the saying, 'Bloom where you are planted.' Maybe you chose this family because you are the only one in it who can be happy. Teach them something."*

I tried to protest. "But I'm a kid, why should I have to—?" But the Angel had disappeared.

The doctors put me on an IV because I had become dehydrated, and it was easier to administer antibiotics. After a few days of this, my fever finally broke, and I was allowed to go home. By that time, I had missed several weeks of school, and my parents were worried that I would have to repeat a grade. My twin was complaining because I didn't have to go to school. I begged to have my teachers send home my lessons so I could catch up.

Being a voracious reader, I quickly got back up to speed and avoided having to repeat the grade. One night, however, I got out of bed to go to the bathroom and slipped on the schoolwork that I had placed on the floor around my bed. I fell, breaking two ribs by landing hard on the footboard pedestal.

My mother heard the loud thump all the way down in the kitchen and came running, already anticipating another accident on my part. She found me curled in the fetal position, holding my ribs, trying to squeeze them back into place. She screamed at me, "What did you do?"

All I could get out was, "I fell, and I can't breathe."

My mother struggled to get me to my feet and walked me down the stairs. She said to me, "Good lord, Gray, are you trying to die? Haven't you been to the hospital enough? Your father is going to be so mad!"

I could only gasp for air; my ribs were throbbing, and it felt like a three-pronged scythe was stuck into my side.

Back to the hospital we all went, for the fourth time in five weeks. I was x-rayed and bandaged, the doctors finding that there had been no damage to my weakened lungs. Having cracked ribs while healing from double pneumonia was extremely painful. I had constant trouble breathing, a condition I carried with me the rest of my life. I had to focus to take a deep breath. Eventually, though, everything finally healed, and at the end of January I was allowed to go back to school. It was the only time I had ever been happy to return to school. Both my Guru and my Warrior couldn't wait to escape my house either.

CHAPTER TEN

Trauma and Teenagers

The traumatic events I experienced during my teenage years seemed to be even more excruciating than those in earlier years. Traumatic events are circumstances that threaten our safety and place our lives or the lives of those close to us at risk. It seemed like when anything unexpected happened, I would go into panic mode, and I couldn't function. I noticed that I tended to bounce back and forth between independence and insecurity in life, which greatly expanded after any traumatic events.

If the trauma is caused by parents or authority figures, teenagers tend to bury their feelings rather than argue with an authority figure whom they don't trust. Teenagers react to trauma differently than children or adults.[11] A child will look for support from close family members. A teenager will look for support from their peers.

Teenagers can experience strong feelings of sadness, anxiety, anger, and terror, which they will repress rather than seem vulnerable and seek help. They tend to overreact to minute irritations and obsess

---

11   "VA.gov | Veterans Affairs," n.d., https://www.ptsd.va.gov/understand/what/teens_ptsd.asp.

over the trauma. They only think about the trauma, which ironically keeps them in Warrior mode. They can't sleep, and they withdraw from family members.

To find some feeling of safety, teenagers are drawn to their peer group for validation and support. Unfortunately, most teenagers can be unkind and are not equipped to deal with the demons of a traumatized friend. If they can't find support from their peer group, they will isolate themselves. They may even regress and reject responsibility or become rebellious.

Some teenagers may seem unfocused and uncaring about their situation, detached, and lost. They may engage in high-risk endeavors, embracing unsafe behavior and habits. Promiscuity and drugs are often used as part of this pattern.

It is believed that trauma shrinks the hippocampus, the part of the brain responsible for storing short-term memories and recalling long-term memories. It also affects the frontal cortex, which diminishes the teenager's ability to learn and retain new information. Teenagers with unprocessed trauma have problems with decision-making, suffer from chronic fear, and can't discriminate between threatening and safe circumstances.

Strong, frequent, and prolonged trauma rewires the adolescent brain and interferes with the functioning of their emotions and body. Not only is the hippocampus affected, but the amygdala can be damaged as well. The amygdala is the gateway to the Warrior and the Guru. It is the part of the brain that assesses whether circumstances are safe or not. If not, the Warrior is activated, and the teenager can overreact, obsess, enter fight-or-flight mode, or freeze.

Additionally, trauma affects the frontal cortex and the teenager's ability to observe and analyze their world and learn new things. It can also impair their ability to think rationally and logically. Connected to the frontal cortex is the anterior cingulate cortex. This part of the brain helps us to regulate emotions. When damaged by trauma, the teenager has problems managing their emotions. Emotions get stuck in their consciousness and linger in their thoughts. Irritation, anger, fear, and other negative emotions are amplified out of proportion to their cause.

The negative effect of trauma on adolescents is multiplied when the parent creates the trauma. I often overreacted to any criticism or guidance from my parents that reminded me of past traumatic events. Ironically, I found myself repeating that behavior with my own children, which made me feel like it was a generational curse.

I was desperate to receive love, support, and a sense of safety from my parents. Instead, whenever I received criticism or emotional and physical abuse, it disrupted my sense of who I was, and I never felt safe around them. As a result, I experienced a lack of emotional management, intense negative emotions, trust issues, fear of rejection and abandonment, negativity, and heart conditions.

I was not aware that these events were laying paths for future problems.

CHAPTER ELEVEN

The Vacations from Hell

In 1966, popular music was dominated by the Beach Boys, the Rolling Stones, and the Beatles. Protests of the Vietnam War were becoming more frequent; the US had five hundred thousand troops in Vietnam. Cassius Clay changed his name to Muhammad Ali and refused induction into the military. The Supreme Court ruled that suspects had to be informed of their Miranda rights before they were interrogated. Miniskirts came into fashion as the women's movement continued to gain momentum. The US Department of Transportation was created. The US and the Soviet Union raced neck and neck to the moon. Ronald Reagan became the governor of California.

When I turned thirteen, it was cause for a huge celebration in my family. We were the first twins in our extended family, and our thirteenth birthday was a big deal socially. My father made it known that he wanted me to be his legacy at the United States Military Academy at West Point. I wasn't so sure about that, but what the hell, that was a long way off and I didn't want to start any arguments. That always ended badly for me.

Instead of having a coming-of-age celebration for my sister and me, my father decided that what his highly dysfunctional family needed was some quality time together. Although he knew little about boats, and even less about Florida, he announced that he was going to take us on a houseboat cruise through the inland waterways of Florida. We were to leave the docks at the north end of Lake Okeechobee and proceed west through the Everglades until we got to the Gulf of Mexico and turned north to Tampa. In keeping with his military background, my father enrolled himself and me in a motorboat course to learn navigation, the rules of the seas, and motor craft maintenance.

The fateful summer of my thirteenth year approached, and we piled into our Vista Cruiser station wagon for the trip to Florida. This would be the longest trip we had ever taken together and the longest period of captivity we had to endure. My Warrior was on high alert, and my Guru busied itself with extra singing and fervent prayers. The drive down to Florida was long, hot, boring, and a foreshadowing of the weeks to come. My father entertained us with descriptions of the adventure we were going to have, the huge and modern houseboat on which we would sail, and the exotic places we were going to visit.

When we arrived at the marina in Okeechobee, we went out to look at the houseboats docked in the marina. There were some beautiful ones and some not-beautiful-at-all ones. My father went in to talk to the harbormaster and take possession of the magnificent boat he had described to the family.

Like a scene from a comedy movie, while we were out admiring the boats we thought we would be getting, the harbormaster took my father to a far dock where an old, worn, somewhat dilapidated houseboat was moored. Upon sight, my mother instantly said, "I am not getting on that boat." My father was caught in a dilemma. He tried to bully the harbormaster into renting him a nicer boat, but the harbormaster stood firm and reminded my father he had wanted a cheaper rental, and this was all he had at that price. My father, with the rest of us anxiously standing by watching, had to decide whether to take what he had paid for, rent a much more expensive boat, or go home. Since there was no refund, my father chose door number one and decided to take the boat offered.

The rest of the family was mortified. Not only was the boat questionably seaworthy, but it also stank, was too small for the six of us, and the air-conditioning unit that had been slapped on the side of the boat didn't work. Besides that, there was only a single fifty-horsepower outboard motor powering the craft, which was woefully inadequate.

Rather than admit defeat or surrender, my father put on a game face and started loading the gear. My mother was horrified. Nothing in her upbringing or adult life had prepared her for this kind of grueling expedition. True to form, she marched back to the marina and bought every bottle of wine the little store had. She even bought a few bottles of bourbon—my father's favorite—because she knew the situation called for extreme measures. You could hear the Warriors of the whole family vehemently sharing their fear about the upcoming trip.

In any event, we got on the boat and cast off. There was one small bed in the aft compartment that barely held two adults. My sisters and I would have to sleep on the couches along the sides of the boat. There was only one bathroom (called the head), which had seen better days and smelled of sewage and bilge water. My father sailed out of the marina before anyone could run to the car and lock themselves in.

Although my father was generous, he was very frugal. (Later a law partner would say that was the kindest word he could think of to describe Dick's love of money.) It drove my mother up a wall and surely contributed to her steady diet of wine and liquor. Even though my mother was extremely wealthy from her inheritance, my father insisted on staying in cheap motels and eating at modest roadside stands when he traveled with the family.

We, the intrepid crew of the SS Minnow, headed south out on Lake Okeechobee on our incredibly adventurous vacation (cue the theme song of *Gilligan's Island*). My father had been warned by the harbormaster that a storm was brewing out on the lake, and he should wait until the storm was over before he went out. He ignored the warning, as that would have added another day to the trip, and he refused to deviate from his plan. When we got to the middle of the lake, the storm hit.

Lake Okeechobee is one of the biggest lakes in the southeast, and the seventh largest lake in the United States. It is also referred to as Florida's inland sea or the "Big O." Surprisingly, it is only nine feet deep at its deepest parts, all of which means that a thunderstorm coming across the lake will generate hellacious waves.

In our case, the waves exceeded ten feet and came rolling in with fierce intensity. It took both Dick and me to hold onto the steering wheel and keep the boat from heading into the waves. If any of the waves had hit the craft broadside, we would have capsized like a rowboat.

It was the most terrified I had ever been. My father kept screaming at us to "hold on!" The rest of the family had retreated into the back bedroom, where one or more of them were getting sick. There was not enough room in the shower-stall-sized bathroom for everyone, so the master bedroom was quickly coated with vomit.

Luckily, we came through the storm unscathed. Much to my mother's dismay, most of the wine had been destroyed, and obviously the bedroom was a mess. If looks could kill, my father would have been fish bait in the first ten minutes after the storm subsided.

Ironically, the storm had blown us so far off course that we lost a day getting back on course. It would have been easier to stay at the marina after all. We got the bedroom cleaned up and put the mattress up on the roof of the houseboat to air and dry out. My mother took out some of her expensive perfume and sprayed it copiously around the bedroom to cover the stench.

Eventually, we got to the western entrance to the Intracoastal Waterway to Tampa. For those who have never been in the Everglades or central Florida, there is absolutely nothing to see for hundreds of miles but swamp and Brahman cattle, which were bred for hot climates and insect resistance. There was a booming business raising cattle for the fast-food industry, and central Florida had some of the largest ranches in the country. As far as excitement goes, it was a total bust.

After the first day trolling along the inland waterway, we were introduced to the mosquitoes and horseflies that make the region nearly uninhabitable. The horseflies had a hideous waxy green head and could bite a chunk of flesh out of any unsuspecting human who unwisely ventured into their realm. This forced us indoors with the malfunctioning air conditioner. After two days of this, my mother's liquor supply ran out, and she started her period. To say things were not going well was a huge understatement.

I had never heard her scream at my father like that before. The volume and profanity increased when she found out there were no hotels for the next 250 miles. The only civilization within that range was local gas marinas that only sold gas and bait. My mother's Warrior was ready to explode, and Its energy caused everyone else's anxiety to heighten too.

It took a week to travel the 250 miles from Lake Okeechobee to the western coast of Florida. The water was brackish and looked more like sewage than the pristine water my father had promised. It wasn't long before the family discovered the water lilies that clogged the waterway from time to time and fouled the propeller repeatedly. Even something so beautiful was a scourge on this cursed trip.

When the propeller became entangled, I was ordered to go into the water and unwrap the lily pad stems from the blade. I was terrified of snakes and alligators, and every time I went in the water, I knew I was going to die. Each time I had to go in, I shut down more and more until I was totally numb.

By the time the boat got to the western reaches of the Florida coast, it was fortunate that there were no weapons of mass destruction on board. My mother was reduced to a sullen mess, hating the small bathroom, lack of shower, and especially the lack of alcohol to dampen the effects of her period and her frustration at the horrific trip. Whatever misery the trip had unloaded on the rest of us, hell has no fury like our mother in that condition.

Eventually, we got to the Gulf of Mexico, and for the first time in ten days, smiles broke out on our faces. The water was clear and warm, and we could anchor and swim without worrying about being blindsided by some amphibious nightmare from below. The next day, when we were returning the boat, we pulled into the marina and all of us got off and kissed the planks of the dock. Our Gurus gave a collective sigh of relief—no one had died or killed anyone else on the trip. As a final punctuation to the misadventure, my father got into a pushing match with the harbormaster, who charged him one hundred dollars more than expected to bring our station wagon from Lake Okeechobee.

We spent the night in a nice hotel in Tampa (my mother insisted) and had a great meal, which I still remember. It was a popular Cuban seafood restaurant, and I had the all-you-can-eat shrimp special. I made my parents proud by eating about three pounds of shrimp with all the fixings. Unfortunately, I spent most of the night in the bathroom throwing up because I wasn't used to the spicy Cuban food. It was the perfect terrible ending to a perfectly awful trip. No one spoke of the great Florida vacation ever again.

One would think that my father would learn from his experiences, but in true military fashion, he decided to recreate the scene of the crime the next summer. In 1967, I thought it was an exciting year to be approaching fourteen in the United States. The first ATMs were introduced. The Vietnam War was escalating. Israel defeated Jordan in the Six-Day War and recaptured East Jerusalem. Thurgood Marshall was the first black appointee to the United States Supreme Court. The first heart transplant was successfully performed by Dr. Christian Barnhart in South Africa.

An old proverb states that the definition of insanity is repeating the same behavior and expecting different results. At the end of my thirteenth year (approaching my fourteenth birthday), my father declared that the problem with the previous summer's vacation was the boat, and he had found a much bigger and grander boat he could rent in Miami. He had decided that we were going to do another houseboat trip, but this time on the eastern coast of Florida to enjoy the sparkling waters of the Keys, far away from the Everglades, cattle, mosquitoes, and horseflies. I had grave concerns about this.

In an overwhelming bout of déjà vu, we piled into our station wagon and headed to Miami for the "reload" of last year's houseboat vacation. My father kept soothing everyone's concerns with promises of a much different experience due to the lessons of last year's debacle. Never one to give up on anything, my father passed around photographs of the new boat we would be renting for the cruise through the Keys.

It was a beautiful houseboat, looking more like a yacht. My father had spared no expense this time, under the merciless eye of my mother. We would be docking at various resorts along the way for air-conditioned rooms, showers, restaurant food, and white sand beaches. Call bribery what you will, the trip sounded more like a vacation than last year's rite of passage.

We got to the marina in Miami, and everyone piled out of the car in anticipation of seeing our luxury houseboat. For some reason, it was a good hour before my father returned, and the look on his face foretold grim news. He gathered us around and reported that the houseboat we rented was in dry dock for emergency repairs. "Don't worry, we have been promised a good boat." I looked at him with some trepidation. What kind of boat would they have?

The family walked down the pier to where the houseboats were moored. As we approached, I was somewhat encouraged by the large, modern houseboats. We got to the slip where our houseboat was moored, and we froze in disbelief. It was an identical version of the houseboat we had rented the year before.

Mutiny instantly ensued. My mother's eyeball dissection of my father's testicles was classic. He shrugged and then bowed up, turning into the commander in chief. "Silence!" he barked. "I know this looks like the boat we had last year, but it isn't. The air conditioner works, and it has two inboard-outboard engines." The reluctant crew climbed on board and, after a cursory inspection, had to admit that it was a bit cleaner, bigger, and more modern than the last boat. We loaded our luggage and food onto the houseboat and shoved off.

To get to the waterway south of Miami, we had to go through the millionaire enclaves that dot the eastern shores of Miami. We climbed up on top of the roof and marveled at all the million-dollar yachts and homes. We had never seen the new wealth of Miami; it was impressive. The yachts and homes of the islands of Biscayne Bay sparkled white in the sunlight.

The impression was short-lived, however, as the idyllic sights and sounds of the affluence of Miami were pierced by a sound that was all too familiar: a police siren. Looking behind us, we could see a harbor patrol speedboat coming up fast with lights flashing and siren wailing. Looking around, we could not see what the police would be interested in; we were the only boat going through the expensive neighborhoods.

The skiff pulled up beside the houseboat, and one of the officers yelled through a megaphone, "Cut your engines!" He did not sound pleased. My father cut the engines, as instructed, and the officers boarded. They demanded identification and registration. My father was extremely nervous; I had never seen him be so meek. The officers asked him if he knew how fast he was going.

My father said, "Not exactly, around fifteen to twenty miles per hour." The officer shook his head and pointed at a nearby buoy and said, "Can you read what is on that buoy?" My father looked and read "NO WAKE ZONE! 5 mph MAX." He turned white; he knew he was in trouble. The officer looked at my father like he was something that had crawled out from under a tarp.

"This area has some of the most expensive yachts in the world. Do you have any idea what a wake can do to these yachts?" The officer yelled at my father.

My father stammered, "No, sir."

The officer shook his head and stated, "This is a very serious offense. You will have to come to the station with us."

My father then did something I had never seen him do before—he groveled. "Please, sir, my family and I are just starting our vacation. I honestly did not know I was going too fast. I was just trying to get to the waterway so we could make it to our hotel before nightfall. If you just give me a warning, I promise I will not go faster than five miles per hour again," my father begged. I was embarrassed. I thought going to the police station would have been fun.

Then my father did the second thing I had never seen him do: he lowered his voice and said, "Surely there is some kind of arrangement we can reach where everyone can enjoy the rest of their day?"

The officer looked darkly at him and said, "I certainly hope you are not offering me what you obviously are offering me. You don't want to make this a felony offense. Right now, you are looking at a fine and a few hours delay, but you could be in jail very quickly."

I thought that would be a fine idea; seeing my father in jail would be exciting. My father bowed his head, defeated. I had never seen him wilt like that. "Sir, I am a respected lawyer in North Carolina. I am a military veteran. I went to the United States Military Academy at West Point, class of 1945. My wife is a respected church circle leader and mother to these children. Please, please let us go, and I swear to you by all that is holy that I will never, ever cause a wake again."

It was my father's lucky day; the police officer knew that if he arrested a lawyer it would be more trouble than it was worth. He overlooked the indirect bribe and wrote my father a ticket with a $1,000 fine. Dick looked at the ticket and his blood pressure spiked.

The officer said, "You will need to pay this fine in two weeks, or a warrant for your arrest will be issued. If you wish to contest the fine, you will need to appear at your preliminary hearing on the date on the ticket."

My father, wanting this embarrassing day to be over, nodded his head and meekly said, "Yes, sir."

The police officer left and shoved off. In a final coup de grace, he turned back to the houseboat and shouted through the megaphone, "NO WAKE!" My father waved his hand in acknowledgment. It was an uncomfortable moment for everyone.

We made our way through the rest of the islands in Biscayne Bay and headed for the open waterway. I had to admit, the crystal water and breeze were much better than the brackish water and stifling heat of the Everglades. We asked my father if we could go snorkeling near some islands to the east, and he pulled over and anchored off the south end of the island of Virginia Key.

The famous Key Biscayne was in the distance. We gleefully jumped in with our snorkeling gear and swam for over an hour. My father had given strict instructions that we could not go more than 100 yards from the boat and to pay attention. He further instructed us that if he blew the horn, we were to return to the boat immediately.

As we were swimming, a fishing boat came by, and the fishermen started shouting at my father. He could not make out what they were saying. They came closer and were very excited. My father came out on deck to hear what they were yelling. "You bloody fool," they yelled, "You are in the feeding grounds of the sharks that live around here. In twenty minutes, the sharks will be coming through here, and your kids will be shark bait!"

He immediately blew the horn over and over to call us back to the boat. I heard the horn, but I had found a school of brightly colored fish and didn't want to return to the boat. Dick continued to blow the horn and started cursing at the top of his lungs, "Goddamn it, you get your asses on board this boat immediately. Quit fucking around and get in this boat!"

I stuck my head up and yelled back, "Why?" which was the wrong thing to say to my already overstressed father.

"Get your ass back on this boat or I will beat you into next week, you idiot!" My father screamed. I swam back to the boat and climbed the ladder up to the deck. Dick grabbed me by the arm and twisted it hard. He hissed, "Dammit, when I say get back here you will obey me! There are sharks in these waters, and you could have been killed!"

It was then that I discovered that perhaps I should have put on some suntan lotion, because I was burned from head to toe. My father's grip on my upper arm was excruciating. It felt like someone had set my skin on fire and poured salt on it. Tears of pain came to my eyes, and I forced myself not to scream. After all, I was almost fourteen years old, and I would not let my father see me cry.

I had third-degree burns over my entire body. It was the most painful sunburn I would ever experience. I didn't want to stay inside, but to go outside I would have had to put on clothes, which was unbearable. I was stuck inside with my mother, who was doing a slow burn herself over being stuck on a boat, which she considered to be beneath her station in life. She had endured last summer; she was not going to endure this. When she found out about the sharks, she almost demanded to be put ashore. Being around her was almost as uncomfortable as my sunburn.

Several days went by without more incidents, and the earlier events were forbidden topics of conversation. I had to admit that motoring down the waterway through Biscayne Bay toward Key Largo was beautiful. Stopping each night at marinas with motels was some consolation, although I was still suffering from my sunburn. While my sisters enjoyed going outside and swimming from time to time, I was a prisoner inside. The vacation was not going very well from that perspective.

Between the episode with the Miami Beach Patrol, sharks, my mother's slow boil, and the stress of commanding a boat with an inexperienced crew, my father's famous temper was simmering nicely just under the surface. Any complaint, any whining, and any criticism of his efforts to make this vacation memorable invited anger and retaliation. He constantly pulled out the guilt card, telling everyone that we were the luckiest family in the world to have him. He repeatedly told them that his father would never have taken his family on a trip like this, so we should be grateful. I swallowed the observation that maybe my grandfather was wiser than my father.

The crowning glory of the trip came off the coast of Key Largo. We were motoring down the coast, headed for our next port of call, a resort on Key Largo. There was a loud clanging, and smoke started pouring out of the engine bay at the rear of the boat. My father turned everything off and went to look. Smoke was rolling out of the port engine. He told me to get a bedsheet and tie it to the banister rail around the upper deck, a makeshift sign of distress. Not only was the sun starting to set, but the tide was taking the boat out to sea. I had visions of a ghost ship washing up on the shores of Ireland, where the great Atlantic Gulf Stream deposits anything caught in its current.

Things were not looking so good for the boat and crew until, at sunset, a Coast Guard cutter appeared and came along beside us. "Ahoy, are you having trouble?" the Coast Guard captain asked.

Although everyone started talking and yelling at the same time, my father shouted everyone down and explained the situation.

The Coast Guard said, "No worries, we will tow you to the nearest marina that has repair facilities." Everyone was greatly relieved, although I would have loved to have seen Ireland.

The Coast Guard threw over a rope, and my father secured it to one of the box cleats. To add insult to injury, when the Coast Guard cutter began its tow, the cleat came out of the deck, leaving a gaping hole. Dick stared at the hole and started cursing under his breath.

The boat was eventually towed back to the nearest harbor on Key Largo. Although it was not their intended destination, it was a nice resort with facilities and, much to my mother's relief, a well-stocked bar. There was a swimming pool and other amenities that agreed with us. The only unhappy person was my father, because we would have to stay there for four days while the engines were repaired. Though unavoidable, it was an unexpected expense, and my father was in a foul mood for the rest of the trip.

Eventually, the engine was repaired, and it was decided to head straight back to Miami. The delay in getting the boat repaired had eaten up the rest of our vacation time, and everyone was ready to get home. My sunburn was starting to heal, causing even more discomfort and itching. There are few things worse than the healing process for skin burns. The itching was incessant, and scratching was painful. I started peeling, and my sisters took great pleasure in seeing who could peel off the biggest piece of skin. However, I did heal, and everyone finally made it home. No one spoke of the great Florida vacations ever again.

CHAPTER TWELVE

Adverse Childhood Experiences

The experiences of my childhood, adolescence, and teenage years had left me sullen and depressed. It was confusing to be told how lucky I was and yet live with the scars from my parents. I truly loved them but was constantly scared and anxious about what could happen.

Studies in the 1990s by Kaiser Permanente and the Center for Disease Control[12] identified a strong connection between adverse experiences in childhood and poor mental and physical health, including heart problems, diabetes, substance abuse, anxiety, and depression.

The experiences were labeled adverse childhood experiences, or ACEs. They include:

- Physical, sexual, or emotional abuse
- Living with domestic violence
- Living with alcoholic parents
- Loss or suicide of a family member

---

12 Centers for Disease Control and Prevention. 2021. "About the CDC-Kaiser ACE Study." Www.cdc.gov. April 6, 2021. https://www.cdc.gov/violenceprevention/aces/about.html.

- Lack of support and bonding in the household

ACEs are not the same as trauma. ACEs usually involve repeated adversities over long periods of time, while trauma may be a one-time, intense event. One of the puzzling aspects of both ACEs and trauma is that every child reacts differently to adversity, including siblings. Twins may experience the same event, and one copes magnificently while the other is traumatized and may experience PTSD.

Probably the most obvious symptom of ACEs is a maladaptive stress response. In a safe household, children learn how to minimize their Warrior response by being supported and validated through their childhood. In households where the children experience long-term ACEs and trauma, children often develop deep-seated insecurity and low self-esteem.

A lack of support and validation results in an inability to deactivate their Warrior response and go into Guru mode. In effect, they get stuck in their Warrior mode, which has long-term physical consequences. They get desensitized to high adrenaline and cortisol levels, which compromises their immune system and causes weight issues, anxiety, depression, and stress. It is the Warrior on steroids. Lacking confidence and coping skills, these children are underachievers and rebellious.

Studies have shown that ACEs will damage cognitive functions, lowering IQ and affecting risk assessment. In other words, children subjected to ACEs are more prone to risky behavior. Being in the Warrior mode affects their limbic system and causes them to react emotionally to events before analyzing them logically. Unexplained outbursts, anger, tears, and inappropriate behavior are symptoms of the damage done by ACEs and trauma.

As adults, ACE children tend to act before they think and find it difficult to explain their behavior. Even a reminder of an ACE will trigger the amygdala and produce a reaction before the frontal cortex is even engaged. This can also lead to an inability to focus, due to the fact that the Warrior is always focused on scanning the environment for danger. In general, children do not react to adversity the same way as adults do; they lack the skills, experience, and knowledge to have perspective.

Having grown up in an environment full of unpleasant surprises, physical and mental abuse, emotional abandonment, and confusing parenting, I had "hidden traumas" that left me confused, depressed, and anxious for most of my life. In my spiritual journey, I discovered that these hidden traumas are called "complex trauma" or "complex PTSD."

Complex PTSD results from repeated situations in which the child has little or no control or any perceived hope to escape.[13] These invisible traumas are usually chronic, occurring repeatedly throughout the child's developmental years, a "drip, drip, drip" of poison that drastically interferes with normal mental and emotional development.

The psychological injuries from chronic hidden trauma often go unnoticed. It left me confused, and I turned to blaming and shaming myself. Even as an adult, I suppressed or denied these painful memories by telling myself that I didn't have it so bad. This was often reinforced when I complained to others and was told I was lucky. As a result, I had problems handling my emotions into my adult years. This was compounded by my sensitivity and intelligence, which knew something was wrong, but could not break through the programming that "I was lucky."

Complex trauma becomes invisible because, on the surface, those who suffer from it look healthy and normal. Our family was considered successful by the public. We had money, good grades, and social standing. My material needs were met. However, the way I felt inside did not match our public image. I appeared to be highly successful, but I didn't feel that way.

Society told me how lucky I was, but my contrary feelings left me confused.

---

13   "CPTSD (Complex PTSD)," Cleveland Clinic, June 2, 2025, https://my.clevelandclinic.org/health/diseases/24881-cptsd-complex-ptsd.

In a healthy family, there should be enough freedom for all members to express themselves as individuals. In families with little tolerance for differences, a child can become the scapegoat, the black sheep of the family. I was the infamous black sheep because I often clashed with family objectives. We were repeatedly told, "Don't do anything to ruin the family reputation."

Fortunately, the brain's neuroplasticity can reverse these conditions with therapy, self-awareness, and training. When we change our thinking patterns from negativity to positivity, neuroplasticity develops new neural pathways and can heal old psychological wounds. Still, it would take me years to overcome the effects of my ACEs and hidden traumas.

CHAPTER THIRTEEN

Duty, Honor, Country

That fall, after I had turned fourteen, my father started his campaign to recruit me into military life. By that time, he had been appointed to the Board of Trustees of the United States Military Academy at West Point, and he traveled to West Point four times a year. He served in that role for thirty-five years.

In 1967, the Vietnam War was in full swing, with more and more recruits sent to fight, many returning in body bags. Gus Grissom, Ed White, and Roger Chaffee were killed in a space capsule fire during training. The American Basketball Association was formed. Numerous demonstrations across the nation protested the Vietnam War. Muhammad Ali was convicted of refusing induction into the US Army and was stripped of his boxing titles. Elvis and Priscilla Presley were married.

As part of his master plan, my father decided it would be a great idea to start taking me along with him to these board meetings at West Point. My first was the fall of 1967. This was one of the most exciting trips of my life, as I got to ride in a plane and stay at the Waldorf Astoria in New York City. For me to be properly dressed for my visit to

West Point, my parents took me to Brooks Brothers on Fifth Avenue to purchase my first suit. I remember it was a glen plaid three-piece suit, and I fell in love with it instantly. I especially loved being measured so the suit could be tailored. My Guru loved the feeling of self-confidence, the assuredness that fitted clothes gave me.

West Point felt cold in every way. Sitting on the Hudson River north of Manhattan, West Point is made up of a lot of gray and forbidding buildings and looks exactly like a military citadel. I took an instant dislike to the place. I could hear voices in my head, the voices of the fallen military soldiers who had returned to their breeding grounds for posterity. By now I was familiar with hearing voices like that, ever since my visit to the halls with the angels.

Not only had that experience connected me to some powerful energy, but it had also connected me to the voices of the beings who watched over me. Hearing their voices had become second nature to me. It was like a constant hum in the background of my mind. Sometimes I would stop and listen, but most of the time I just wished they were quieter, if not silent. When I stepped onto the grounds of West Point, all I could hear were voices telling me to run away. I had never had that kind of feeling before, like something terrible was going to happen. The fine hairs on the back of my neck prickled, and my Warrior stayed on even higher than usual alert.

I could see that my father was excited that I was with him at West Point. He was telling stories about his time there as a cadet. He described hazing, abusive treatment by upperclassmen, and strict discipline, told as if these were fun campfire stories. I could not wait to leave the place. Repeatedly, he asked me if I liked West Point and "Wouldn't it be fun to go to school here?" I would just grunt noncommittally and keep my head down. I was repulsed by the energy of the place.

Dick heard what he wanted to hear and believed that I was interested in going to West Point. I did not disabuse him of his misconception. I had learned long ago it was wise to play up to him and not disagree. I was conflicted, to be sure, and I didn't know how to tell my father that voices were telling me to leave that place. I decided to keep quiet, as it was the safer course of action by far.

We returned home, and I promptly forgot the whole affair. It was my ninth-grade year, and I was busy enjoying being in the graduating class of my private junior high school. I had gone to Summit School, only 500 yards from my home, since I was four years old. Summit was an exclusive private school that had been founded by the city elite for their children.

Public schools had become problematic during those years, as the civil rights movement had many people uneasy. Summit provided the city's wealthy families a haven and private education. From my perspective, it was unfortunate that Summit only went through ninth grade. I had never gone to public school; high school was a daunting prospect.

The classes at Summit were extremely small, and my graduating class only had twenty-two students. The individuals in the class had changed from time to time as students came and went, but there was a core group of us that had been together since kindergarten. It was a time when we were starting to think about who we "liked," and a few of the students had paired off and were "going steady."

Around this time, I started sleepwalking. Sometimes I would find myself outside; other times I would find myself in the basement with no idea how I got there. I started having nightmares about being stuck in the basement with a malevolent presence, and I would wake myself up screaming.

I was completely uncomfortable around girls. Despite (or because of) growing up with my sisters, I hadn't had much contact with them and couldn't understand the way they thought, and my Warrior found them confounding. Most of them paid no attention to me at all, which was fine with me.

My parents decided it was time that we became more social. Up until that point, they had not allowed any of us to spend much time away from home. I remember an occasion when I had gone to the movies and ran into my cousins. I asked the friends I was with to call my parents and let them know I was staying to watch the movie a second time.

After all, being away from my parents was a gift, and the movie was *Hercules and the Vampires*, a movie bloody enough for a fourteen-year-old's taste. About halfway through, an usher moved through the theater yelling my name, "Gray Robinson! Gray Robinson!" Thoroughly embarrassed, I slunk up to him, and the usher stiffly escorted me to the lobby.

Waiting there, his famous temple throbbing, my father stood looking like he had learned I had committed a mortal sin. He grabbed my ear and twisted it hard, pulling me outside. He launched into his typical style of berating, yelling at the top of his lungs, oblivious to passersby. "How dare you do this to us!" "We were worried sick!" "We looked everywhere for you!" and so on. He shoved me roughly into his car and screamed at me all the way home.

Apparently, my friends hadn't called my parents to let them know about my change of plans. I attempted to tell my father that I had asked my friends to call, but he would hear none of it. On and on and on, he lambasted me with accusations that I was selfish and uncaring, and that I had caused my mother to be on the verge of a heart attack. That cut short any sense of independence budding in me, and I completely shut down. My Warrior seethed from Its perch on my shoulder.

After that, my parents started nagging me about who my friends were and why I didn't invite them over to play. That seemed completely disingenuous to me. As a teenager, I cringed at the phrase and attempted to tell my parents that my friends did not "come over to play."

The communication gap was widening rapidly. My parents decided that it was time for us to have a dance party. Dance parties in those days were mostly teens sitting around listening to 45-rpm records. As we didn't yet have any of those adolescent trappings, my father was forced to go buy a record player and some records. My mother called all the parents and invited the ninth-grade class over for a dance.

I had no idea what to do. For me, lacking in any social confidence, having my classmates over for a dance felt like taping my lips to a bus exhaust. This was one of the first dance parties we had all gone to, and everyone was a bit uncomfortable and shy. After about an hour, I said to myself, "What the fuck," and asked one of the girls to dance.

I was tired of everyone sitting around looking at each other. A few people started dancing, and things started to loosen up. We were in the basement playroom, so someone went and turned off some of the lights so people could relax or make out in the corners. I was starting to feel a bit more comfortable.

While I was dancing a slow dance with one of the girls, I felt a hand tap me on my shoulder. I looked up and was shocked to see my mother standing there. It was obvious that she had been drinking quite a bit. Wobbling slightly, she coyly asked, "May I have this dance?" Neither the girl nor I knew what was happening, as neither of us knew what "cutting in" was. I thought I was in a nightmare as my mother put her arms around my neck and started slow dancing with me.

I could hear the others whispering and snickering at us. My Warrior was aflame with embarrassment. I couldn't understand what she was doing there and why she was holding me so tightly. I wouldn't understand any of it until much later in life. If our relationship had been healthier, or my mother less drunk, perhaps it would not have felt so boundaryless, but as it was, I felt violated. My Warrior was enraged, and my Guru dismayed. I would never dance with my mother again.

That summer, my parents sent Kitty and me on the Grand Western Tour, a bus tour of the western United States that was organized by a local couple. Approximately sixty teenagers were put on two Greyhound Streamline buses for six weeks and taken around the western states as a rite of passage of some sort. While the rich children of my mother's generation were treated to a tour of Europe, she would not allow us to leave the continental US. The western US would have to do.

The most memorable part of the trip for me was walking around the Haight-Ashbury area of San Francisco and seeing the counterculture that had been incubating there during the 1960s. The head shops and smell of marijuana were everywhere. One of the boys bought a bag of some sort of green vegetable matter. I couldn't smoke tobacco, as the damage to my lungs from the double pneumonia made it too toxic. However, I loved the feeling of smoking pot. I felt like I was doing something exotic and exciting. It felt rebellious and naughty and grown up. My Warrior and my Guru both danced with it in different ways, my Warrior always on alert, as it felt delightfully out of control. I would chase that feeling for the rest of my life.

CHAPTER FOURTEEN

Negative Thinking and the Brain

I was a nervous wreck. Not only did I lack any social confidence, but I also had no idea why I was so depressed and anxious. My parents often commented on my negative demeanor. I just wanted to be left alone.

Children who are subjected to abuse, trauma, and neglect suffer a profound sensory impact. Their sense of safety can be destroyed by frightening visual stimuli, loud noises, violence, and physical abuse associated with an unpredictable, terrorizing event. These memories tend to surface through nightmares, sleepwalking, and unconscious behavior seeking to recreate the event. They believe their negative thoughts and emotions can become real, producing a nightmarish existence.

Children usually lack the experience to anticipate danger or know how to be safe in a frightening situation, and they blame their parents for letting these circumstances occur. These occurrences result in misinterpretations of reality, which reinforce their negative mindset. Children who are subjected to ACEs can experience a reduction in the size of their frontal cortex.

The frontal cortex is responsible for many complex functions, including memory, attention, perceptual awareness, thinking, language, and consciousness. These changes may affect IQ and the ability to regulate emotions, and the child may become more fearful and may not feel safe or protected.

Exposure to ACEs changes the brain. The part of the brain that regulates the autonomic nervous system, particularly the Warrior, can overdevelop, which leads to inappropriate responses to imagined threats. The limbic system, which controls emotions, memory, and risk assessment, can be underdeveloped and stunted. This is one reason why children exposed to toxic stress don't remember their childhood.

The inability to regulate emotions can create a constant negative loop between the child's mindset and the Warrior. The inability to downregulate negative emotions will keep them trapped in the Warrior mode, which reinforces the negative emotions. The child can become needy, fearful of new situations or environments.

When subjected to chronic negative thinking, children can be difficult to control, easily frightened, hard to comfort, aggressive and impulsive, and nervous sleepers. They can find learning difficult, bully and abuse other children, have problems making friends, lack self-confidence, and blame themselves for being abused.

These children can act out and behave inappropriately, especially if the abuser is an authority figure or parent. They can experience overwhelming stress without the ability to communicate what they are feeling or what they need. Unexplained symptoms and uncharacteristic behavior may plague the negative child.

Long-term negative thinking patterns become normalized, and neural pathways that reinforce these patterns are formed. The ability to heal these destructive patterns becomes more and more difficult the longer they exist. These patterns diminish the brain's ability to reason, think, and form memories.

Negative thinking also leads to depression, anxiety, chronic worrying, and obsessive-compulsive disorder. Thinking negatively causes the limbic system to respond accordingly, thus causing children to feel negatively as well. They have low self-esteem and feel ineffective and hopeless. They are reluctant to communicate and connect with others because they expect a negative outcome for whatever they do. A favorite saying for these traumatized individuals is "no good deed goes unpunished."

Negative thinking inhibits acting on potential opportunities, primarily because negative thinking will make goals seem farther away and harder to accomplish. Negative thinking interferes with our self-image and self-confidence. Negative thinking drains our mental and physical resources, and we feel exhausted most of the time. People with high levels of negativity can suffer from brain disease, digestive disorders, heart problems, lowered immunity, and longer healing times.

I've found that negativity can manifest itself in numerous ways. I experienced a general negative opinion of others and found it hard to establish trust. I became a loner and found myself unwilling to make any effort to develop friendships. I developed an all-or-nothing attitude towards people and focused on negative aspects of relationships, even if they were generally positive. I tended to judge people unfairly and throw them under the bus if they did not live up to my unrealistic standards. I became a card-carrying victim, assuming the worst would happen no matter how hard I tried to avoid it.

Everything that happened in life that I did not like was someone else's fault, and I had a systemic inability to accept responsibility for anything. I believed that hard work would bring great rewards, but when that did not happen, I felt betrayed and abandoned. My emotions took over my objectivity, and I often judged events by how I was feeling rather than impartial perception. When I was feeling depressed or angry, my memory of an event was often inaccurate. Even worse, I tended to dismiss events that occurred when I was happy, while exaggerating those that happened when I was feeling negative emotions.

The worst trap that my negativity set for me was believing that if my circumstances changed, I would be happy. I divorced, quit jobs, and dismissed friends, believing that if I could find the right circumstances, I could be happy. The problem was the negative mindset that was operating my life. I did not realize that I had to change how I felt about myself, not my circumstances, in order to find happiness. That meant changing the neural pathways in my brain.

The consequences of long-term ACEs include behavior problems, disease, obesity and diabetes, depression and anxiety disorders, criminal behavior, substance abuse, and risky sexual behavior. I was guilty of all of that.

CHAPTER FIFTEEN

What Doesn't Kill Us Makes Us Stronger

1968 was an uneasy year in the US. Both Robert Kennedy and Dr. Martin Luther King Jr. were assassinated, and student protests of the Vietnam War became more frequent and violent. US soldiers massacred men, women, and children in My Lai, Vietnam. McDonald's introduced the Big Mac for forty-nine cents. Japanese cars began dominating the US auto industry. The Soviet Union invaded Czechoslovakia and arrested Alexander Dubček, the head of the Czechoslovak Communist Party, for straying from strict communist doctrine. The Zodiac Killer went on a killing spree in California and was never caught or identified. Aristotle Onassis wed JFK's widow, Jacqueline Kennedy. Tommie Smith and John Carlos raised their hands in the iconic Black Power salute at the Mexico City Olympics.

I decided to go to public high school for the next three years of my life. It was an excellent public school, built by the Charlotte elite as a haven of wealth and education. It had an auditorium that resembled a New York theater and was often used for arts, drama, and music presentations for the city. I went from a class of twenty-two to a class of one thousand. My Guru and my Warrior did their best to keep up with this drastic change.

Several milestones occurred during my sophomore year. First, I turned sixteen and got my driver's license. The second was when Kitty went away to boarding school. I suspected that she was just trying to get away from all of us. She had grown more and more withdrawn from the family over the years, saying that she hated our money, our "status," and our family name and expectations.

I was surprised my parents let her go, but other than that, I couldn't have cared less. I was excited that I didn't have to share the Jeep Wrangler that my father had bought us for our birthday and happy to have one less person around to fight with. My mother cried when they took Kitty to school; her firstborn was leaving the nest. I, on the other hand, could hardly contain my joy.

In November 1968, Richard Nixon was elected president, much to the relief of conservatives like my father. Nixon promised to win the conflict in Vietnam, and neither defeat nor surrender was acceptable in our household. I kept asking my father why the US cared about Vietnam. Eisenhower had started the mess, and Johnson escalated the US involvement. My father ignored my questions and resumed lobbying me to go to West Point. He saw the war in Vietnam as a career worthy of me. I thought of it as nothing short of insanity.

The Vietnam War was raging in 1969, and despite my father's continued mentions of West Point, I did not want any part of the military. I had decided to focus on playing golf, a far cry from giving my life to protect my country. Golf was enjoyable; war was despicable. I was good at golf, and nothing felt better to me than discovering something I could do well.

In December 1969, my parents took me back to West Point for the winter meeting of the Board of Trustees. By this time, I was tired of pretending that I was interested in attending. When I stepped onto the bleak gray campus, all I could hear were the voices saying, "RUN AWAY!" I played one game of golf in the freezing rain on the West

Point golf course, and my mind became even more sure that I did not want to go to school at such a cold and forbidding place. My Guru and Warrior both hated it, and at that point, there was little that they agreed upon so intensely.

On Saturday night, the commandant of West Point, who was a three-star general, held a reception for the Board of Trustees in the great dining hall where General MacArthur had given his famous farewell speech. I dutifully stood in line with my parents as we made our way through the receiving line to the three-star general Samuel William Koster. (Koster would later be demoted and drummed out of the Army for covering up the My Lai massacre.) When we approached the commandant and his wife, Mrs. Koster gushed at me and said, "What a good-looking young man. You look like the kind of cadet we would like at the Academy. Are you considering applying for an appointment to the Academy?"

I considered my options, including lying to make my father look good, but I knew that if I lied and said yes, I would be going down a road I might not be able to get off. In an unusual fit of courage, I simply said, "No, ma'am." Mrs. Koster dropped my hand like it was a rotten fish and turned to the next in line. My father was livid. My Guru smiled more broadly than It had in some time.

When we finished the receiving line, my father hissed, "You could have at least lied."

I shook my head and used his own rigid principles against him: "You told me never to lie."

My father had no response, but my mother interjected, "Well, at least you said 'ma'am.'"

It was a strained meal afterwards, to say the least. I found small entertainment watching the vein in my father's forehead throb uncontrollably.

CHAPTER SIXTEEN

The Brain on Eggshells

I felt like I was in a prison from which there was no escape. To be sure, it was luxurious, with lots of toys, but a prison nonetheless. Surprisingly, families do not primarily communicate by language. The most far-reaching consequences occur between parents and infants through tone of voice, facial expressions, touch, scent, and body posture, not language. Most communications occur through emotional attunement, when we match the emotions of the people we love.

When children are raised with trauma and abuse, their primary mode of defense is to walk on eggshells. Walking on eggshells essentially means tiptoeing around family members to avoid emotional blowups, mood swings, criticism, forms of disapproval, or put-downs.

In our constant efforts to tiptoe around someone else's moods, we constantly edit what we say and do. We second-guess our own judgment, our own ideas, and our own preferences. We begin to question whether the way we think is valid and right. Ultimately, our perceptions of reality and our sense of self change for the worse.

When we are tiptoeing around, attempting to anticipate the minefields in family relationships, we must be ready to change our personality on a moment's notice. This erodes our self-confidence and sense of self. We become truly codependent, not allowing ourselves to be happy until our family members are happy. We focus on their needs instead of our own.

When our authority figures are upset, we internalize that as our fault. We do whatever we have to do, sacrifice whatever we must sacrifice, to make them feel happy. Many times, we sacrifice our dreams to fulfill the dreams our family has for us. Everyone in a walking-on-eggshells family loses their sense of self, their dignity, and their independence. We focus on fulfilling the parents' needs instead of our own.

Eggshell children are prone to anxiety and depression.[14] Childhood depression presents as isolation, boredom, lack of interest in normal childhood activities, and an absence of excitement. They can show aggressive tendencies, hyperactivity, and high emotional activity (especially negative emotions) or no emotional engagement whatsoever. They would rather feel nothing than the pain of walking on eggshells. As adults, they are resentful, angry, and emotionally abusive.

Parents who are the black holes that suck all positive emotions out of their children cope with their children's behavior by blaming it on others, denying responsibility for their actions, or avoiding feeling the consequences of their children's behavior by using alcohol, drugs, or other addictive behavior. The most common trait shared by all family members is a lack of self-esteem.

Another result of eggshell environments is enmeshment trauma. Enmeshment happens when parents or authority figures disregard their children's boundaries and micromanage every aspect of their children's lives. We call it "helicopter parenting" today. Parents make all the decisions for their children, believing that children don't have the proper experience or knowledge to decide which activities, friends, or education they will experience. I was subjected to this constantly,

---

14 Michael Vallejo Lcsw, "What Is Eggshell Parenting?," Mental Health Center Kids, June 25, 2025, https://mentalhealthcenterkids.com/blogs/articles/eggshell-parenting.

and I eventually quit thinking for myself because my decisions didn't matter. Children who experience this may feel like their emotional needs weren't met, due to a lack of individuality or proper roles within enmeshed families.

It may not be until adulthood (if ever) that someone is able to recognize how these relationships impacted their ability to process emotion and function in general. People can have many different responses to emotional trauma, but it is most important for them to recognize these enmeshed relationships as being manipulative and potentially abusive.

Enmeshment exists on a spectrum. Some people can set boundaries more easily than others, depending on their circumstances and experiences. In poorly functioning family units, children may resist conflict by performing a "fawn" trauma response in which they give in to meet the needs of others. The fawn trauma response in enmeshed relationships aims to please or pacify to avoid arguments or blame.

Children who experience enmeshment trauma exhibit several common traits:

- Over-identification with parents. Parents attempt to relive their childhood through their children and focus primarily on what they wanted in childhood that they didn't get, instead of focusing on what the child wants or needs. The child ends up sacrificing their wants and needs to keep the peace or get attention from their parental figures.
- Lack of boundaries. Parents allow no privacy for the children and are constantly micromanaging the children's lives. They make decisions for the children to the point that children lack decision-making skills, and are often frustrated or embarrassed by the lack of individuation. Children are trained to live up to their parents' expectations, not their own.
- Conflict avoidance. Children and, later, adults avoid conflict, disagreement, or confrontation in any form out of fear of rejection,

abandonment, or blame. They must repress negative feelings because they are not allowed to be expressed.

- Family über allies. The family is everything. Children must stay within the confines of the family and are discouraged from trying anything outside the family. Children are expected to participate in the family business and are perceived as traitors if they don't. The family takes precedence over all aspects of the child's life, including any families the adult child may create. The adult child gets stuck in the middle between competing family interests and feels guilt, shame, and unworthiness.

- Overparenting. Also known as "helicopter parenting," this is when the parent micromanages everything in the child's life. Parents justify this behavior as a desire for safety and a response to the child's lack of maturity. Ironically, it is the high level of control exerted by the parent that prevents the child from individualization and emotional growth. The child is trained that they are not allowed to disagree or say no.

- Poor interpersonal skills. Children who grow up with enmeshment trauma often fail to develop the skills necessary to have a healthy relationship outside of the family. With all the focus on the family of origin, any interpersonal relationship outside the family suffers for lack of attention and intention. Their partner can resent the overbearing relationship with the family.

- Trauma bonding. Many times, the parent and child in an abusive trauma relationship form an unhealthy bond, which keeps the child coming back for love, nurturing, or validation that is not available from the parent. The parents or other family members are irreplaceable by design. When separated from the enmeshed family, both adults and children have difficulty making decisions or forming healthy relationships.

There is no uniform manual on how to raise children. Each generation seems to apply different rules, many of which are in reaction (rebellion) to how they were raised. The Greatest Generation was raised with physical discipline and strict socioeconomic rules. They lived through World War I, the Great Depression, and World War II. They were described as patriotic, hardworking, driven, frugal, career-oriented, and team players. The man was the head of the household and usually the sole provider for the family.

The baby boomers were the generation after the Greatest Generation. They are characterized as reformers, living through the Cold War and the various unpopular military engagements during that time. They instituted the civil rights movement and ushered in the sexual revolution. The Greatest Generation sold them the "American Dream," and they pursued material prosperity, often to their mental, emotional, and physical detriment. They are the hippies of the '70s and the yuppies of the '80s. They did not trust the Greatest Generation.

Generation X was the offspring of the baby boomers. This was a time of single-parent families, two-income families, latchkey kids, Y2K, the end of the Cold War, Mom going to work, and an increasing divorce rate. This generation's perceptions were formed by looking after themselves more than any other generation. "Politician" became a bad word as trust declined. This generation was the first that did not do as well financially as their parents, even though they were known for individualism, ambition, and a solid work ethic.

Millennials (Gen Y) were the children of the latchkey kids. They were put on schedules and driven to soccer games and music lessons. Their parents were determined to give them a better life through wealth. Many were children of divorce. They were the first "digital natives," growing up with computers and virtual worlds. Millennials were dissatisfied with the world given to them by Generation X. They were the generation of protected feelings, participation trophies, and lack of ambition. They were labeled the "me" generation and accused of being lazy, narcissistic, and spoiled. For the first time, a generation had trouble finding work.

Generation Z arrived with a smartphone and tablet in their nursery. The internet has completely changed how the world operates and how people connect and communicate, dramatically affecting interpersonal relationships. Images of people sitting around the dinner table on their smartphones have become common. People have lost some ability to relate to each other. This generation gravitated toward digital and knowledge-based jobs, and trades suffered a large exodus of workers. They could multitask but had reduced attention spans.

Each generation is the product of how the children were raised. Each generation rebels against how they were raised. It is fundamental that we study (not rewrite) history so we can determine what is working and what is not working.

How we parent will dictate our children's adult relationships to the world. It is said that parents are the ghosts of their children's future. Children will either try to emulate their parents or reject them. While it may take a village to properly raise a child, their well-being and future are often dictated by how their parents relate to society and reality. Fortunately, parents are not limited to what they experienced. The internet has provided resources for every possible scenario for parenting children. The "village" is now digital.

And what of the Guru and the Warrior in the digital age? What adjustments must they make for this new landscape of human culture? We are discovering it as we go along.

CHAPTER SEVENTEEN

A Battle of Willpower

In 1969, Richard M. Nixon was sworn in as the president of the United States. Yasser Arafat was elected leader of the Palestine Liberation Organization. The first commercial flight of the Boeing 747 was launched. The first test flight of the Concorde was conducted in France. Golda Meir was elected the first female prime minister of Israel. John Lennon and Yoko Ono got married. The first artificial heart implant was achieved. One of the earliest documented AIDS deaths occurred. Apollo 9 and 10 successfully paved the way for a lunar landing that was accomplished by Apollo 11 on July 20, 1969. Nixon announced the first withdrawal of American troops from Vietnam. Sharon Tate was murdered by Charles Manson and his followers. The music festival known as Woodstock was held on Max Yasgur's farm in Bethel, New York. Muammar Gaddafi came to power in Libya. *Sesame Street* debuted on TV. The My Lai massacre in Vietnam was revealed to the public. The hippie movement waned.

With the tumultuous events of 1969 as a backdrop, I had my own mini revolution over my body with my parents. I played football in my junior year of high school and ballooned to nearly 200 pounds. I was only five feet, eight inches, which elevated me from "husky" to "obese." As a junior in high school, I was well aware that many of my classmates were entering into relationships with their "sweethearts." Many people had girlfriends and boyfriends. Given my weight and body image, I felt unattractive and unpopular. I became extremely depressed and decided I needed to lose some weight.

To motivate my weight loss, I joined the wrestling team. I started losing weight (mostly baby fat) rapidly and got down to 165 pounds by the end of the year. I was feeling much better about myself. I was getting absolutely no support from my parents. They thought that I was starving myself and looking unhealthy. They were always demanding that I eat what was on my plate and quit wasting food. I was continually arguing with them about my desired weight and not wanting to stay fat all my life. It was a constant source of stress, but I was determined to become attractive and maybe get a date at some point.

In wrestling, there are weight classes. At my height, the possible weight classes available to me ranged from 175 down to 145 pounds. The only weight class in which I had any hope of making the team was 145 pounds. This required me to eat extremely little, as in a hamburger patty and some salad per meal. My parents thought this was unacceptable and hounded me for weeks to eat more. In my first act of true defiance, I continued to starve myself and eventually made my weight class of 145 pounds.

I vividly remember wrestling in meets for my high school. I did well, only losing at the last minute to wrestlers who were much more talented than me. I didn't care; I got to wear the letter jacket and was loving the notoriety.

I gathered up the courage to put my toe in the dating pool, with painful results. Melody was the daughter of some friends of my parents, who attended the UNC School of the Arts. My parents invited her to our house several times, and I finally worked up the courage to ask her out. She agreed, and we made plans.

I was very excited; Melody was cute and seemed to like me. I was playing golf for my high school at the time, and on the day of our first date, I had to cut practice short. My coach didn't like it, but I didn't want to be late. When I got home, I quickly showered and rushed to the door; it was going to be close timing.

My mother stopped me on my way out the door. "Where do you think you are going?"

I reminded her, "This is the night I am going out with Melody. I'm in a hurry."

My mother looked at me and insisted, "I made you supper, you will have to sit down and eat it first."

I couldn't believe my ears. "Mom, I don't have time to sit down and eat with you. I want to go on this date." I was pleading.

My mother, who had been drinking, shook her head and told me to sit down. I was in a dilemma. I knew if I defied my mother, I would pay later to my father, but if I was late, Melody would surely be upset. My mother seemed to read my mind and said, "Any girl who really cares for you will understand if you are a few minutes late."

I was between a drunken rock and a hard place. I dissociated, feeling numb and disconnected from reality. It felt like I was moving in slow motion. I stayed and shoveled the food down my throat even though I wasn't hungry. Inside, I was raging, and my Warrior was chomping at the bit to get the hell out of there.

When I stood up to leave, my mother said, "You'll have to wait until I'm finished too. You know better than to leave the table without permission."

I looked at her and said, "Why are you doing this? You've been bugging me for months to get a date, and now that I have one, you are doing everything you can to screw it up."

My mother sat up straight and gave me the evil eye as hard as she could. "How dare you talk to me like that?!" she screamed.

I refused to back down and shot out, "I'm out of here. If you want to get Dad on my ass, go right ahead." I felt the laser beams of her eyes boring into my back as I left.

I drove as fast as I could to Melody's campus and ran into the dormitory where she had told me to meet her. I didn't see her anywhere, so I asked the front desk to ring her room. Unsurprisingly, there was no answer. My shoulders dropped, and my heart followed. Not only was I going to be disciplined by my father, but I had also missed my first date. I felt like someone had kicked me in the stomach.

I drove home, defeated, my Warrior gearing up to defend me from my father. As I expected, he met me at the door and screamed at me for thirty minutes for being disrespectful to my mother. As a result, I lost my car privileges for thirty days to "teach me respect." All I felt was betrayal, fury, and resentment. I knew I would never be able to date anyone while living with my mother, who drove me everywhere for thirty days. The rides were as icy cold, silent, and barren as the Alaskan wilderness. I could no longer muster up any feelings for this woman who had let me down time and time again. I moved, with few regrets, into not feeling anything for my mother at all.

I quickly gained all the weight back that I had lost for wrestling. I was extremely stressed and depressed. I felt like I couldn't win and that my parents were trying to sabotage any happiness in my life.

CHAPTER EIGHTEEN

The Curse of Cortisol

I have always had problems with my weight. Not only did I overeat in times of stress, but I also found that I had to starve myself to lose any weight. What I didn't know was the role cortisol was playing in my life. One of the blessings and curses of engaging the Warrior mode is that our bodies are flooded with cortisol. Known as the stress hormone, cortisol is released by the adrenal glands when the brain detects stress or low cortisol levels. Cortisol primarily works with our brain to regulate mood, motivation, and fear. It also manages how the body uses proteins, fats, and carbohydrates, as well as increases blood sugar levels to enable muscles to fight or run away.

The Warrior mode can be limiting. When our body responds to stress, we go into survival mode and make decisions based on avoiding pain rather than creating pleasure. Our body is designed to return to Guru mode when stressors pass, but when we perceive threat from all directions and we constantly feel under attack, the Warrior mode will not turn off. Our neuroplasticity normalizes the stress response, and survival mode becomes the new normal. If adrenaline and cortisol levels start to drop, something feels wrong. Long-term exposure to stress hormones can cause anxiety and depression, headaches, high blood pressure, memory and concentration problems, digestive disorders, irritability, weight gain, and trouble sleeping.[15] I suffered all these symptoms from time to time, but never thought they could be related to cortisol and adrenaline.

I will discuss strategies for managing cortisol later in this book, but it is important to be aware that many physical symptoms of stress are due to elevated levels of adrenaline and cortisol over long periods of time.

---

15 "Chronic Stress Puts Your Health at Risk," Mayo Clinic, n.d., https://www.mayoclinic.org/healthy-lifestyle/stress-management/in-depth/stress/art-20046037.

CHAPTER NINETEEN

Civil Rights

In 1970, Boeing unveiled the 747. Paul McCartney left the Beatles. The Apollo 13 crew successfully returned to Earth. Four students were killed by National Guard troops at Kent State. Two students were killed by state law enforcement at Jackson State University. Thor Heyerdahl successfully sailed from Morocco to Barbados in a papyrus boat. The Aswan High Dam was completed. Jimi Hendrix and Janis Joplin died from drug overdoses.

In 1970, during my senior year of high school, the school board instituted busing throughout the county. Our predominantly white school was suddenly 75 percent white and 25 percent black. Racial tensions became more tangible and public. Fights broke out in the common area during lunchtime. I was never present to see what torched off the altercations, but we all were feeling the growing tension.

The black students blamed the white students, and the white students blamed the black students. It became intolerable to the white administration, who closed the common areas and ordered that students were not allowed to "hang out" in groups anymore. The atmosphere was becoming dangerous for everyone.

I never knew what it was like for any of the black students. Back then we didn't intermingle, so I didn't have any personal account or insights into how it was for them. I knew that from my side it felt like there were atrocities, but I was smart enough to know that when they looked at it from their side, things were just as bad, if not worse.

Even at that age, it felt to me like a setup. When I looked at the fundamental details of our lives, they seemed to be the same. Black people had families they cared about, went to school and church, celebrated holidays, and cared about their friends and pets. They had been born here, just like me. So, what was so different about us? Why did it seem like we were against each other all the time?

Violence amongst blacks and whites was common. After a particularly gruesome event at my high school prom, whites rode around in cars with weapons searching for young black males to kill, something that was known in the Deep South as "riding to the hounds." Curfews were set by the city authorities until the emotions died down. I didn't know how to react or respond. I was outraged on a deep level, joining my Warrior in the most wretched of thoughts, but unable to do anything about it. My sense of morality felt trapped with nowhere to go, and my anger and helplessness were overwhelming. I couldn't wait to graduate and get out of Charlotte.

Kitty came home after graduating from her academy. She had completely changed. Her hair was now waist-length, and she wore it and all her clothes in what I would call a "flowy" state. Which was a lot nicer than what I overheard my father call it: "hippie-dippy bullshit." She spoke passionately of activism and civil rights and other things that made the predictable vein in my father's temple jump and twitch at the dinner table. She had been admitted to UC Berkeley, where she planned to study human rights and holistic medicine. My parents spoke in low tones at night of their belief that she might be in the early clutches of some California cult.

Our relationship graduated into one of silent tolerance. The longest conversations we had were over who would get to drive the Jeep.

To me, a total stranger had come home, and I felt more isolated than ever. I tiptoed around my home to avoid her and my parents, although it felt equally volatile outside the home. Peace remained elusive, everywhere. My Warrior saw no opportunity to let down Its guard, as my nervous system became more and more accustomed to a life of chaos.

My nightmares and sleepwalking started occurring almost every night. The nightmare was generally the same: I would find myself in the basement of my house in the dark. There was an evil presence with me in the dark, and I had to escape to avoid being seriously injured or killed. As a result, I often found myself sleepwalking around the house or outside, with no recollection of how I got there. Sometimes I found my way back to bed; other times, family members would find me and wake me up. To say the least, this was entirely disconcerting, and no one knew what to do about it.

CHAPTER TWENTY

Nightmares and Sleepwalking

Episodes of undesired events during sleep are called parasomnia. They can include night (or sleep) terrors or nightmares and can be associated with sleepwalking. Terrors are different from nightmares in that individuals who have terrors won't wake up, while those who have nightmares will wake up and remember the dream.

It is believed that about 40 percent of children and adolescents have nightmares or night terrors.[16] The symptoms of trauma can also cause sleepwalking or night terrors. Inconsistent sleep, depression, anxiety, stress, and alcohol abuse (in adults and adolescents) can cause nightmares and night terrors. The sleep disruption of sleepwalking and night terrors adds to the symptoms of trauma, and they can feed on each other.

I have experienced both sleepwalking and night terrors throughout my life, up to the present day. I attribute these symptoms to stress, anxiety, and negative emotions, and I interpret these events as my brain's

---

16 Jay Vera Summer and Jay Vera Summer, "Night Terrors: Causes and Tips for Prevention," Sleep Foundation, February 29, 2024, https://www.sleepfoundation.org/parasomnias/night-terrors.

way of telling me I need to heal some part of my subconscious mind. As I heal, I have stopped sleepwalking, but still experience nightmares and night terrors, often waking up at night screaming. As far as I have come to master my mind, I have a long way to go.

Generally, my nightmares involve being in a dark place with an evil presence, being restrained or trapped, being abandoned by a loved one, or being naked in a public place, often in a courtroom. These are all trauma-related and will probably be with me until I completely heal my subconscious trauma. I usually wake up moaning or screaming, or thrash about trying to get out of bed. When I wake up, I am confused and disoriented. All of these are classic symptoms of nightmares and night terrors.

CHAPTER TWENTY-ONE

Lead Balloons Don't Fly

The year 1971 marked the introduction of the microprocessor, which defined the digital age. NASDAQ was introduced, and the Walt Disney World theme park opened near Orlando, Florida. Forced integration through school busing was affirmed by the US Supreme Court with drastic consequences in the South. The carrier service Federal Express began operations. Tobacco advertising on TV was banned. Idi Amin took control of Uganda. NPR began broadcasting. Qatar and Sierra Leone were granted independence from the UK. Apollo 14 landed on the moon.

I was admitted into a small liberal arts college in Davidson, North Carolina known as Davidson College, only thirty miles from Charlotte. It had a small, all-male enrollment of approximately 1,100 students. I had almost no preference about where I went to college. As long as I could get away from my parents, it could have been anywhere. The universities in North Carolina didn't appeal to me. The main thing I wanted to avoid was more incidents like what had happened in high school, and in 1971 the larger universities were experiencing racial violence. Strangely enough, I was a bit of a prodigy in chemistry, having scored high enough on my advanced placement tests to place out of the first two years of chemistry at Davidson. Although I did not apply myself to academics, I did well in high school, graduating in the top 10 percent of my class. My college SAT scores were also remarkably high, so I could have gone wherever I liked.

I had never heard of Davidson College, but I knew some boys from Charlotte who were enrolled there. Davidson College was for smart rich kids and had a strong history of placing its graduates in top graduate schools. The word was that it was a prep school for doctors and lawyers. The one thing I did like about it was the small class size. I never even visited the campus; I just applied and was accepted. Although my father wanted me to go to West Point, at least he was thrilled that I was going to an elite school.

Davidson was not a particularly happy experience for me. Being away from the micromanagement of my parents created a backlash of biblical proportions. Alcohol and other mind- and mood-altering substances were in generous supply, as the hippie movement of the 1960s was still in full swing. It was certainly eye-opening and mind-expanding, but my commitment to all things scholarly was sorely lacking. My Guru and my Warrior both loved different things about the altered states I chose, the Warrior being able to occasionally relax a little bit, and my Guru loving that I would forget about my insecurities and laugh and dance freely. I would always regret not applying myself to my studies, but my Warrior was too busy rebelling against discipline of any kind.

The fall term started on a positive note: I avoided the draft. In 1971, it was a lottery system, and my birthday ended up being a very high draft number. There was no chance that I would be selected for military service. Several of my hometown friends received low draft numbers, so they enlisted in the Navy and spent their two years docked in Norfolk, Virginia. I was extremely grateful that I never had to deal with the military in my life. My father wasn't thrilled because he thought that if I was drafted, I would be forced to reconsider my refusal to go to West Point. He was tenacious, to say the least.

I tried out for the golf team, which was more of a golf club than a team, and I played in several matches. Two events ended my college golf career. The first was my introduction to alcohol and drugs. The second was joining a fraternity. In 1971, Dr. Sam Spencer was hired by Davidson College from Baldwin College, an all-women's college in Virginia. His claim to fame was that he had dismantled the sorority system and made all sororities voluntary and open to whoever wanted to join them. It was a bold move met with mixed reviews, but since Davidson College was progressive to a fault, he was encouraged by the Board of Trustees to do the same to Davidson's fraternity system.

When Dr. Spencer came to Davidson, he enacted the rule that anyone could join any fraternity they wished. There were eight fraternities, and they responded in different ways. Three of the fraternities lost their national charters and disbanded. Four accepted the change publicly but privately made every effort to let interested freshmen know they would not be welcomed, and their lives would be hell if they joined. One fraternity, Sigma Phi Epsilon (SPE), decided to move off campus and keep its exclusivity.

In the SPE fraternity, I had finally found a group of men who would be my brothers, and SPE found a rich kid who fit into their social structure. It was a match made in heaven. I immediately pledged the fraternity in the first trimester of my freshman year, and my fate was sealed. Not only could I get a steady supply of alcohol and recreational drugs, but I also quickly formed bonds with men who shared my political and social views.

I was assigned a "big brother" whose name was Dan Thompson. I loved the idea of having a big brother, an experience I had missed out on growing up, and we became lifelong friends. Dan was the social chairman of SPE, so I had a crash course in how to party—something that I had great skill sets for but no experience. My early days of risk-taking and a taste for the thrill prepared me for it in ways I didn't see coming. Both my Guru and my Warrior worried from the start that I would take it too far.

The fall trimester was less than spectacular, but not dismal. I had a 2.9 average, two Bs, and a C. My father wasn't happy but accepted the scores as a learning curve and thought I would do better the next semester. I had every intention of bringing up my grades, but because I was a chemistry major and taking advanced classes, this would require dedication and focus, commodities that I held in very short supply. I was more interested in partying than studying, and although my faculty advisor was warning me that I needed to "buckle down," I had other ideas. My Warrior began to prepare for the worst.

Towards the end of the fall term, I was invited to attend a meeting introducing transcendental meditation (TM). TM was a meditation technique introduced to the West by Maharishi Mahesh Yogi, an Indian spiritual leader. Although the fees charged to adults were quite expensive, student fees were minimal. I was curious about meditation, and since it was cheap, I decided to attend. I had no way of knowing what a huge difference this would make in my life.

When I was taught the technique, I immediately went into a deep trance. It felt like I was floating underwater, where everything was peaceful and calm. The meditation technique lasted twenty minutes, twice a day. When I was meditating, it felt like a being, or a group of beings, were trying to talk to me, but I couldn't quite make out what they were saying. The more I meditated, the closer I felt to hearing their messages. It reminded me of the energy and feelings associated with my early out-of-body experiences. My Guru luxuriated in my new habit, taking deeper sighs than It had in years.

My Warrior still believed It could never get too comfortable, and soon Its vigilance would be validated. The annual SPE scavenger hunt consisted of teams of pledges who went around campus with a list of items to be found, and the first team to return with a complete manifest of treasures won the day. Our team, fortified with large quantities of alcohol, was breezing through our list until we ran into an item that had to be retrieved from a fraternity brother's room.

The fraternity brother was at the fraternity house and would not give the pledges a key to his room. I asked the dorm manager if he could let us in, but he refused, stating it would cost him his job. So I did what any intoxicated eighteen-year-old with no impulse control would do: I decided to climb up to the window of the room and break in. My Warrior came fully to life, pushing my protesting Guru aside.

The room in question was on the top floor of Richardson Dorm, a five-story building of Georgian architecture. Fortunately, the window was not far from a balcony that was a common area for students to use, so I only had to inch my way about ten feet along a four-inch-wide ledge to make it to the window. Although it was about sixty feet to the ground, I was feeling immortal and bulletproof. With drunken yet catlike reflexes, I managed to make it to the window, only to find it locked. Then old Murphy, that cynic with his wretched universal law, came to visit as I was trying to force the window open. My foot slipped, and I fell off the ledge.

Sixty feet is a long way to fall, especially with a brick-lined culvert directly below me. At the angle of impact, I landed on the edge of the brick wall on my left side, starting below my rib cage. The impact knocked me unconscious, but my descent scraped all the skin on that side of my body off, and my head hit the brick wall, ripping all the skin off the left side of my face. The whiplash of the impact permanently injured my neck, which would bother me for the rest of my life.

"Where am I? I don't seem to be in my body." I thought.

"*What are you doing here?*" The Angel asked.

"You aren't supposed to be here." I thought, "This is really weird. I can see you. You are a blob of light."

The Angel replied, "*You are in a different dimension. This is where you go when you leave your body, usually permanently.*"

I said, "What does that mean, 'leave your body'?"

The Angel replied, *"When you die, or have a catastrophic event that knocks you out of your body, your consciousness, or awareness of what is, is disconnected from your physical body. Some people describe it as floating and looking down on their body. Some people experience traveling to different places without their body, sometimes called astral projection. When you hit the ground, you were separated from your body. You could be dead, or not."*

I pondered this, while also wondering, "Where have you been? I haven't heard from you for several years."

The Angel replied, *"As I recall, you told me to 'shut the fuck up.' I was doing as requested."*

"Well, since I can see you now, do you have a name?"

The Angel said, *"You can call me Bob."*

"Bob?" I had to laugh. "That isn't very dignified."

The Angel responded, *"My real name is long and hard to say, so let's keep it simple. Bob will do."*

"Okay, Bob, am I going to live?" I asked.

This time it was Bob's turn to laugh. *"Oh, yes, you don't get out this easily."*

I was distinctly outside of my body, looking down on its broken, injured frame. I saw that it was lying at the bottom of a window well in a gathering pool of blood. The window well was hidden behind a row of bushes, and I could see my fraternity brothers running around calling for me. At that point, I was immersed in a floating sensation, a suspended state where I was no longer in pain. It felt like I was meditating, but even more pronounced. I felt my Guru near me, although it felt nebulous and out of reach.

There were several beings floating around me that were more like light bodies than physical bodies; they didn't have arms or legs but looked more like elongated eggs. They were talking to me in a musical language that I strangely understood.

They were laughing at me, telling me that I could not escape my destiny so easily. There was no sense of anxiety or fear, and for the first time in a long time, I felt stress-free. My Warrior was nowhere in sight. I was completely disconnected from my past and free from all the negative beliefs, thoughts, and emotions that almost always crowded my psyche. I asked them if they knew Bob but got no response. I wanted to ask these beings many questions, but before I could, they came together and pushed me, hard, back into my body.

Suddenly, I was aware of someone yelling my name and asking if I was alright. All I could choke out was a garbled "no." I couldn't take a deep breath, and my left side felt like it was on fire. My Warrior was back and was roaring at the top of Its lungs, desperate for someone to find me. My fraternity brothers arrived and together grabbed my left arm and started pulling me out of the well, which hurt like hell.

When my fellow pledges got me out and got a look at me, one of them threw up, and the others looked worried. Gingerly, as though I might break all the way through, they lowered me into a car and took me to the campus infirmary. There was no doctor on duty, only a nurse. Due to the late hour, the nurse decided to sedate me and call for an ambulance in the morning.

I woke up the next morning wrapped head to toe in gauze, which was starting to bleed through. I felt like I had stepped in front of a speeding bus. I couldn't see out of my left eye, which I later found out was covered by bandaging, much to my relief. The nurse told me the doctor was on his way and that I would have to be taken by ambulance to a Charlotte hospital.

I asked if she could call my parents, which she did. She came back and reported that they were out of the country. This news caused me to laugh out loud, which I immediately regretted as pain shot excruciatingly up my side.

The doctor arrived and examined me. Taking off the bandages was almost as bad as the impact of the fall, as the blood had congealed and required some tugging to get off. My Warrior was beside Itself, trying to hold back the pain with Its mighty shield. After a few minutes of poking and prodding, the doctor informed me that I had significant damage to my ribcage and possible interior damages as well.

My face would probably require surgery, but he couldn't tell under the bandages. I told him I wanted to go to Charlotte, so the doctor arranged for an ambulance to take me to the hospital. He also gave me some heavy-duty narcotics for the pain, which suited me just fine.

When I got to the emergency room, all I could think about was how this was the hospital where I was born, and I wondered if this was where I was going to die. At that point, I heard the musical voices in my head, the same ones that I had heard while floating outside of my body.

They told me not to worry, that I would live a long and important life. They also asked me if I was ready to stop going to the hospital so many times. I couldn't fully commit, so I simply thought, "We shall see." I was x-rayed from head to foot before the team of surgeons came into my stall in the emergency room.

The lead surgeon began, "Well, the good news is we don't have to operate. But you have significant damage to your ribs and face, not to mention the loss of skin on your side and face. Surgery won't help anything; we are just going to give you a rib harness to hold your ribs in place so they can heal.

"You have two dislocated ribs and five cracked ribs and are lucky that nothing internal was punctured. The skin on your face will grow back eventually, but it may look bad for a while." I lay back down in relief. I had not been looking forward to surgery. Gingerly, I asked, "Can I go home?" The surgeons nodded their heads in approval. I considered telling them about my experience of floating over my body but thought better of it.

Mrs. O'Neill picked me up and took me home. I was glad to lie down in my familiar bed; it had been a brutal two days. If I could stay medicated, I felt that I could survive. I even felt calm enough to face my parents when they returned the next day. Luckily winter break had started, so I wouldn't miss any classes.

Davidson had a no-cut policy, but I felt sure that, as medical circumstances had warranted it, I could get by. I continued to meditate, which made a significant improvement in my healing. It seemed like every day the soreness and wounds were substantially better. I was quite surprised that meditating would have such a profound healing effect. What was most remarkable was the similarity between the feelings of deep meditation and the feelings of being out of my body without a care in the world.

The next day, my parents got home, and I had to pay the devil for the dance that I had called. Of course, my father read the riot act about fraternities and irresponsibility. My mother weighed in about image, gossip, and embarrassing the family. Fortunately, they were so shocked at the sight of me and extremely concerned about my injuries that it tempered some of their usual dogmatic lecturing.

I realized that even though they were very unhappy with me, they cared about me. I was still lost in wondering about the voices I was hearing in my head and my near-death experience while in the window well, but those questions would not be answered for many years.

I stayed in bed the entire winter break. My father would not hear of me missing school unless my condition was critical, so I was met with a hero's welcome when I returned to school. Dan, my fraternity big brother, just looked at me and handed me a joint. After a few puffs, I started to feel very glad to be back at school. With the help of meditation, I was healing extremely fast. My face was almost completely restored to its normal state; no one could tell I had lost skin. My ribs were still hurting, but I didn't need a harness.

I could only attribute the rapid healing to the fact that I was meditating for long periods of time. While I meditated, I would get glimpses of the light beings that I saw while I was out of my body in the window well. They would whisper to me, but most of the time I couldn't understand what they said. When I meditated, I could viscerally feel my body healing much faster. The results astounded the doctors, who said they had never seen anyone heal that quickly. I was up and running in no time. Again, both my Guru and my Warrior were pleased.

CHAPTER TWENTY-TWO

Near-Death Experiences

It would be many years before I would realize that I had a near-death experience. With all my prior injuries, I chalked it up to just another event I survived. It didn't even occur to me that I had experienced something potentially life-changing. Near-death experiences (NDEs) are often defined as an event involving a serious medical condition resulting from catastrophic injury that involves loss of consciousness or life functions. It often involves significant head or bodily injury (trauma) and a dream-like experience involving an afterlife interaction with supernatural beings. Depending on neurology and beliefs, people may experience positive visions, dreams, or out-of-body experiences as well as hellish, negative experiences. I have made a documentary about NDEs, called *Beyond Physical Life*, which was released in the spring of 2025.

When the frontal cortex is compromised due to unconsciousness or injury, our innermost biases, beliefs, and dreams come to play. NDEs are quite common, with eight hundred to nine hundred NDEs reported every day in the United States. Surveys have established some common themes and experiences during the near-death experience, many of which I encountered myself. They include: an altered consciousness or awareness of death; a feeling of peace and calm with other positive emotions; an out-of-body experience that involves seeing your body from above; a tunnel experience; movement towards a bright light; conversations with beings of light or without form; reunion with deceased friends and loved ones; going through a life review; suspension of time and space; gaining new understandings of life; acquiring talents or powers not present prior to the NDE; and a decision to return to your body. [17]

I can personally attest that NDEs often result in changes in personality and mindset, as well as gifts or powers not experienced before. I experienced:

- Greater appreciation for life and myself
- Greater compassion for others
- Heightened sense of purpose and self-understanding
- Desire to learn
- Elevated spirituality
- Feelings of being more intuitive
- No longer worrying about death

Spoiler alert: This would not be my last NDE. I would go on to have repeated NDEs, which would change my relationship with the world. I would develop a different perspective on life and would often wonder why people felt and believed differently. At times, I would think there was something wrong with me. I imagine that you have felt this way before too, but as you continue reading, you will see that there is nothing wrong with you. Some unlearning and relearning may need to take place, but you have reasons for all the choices you've made. As you begin to understand them, you can also learn how to make new ones that serve you best.

---

17   Jeffrey Long and Paul Perry, *God And the Afterlife: The Groundbreaking New Evidence for God and Near-Death Experience* (Harper Collins, 2016).

CHAPTER TWENTY-THREE

Alternate Realities

Another milestone in my freshman year life was my introduction to psychedelics. Timothy Leary was getting quite a bit of underground press, and his motto of "tune in, turn on, drop out" was a favorite line of the counterculture at Davidson. My first experience wasn't intentional. Dan was friends with an upperclassman named Bob Mendleson, an intellectual who was as counterculture as it got in North Carolina.

While the SPE political posture was conservative republican, Mendleson favored anarchy and chaos. On one occasion, I went to a meeting where Mendleson and some off-campus men were planning how they would blow up local bridges. I thought they were nuts. One night, Don and I stopped by Mendleson's room to visit. Two lava lamps lit the room eerily, and Mendleson sat on the edge of his tousled bed, drinking wine from a bottle. I asked if I could have a drink, and he said, slowly and deliberately, "Sure, but it has acid in it."

I assumed he was kidding. Immediately, I took several big swigs from the bottle and smirked, announcing, "I don't feel anything." Mendleson just laughed and lay back on his bed, sinking into his covers. After a while, he raised himself up on his arms with the most peculiar blissed out look on his face and passed me a joint. When I inhaled, the world exploded. I had never felt that way before. My body started tingling from head to toe, and everything was obscenely funny. Before long I was giggling uncontrollably.

It was like the veils of reality had parted, and I could see something hilarious on the other side, although I couldn't get my head around what it was. Feeling no pain, my body felt euphoric in a way I had never experienced. School, parents, my past, all faded away, and time collapsed into the chair I was sitting in with Dan and Mendleson. Mendleson looked at Dan and said, "You better get him to his room, he won't be able to find it later." So Dan took me back to my room, and I went to bed.

My freshman roommate was a straightlaced young Christian man from Atlanta named Michael Pecan. Michael was on academic scholarship and was quite fed up with my social life and lack of scholarship. Michael had asked twice for a change of roommates, but the dean of students wouldn't allow it.

We were stuck with each other until the end of the school year. When I returned to our room that night, Don simply led me to my bed, and I fell in. The lights were out because Michael went to bed early. I turned on my back and experienced six hours of alternative reality.

About three hours into the effects of the drug, I was looking at the ceiling, and a window appeared, revealing venetian blinds that were closed. Suddenly, the blinds opened, and a huge eyeball appeared, looking through the window directly at me. I thought it was the eye of God. Even worse, I wondered whether it was me looking at myself.

I tried closing my eyes, but the open window with the gaping eyeball was there whether my eyes were open or closed. My body prickled with feelings of anticipation, exhilaration, and something I couldn't name. The window expanded to a grand portico, like those of classic Southern homes, with columns and balconies wrapping around a huge and beautiful building. My view expanded to include thousands of similarly stunning, starkly white buildings. It occurred to me, in my sensory-heightened state, that this was what my vision of heaven was like. It took my breath away.

Then I saw him, hovering above it all. He lowered himself down to me slowly, unhurriedly. "Bob, is that you?"

Bob answered back, *"It is,"* and smiled that beatific smile of his.

I sighed deeply. "Bob, I am not having such a good time here in this school."

"Patience, my boy, patience. Sometimes getting an education is not about having fun. You need to focus more."

I couldn't hold back my disdain, even there in my version of heaven. "What in the world will I learn here that I will remember in twenty-five years?"

Bob replied thoughtfully. *"Hopefully you will learn how to write so you can tell your story one day. You might learn some history so you can gain some perspective on where you are in the world. If you stop being self-absorbed, you may make some friends. Finally, you may even learn that escaping reality is just a waste of time. Getting high may feel good, but it basically puts your life on hold and can get you into hard places, physically and mentally. It can become a very destructive habit. Just remember that fools never learn, smart people learn from their mistakes, and wise people learn from other people's mistakes."*

That was a lot to swallow, especially in my current state. I switched gears. "Bob, was that your eyeball I saw looking through the window?"

Bob laughed. *"Yes."*

"That was a little dramatic, wasn't it?"

Bob replied, *"Everything you perceive is a projection."*

I couldn't help myself. "What the fuck does that mean?"

"Everything you witness is simply data. What you perceive is how you interpret that data. So, if you think something is bad, that is because you perceive it to be bad. Your mind labels it as bad. That is the same thing with all judgment, bad or good, right or wrong. When you can see things objectively, without projecting your opinion on them, you will be a

lot more effective, and happier."

I mused on that for a second and exhaled loudly. "I'm too fucked up to understand that."

Bob smiled again. *"That's okay, I'll keep reminding you."*

After a few hours, the effects of the drug started to wear off, and I was able to fall asleep. In my dream, I was back with the light beings I had seen when I fell off the dormitory. It was so vivid that I wasn't sure whether I was reliving it or dreaming it. The beings kept whispering to me in lilting tones, the same ones I was starting to hear in my mind most of the time, like bewitching elevator music. It was beautiful, even if I couldn't understand what they were saying. I felt safe and cocooned. My Guru lay beside me, humming Its own reassuring tune and stroking my hair. I didn't want to ever wake up.

The next morning, I realized I had a German test. I went to the professor and feigned food poisoning to get out of the exam. It would not be the last time I would shirk responsibilities because of an interaction with alcohol or drugs. In fact, there would be more times than I could or cared to count. Instinctively, I knew it was counterproductive, but the short-term exhilaration that I felt gave me a break from the demons in my mind. And that was incredibly hard to resist.

Substance abuse was an escape from the negative feelings, emotions, and beliefs I had about myself. Whenever I was high, I felt like a great weight was lifted from my psyche. Life was fun, responsibilities were avoided, and the painful memories of my childhood evaporated like the morning mist. Unfortunately, the guilt and shame, which inevitably followed the substance use, made me feel worse. My self-hatred only intensified. Nothing I could do would ever shake the underlying belief that I was a mistake and shouldn't be on this planet.

After I experienced my first drug trip, things began to get back to more of a routine. I started studying a little bit, as my father was calling every week to get a report of my progress. The poor report card was a bit of a wake-up call. I had always been at the top of my class, and I wasn't used to being regarded as a shoddy student. I couldn't accept the idea of letting go of one of the only things that I was proud of—and that my father respected. That galvanized me to study harder and go to class. Things were looking up. Then, just as it seemed that I might be getting a handle on my life, my hopes and dreams about the opposite sex came true.

Her name was JoAnn Wilson, and we were set up on a blind date by one of my fraternity brothers. She was a freshman at UNC Greensboro, which was known for having attractive students. When we looked at one another, it was lust at first sight. We slept together our first night, and I felt like I had found my soulmate. I had known her for all of three hours. We were inseparable over the weekend, and I was brokenhearted when she had to go back to Greensboro. My Warrior wept into my notebooks, already fearing abandonment, as I tried unsuccessfully to study.

I fell head over heels into sexual attraction, and my world became focused on her. I began to travel to Greensboro every weekend to see her, and on the way, my Guru bounced on the leather seats of my car in excitement. Love and sex felt so good! I even stopped my extracurricular substance abuse. My fraternity brothers thought I had lost my mind, but I had simply lost perspective, as so many new lovers do.

I even took her home to meet my parents, which was an ill-fated affair. My mother took an instant dislike to her, probably even before they met. To my mother, no one was good enough for me, especially some tart from Greensboro. JoAnn was adopted and therefore flunked the pedigree test. My father was horrified to learn that UNCG had an open-door policy, which meant that visitors could sleep with the girls in their dorm room. The old vein in his forehead that I remembered so well from my childhood took to pulsing again any time the subject was raised.

I certainly didn't tell them what I had been doing for the last month, climbing into JoAnn's bed on the weekends and ravaging her every chance I got. My father started cross-examining JoAnn about her background as only a judge could do. I was thoroughly embarrassed, and JoAnn was devastated by my parents' treatment of her. As I was driving her back to UNCG, she informed me that she would never do that again. I couldn't blame her and wished, as I had many times in my life, that I had come from a different family. My Warrior couldn't have agreed more.

Spring term finally ended, and I went home with a B average. My parents weren't satisfied, but at least I'd improved. All I'd been thinking of was being with JoAnn over the summer, and I couldn't wait to call her the day after I got home. I was shocked and brokenhearted to find out the number she had given me was a wrong number. I called information, but there was no listing for her.

I called UNCG student affairs and asked for her contact information. I was told that it was confidential and could only be shared with the authorization of the student. With every dead end, I felt like the earth was caving underneath me, and I clung desperately to the hope that I could call her when she got back to school the next fall. Except she did not return to UNCG. I would never see her again.

I felt like the world had collapsed in on me. I had never felt so depressed about anything in my life. She was pretty, smart, and now a ghost. All the negative thoughts in my head started playing repeatedly. The Greek chorus of "you are a loser," "you will never have a girlfriend again," "you are unlovable" was incessant. I just wanted to crawl into a fetal position and die. My Guru was nowhere to be found, while my Warrior bellowed and growled without stopping.

I hired a private investigator to try and find her, but she had disappeared off the face of the earth. I began to wonder if I had hallucinated the whole story in some sort of hallucinogenic flashback of epic proportions. My parents assured me she was real, even if they didn't think she was "good enough" for me. I almost wished that she had been an acid dream, because then I wouldn't have to feel so abandoned and rejected. My mind scrambled constantly, trying to understand why she disappeared, and my heart felt like it would never be able to close the gaping hole she left behind.

CHAPTER TWENTY-FOUR

Scapegoating

I was labeled the black sheep of the family when I refused to go to West Point. My father took it personally and would repeatedly let me know how disappointed he was that I chose not to go to the military academy that had made him into what he had become. Years of therapy and research have taught me that people resort to making a scapegoat of a child to avoid dealing with their own emotional turmoil. As soon as someone is scapegoated, the family will try to make it stay that way so they do not have to deal with their own problems or vulnerabilities. When we try to change or leave, we may be emotionally blackmailed or manipulated. That was exactly my experience whenever I sought to live my own life and explore what I wanted.

This exhibited itself in a number of ways: I was criticized for being different; I was treated differently from my siblings; I was never allowed to forget my mistakes, and my punishments were often harsher than my siblings'; I felt bullied by my parents; and my achievements were often dismissed.

Proper parenting includes acknowledgment and validation. I needed to feel wanted and welcomed by my parents, not the constant criticism I experienced. Grades can be a source of pride or shame, but when anything less than an A+ was a source of shame, I always felt like a failure. It felt like my inner critic was a monster who knew no limits, while my inner child felt abandoned and rejected. When we are constantly disciplined by our parents, we lose our sense of self-worth and the ability to manage stress and setbacks. I felt like no matter what I did or how well I did it, it wasn't good enough.

Parents who are overprotective and controlling of their children's social interaction interfere with the child's socialization and individuation. I was not allowed to play with classmates on a regular basis, and I was not allowed to have unsupervised social time with friends. I had few friends and never went out with girls until college. It was not allowed. I suspect that my parents' need to maintain control came from their fear of being dispensable. They tried to use me to fill a void they felt from being displeased with their own lives or relationships.

It was obvious to me that my parents' need for control overrode my need for independence. Therapists told me that my sense of self was based on what my parents wanted. This kind of dynamic results in a relationship where people become excessively involved with each other.

My family boundaries were blurred or nonexistent. A switch in my parents' mood quickly affected the whole family. Since I did not grow up with firm emotional boundaries, I struggled to set them as an adult. I found it difficult to differentiate between my feelings and the feelings of those close to me. I felt the need to help others, often compulsively.

The erasure of boundaries is an insidious, toxic family dynamic because it often occurs under the guise of love, loyalty, family, or unity, which makes it even more deceptive. I felt like I was imprisoned in a web of family needs and wants rather than focusing on my own needs and wants.

My parents were my first role models. When they criticized me for my accomplishments or put me down, I began to develop low self-esteem and hate myself. As an adult, I felt guilty or ashamed of my accomplishments. I even struggled with the need to sabotage myself, stay average, and purposely underachieve. As a result, I often felt like an impostor or defective. I felt dead inside, anxious, needy, and insecure. I was wary of relationships and doubted people's motives. I was conflicted between needing support and connection and fearing contact. I carried grudges and became resentful and suspicious.

These are the consequences of being the black sheep of the family.

CHAPTER TWENTY-FIVE

Don't Change Dicks in the Middle of a Screw— Vote for Nixon in '72

The year 1972 was a year of violence. Israeli Olympic athletes were executed by Palestinian gunmen in Munich. The US was testing nuclear weapons in Nevada, and the Irish conflict literally blew up, with many casualties on both sides. The Watergate break-in occurred on June 17, 1972, but Nixon was reelected anyway. Roe v. Wade was decided. OPEC reduced the flow of oil to the US, and gasoline prices soared. The American Indian Movement occupied Wounded Knee, with gunfire between them and US federal agents. The last US troops were withdrawn from Vietnam. Alabama Governor George Wallace was shot three times and paralyzed. *The Godfather, Dirty Harry, The Last Picture Show*, and *A Clockwork Orange* were the big movies of the year.

My sophomore year was much calmer and more pedestrian than my first. Ironically, I was asked by an upperclassman fraternity brother to live with him in the very basement room where I had fallen into the window well. I reflected that sometimes life predicts itself.

The voices in my head were now belly laughing. I decided to clean up my act. I started taking karate from another student, George

Stavros. George was a huge fellow from Long Island and had a black belt in Shorin Ryu karate. I had no idea what that was, but my sister was taking tae kwon do at Berkeley, and I somehow couldn't shake the feeling of competition our relationship always spurned.

Shorin Ryu karate was not fancy. It was basically boxing with some kicks thrown in. I enjoyed karate; it was weird enough to satisfy my rebellious nature. It also got me into better shape, and I started slimming down. My Warrior loved the opportunity to blow off steam, and my Guru loved how it felt to be strengthening my body.

With my newfound love of karate, I straightened up my lifestyle. I stopped drinking and other mood-altering activities and concentrated on my studies. For once it was a relatively calm year. I didn't date much, as my Warrior guarded my heart night and day, still reeling over JoAnn's unexplained disappearance from my life. I even drove to UNCG to see if I could get some background information on her, to no avail. In many ways, I was doing better, but I also started feeling depressed, which was a cloud that would cast a shadow over my life for many years to come.

My depression crept around corners in my mind in ways that my Guru longed to chase away. My mind, while still often wallowing in pain, also began to find other ways to fill the space drinking and drugs had taken up. My creative nature began to flourish. I started painting and, in my typical overzealous fashion, painted everything I could get my hands on. I painted our entire dorm room with the interior scene of the Yes album *Close to the Edge*, which had islands floating in the sky and waterfalls of brilliant colors. I used dayglow paint for an even more eclectic feel. Students from all over campus would come to see our room. I was settling down into a dull routine, which in ways was a welcome break from the last few years. It was a brief period of what felt like growing up.

Towards the end of the school year, I had a karate test to advance to green belt. I had already earned a yellow belt and wanted to get my green belt as quickly as possible. My sensei, George, was a hot-tempered young man who loved to go into bars on Long Island and pick fights. He slept with his legs in a sling to increase his kicking flexibility. He was unpredictable and a bit of a nut. My Guru never trusted him. However, I wanted a green belt, so I asked to be tested. George thought I wasn't ready, but the test would tell. My Warrior was itching to prove him wrong.

The green belt test was a series of choreographed karate punches and kicks called katas. There were seven katas that I had to do perfectly, without any missteps or losing my balance. Each kata had to end in the same place it started, and each technique had to be flawless. Most people failed during the kata sequence, because it is very exhausting, and each one becomes more and more difficult.

However, to everyone's surprise, especially mine, I passed. George wasn't happy about it because he wanted to maintain his image as the only upper-level rank karate master at school. There remained one final test: I had to spar with George. Sparring was supposed to be non-contact. That was part of the test—to throw the punch or the kick as close to your opponent as possible without touching them.

I was doing well until I executed a flying jump kick at George's stomach at the exact instant George stepped forward to deliver a punch. I knocked the wind out of him, and he went down to one knee. I could hear the audible gasp from the class. It was the first time they had seen George hit in any way, and for him to go down was unexpected.

Given George's temper, everyone (including me) knew I was about to get my ass kicked. I didn't have to wait long. I bowed to George, and while I was bent over, George executed a spinning roundhouse kick that caught me just above the ear. I went down like a sack of wet sand.

"Bob, are you there?" I thought.

"Yep, I'm here." The voice cut through the darkness.

"Bob, am I dead?"

"No," said Bob, *"but you obviously have left your body."*

"Why did this happen?" I asked.

Bob replied with a question of his own. *"Why did you take karate?"*

I said, "To learn how to protect myself."

Bob said, *"Go deeper. What was the real reason you took karate?"*

I thought about that and answered honestly, "Because Kitty was bragging about taking martial arts, and I wanted to beat her."

"Why do you have to compete against your sister all of the time?" asked Bob.

"It's what I was raised to do."

"Well, can you see how your programming may be causing you pain and suffering? And I am not just talking about physical pain and suffering like you are experiencing today," answered Bob. *"Wake up."*

I was told later that they had to do CPR to get me breathing again. The instant I heard "wake up," I was suddenly back in my body with a massive headache. The other students stood me up and asked me if I needed to go to the hospital. I asked if I was bleeding, and when the surprising answer was no, I declined. I felt that my parents had seen me in a hospital enough for the time being. I was probably concussed, but I was used to that. I could imagine my father saying, "I hope it knocked some sense into him." I didn't need him adding insult to my injury.

George was nowhere to be seen. I didn't return to the karate class, and I never saw George again. Several years later, I heard that he was seriously injured in a bar fight that he had started. Rumor had it that he was paralyzed, but I never tried to find out. I remembered the old saying, "He who lives by the sword shall perish by the sword."

If only I could get my Warrior to understand the meaning of the phrase.

CHAPTER TWENTY-SIX

Functional Neurological Disorder

I began to experience acute depression and panic attacks. Whenever my father criticized me or yelled at me, I would completely shut down. The brain is a sensitive and complicated machine, and sometimes it malfunctions for unknown reasons. As a result, individuals can experience stress- or trauma-related symptoms. These include:

- Chronic pain
- Fatigue
- Insomnia
- Anxiety
- Panic attacks
- Depression
- Loss of motor control
- Loss of memory
- Sensory dysfunction

- Dizziness
- Functional seizures

The causes of functional neurological disorder (FND) are unknown, though childhood abuse is a common denominator for people diagnosed with FND.[18] Some preexisting conditions can bring on FND symptoms, including physical injury, panic attacks, abuse, or severe headaches.

FND has traditionally been defined by psychologists as a disorder in which repressed psychological stress or trauma gets converted into a physical symptom. This is where the term conversion disorder comes from. Psychological disorders and stressful life events, both recent and in childhood, are risk factors for developing the condition.

Anxiety disorders and depression can sometimes cause physical symptoms that overlap with FND symptoms. For example, panic attacks can present with symptoms such as pins and needles in the fingers or mouth, and depression often causes poor concentration or fatigue.

Anxiety, panic attacks, and depression are common in patients with FND. Other psychiatric conditions include PTSD and emotionally unstable personality traits (often related to past trauma).

---

18 "Functional Neurologic Disorder," National Institute of Neurological Disorders and Stroke, n.d., https://www.ninds.nih.gov/health-information/disorders/functional-neurologic-disorder.

CHAPTER TWENTY-SEVEN

On the Outside Looking In

In 1973, the United States ended its involvement in the Vietnam War after the signing of the Paris Peace Accords. OPEC instituted an oil embargo in retaliation for US support of Israel in the Yom Kippur War. Gas prices skyrocketed as much as 200 percent, and gas shortages were experienced all over the US, beginning the first oil crisis. The Watergate scandal erupted. Roe v. Wade caused the US Supreme Court to rule abortion a constitutional right.

In my junior year, the opportunity arose to live off campus at the house SPE leased for their fraternity house. Rather than live in the large fraternity house, I opted to rent a small room in the "dollhouse," a small building at the back of the fraternity house. My room was eight feet by eight feet with a small attached living room. There was one other person living in the dollhouse, Preston Clark, who was not a member of the fraternity but was friends with many of my senior fraternity brothers.

In a strange twist of fate, I was elected the fraternity president. It certainly wasn't expected, as I was put on the ballot purely as a joke. No one really expected me to win, but as I was the "counter candidate," that seemed to strike a chord with most of my fraternity brothers.

So, I had a lot to look forward to as I drove to Davidson for my junior year. The summer at home had been uneventful. I spent the months at a temporary job in the trust department at Wachovia Bank.

It was meaningless, boring work, but it got me out of the house and away from my parents and sisters. After finishing, I would go straight to the golf course and not return home until after dark. Interaction with my sisters was infrequent. Kitty had moved to a room in the basement to get away from me, so an uneasy truce prevailed. It was the quietest summer my Warrior ever had.

When I arrived at the off-campus fraternity house, there were police everywhere. I was wondering what the hell was going on. I went into the main house, where I was questioned by police detectives about a friend, Bill Walker, a black student who was popular with the fraternity members. I didn't know him that well, but we were always friendly.

The detectives finally informed me that Bill had gone into my room in the dollhouse at about 2:00 a.m. and had blown his brains out of his skull with a .30-06 hunting rifle stuck in his mouth. No one had any idea why Bill ended his life, or why he had chosen my room to do the deed. He didn't leave a suicide note. His corpse was removed later that morning, and I was there to see it taken away. Even my Warrior could barely stand the sight. I had never seen what a large-bore, high-velocity bullet could do at close range, but the term "blew his head off" was accurate. I was sick to my stomach, while my Warrior bellowed inside of me.

The police finished their investigation, and I was allowed to move into my room later that evening. As the body had sat there for nearly twenty hours in the hot August weather, the smell was nauseating. Over and over, I went into the small bathroom and threw up. I spent the rest of the evening picking skull fragments out of the four walls of my room. Even bleach did not eliminate the smell left by Bill's corpse. My Guru and Warrior were both climbing my interior walls to escape it.

"Why is there death?" I asked.

Bob replied, *"Because life would be so boring without it."*

I thought about that and said, "It seems like such a waste to me."

Bob said, *"There is nothing wasted in the Universe. Matter simply changes to energy, and energy changes into matter. Humans are born, and they die, and then they are born again. Nothing is wasted. When people die, they are just putting on different clothes. They continue to exist.*

"Humans are so melodramatic. The beings in my dimension think it is quite funny. You simply don't have the larger perspective. You have already experienced what it feels like when you die."

"What do you mean?" I asked.

"When you fell off the building, that is what it feels like. When you were knocked unconscious, that is what it feels like."

"Then why are we so afraid of dying?"

Bob sighed. *"It is because humans have forgotten that death is not the end. Death exists to make living more rewarding. Most people are so afraid of dying, not realizing that they are barely living. Many people needlessly chase their lost youth when they should be enjoying every stage of their life. That is why so many people are afraid of getting older and obsess over avoiding it. Just live your life as much as you can every day and forget about the dying part. It is just another part of living."*

Something changed in me that day. For some reason, the idea that death may visit at any time suddenly clicked and sent my mind spinning. It is one thing to contemplate it hypothetically; it was something completely different to see a still-warm corpse. And what was my response?

I started to party in earnest. I decided that the Bible was right: "Eat, drink, and be merry, for tomorrow we shall die." In a bit of synchronicity, I was taking a course on the history of philosophy. The ancient writings of Aristotle, Nietzsche, and Voltaire—all the classics—brought me comfort. I got an A in that course; the only A I earned at Davidson.

I started using recreational drugs again occasionally, but I pretty much stayed drunk every weekend. The fraternity had beer on tap, and I ran up an $800 bar tab, which I could not pay. I had to call my father for more money, resulting in him going ballistic. I eventually got the money by threatening him that I would get a part-time job, and my grades would be what they would be. Always preoccupied with keeping up appearances, my father sent me enough money to cover the bar tab with a stiff warning to watch my expenses.

I formed a self-defeating philosophy that I needed to get drunk and see how I performed while impaired. Academics, sports, and life in general were boring, so I told myself that I needed to get buzzed to see if I could do as well as when I was sober. It was a flimsy excuse to avoid finding out how well I could do. If I wasn't great at something, I had a built-in excuse. If I did well, being buzzed made it adventurous. My Guru and my Warrior were both confounded by these antics.

My father was fully focused on my future, which was the furthest thing from my mind. He hoped that since I didn't want to be a soldier, perhaps I could follow in his footsteps and be a lawyer. His father had been a lawyer and judge, and my father thought it would be the next best option for me to follow in the family tradition.

I, on the other hand, had started thinking about being an Outward Bound counselor. I had no interest in being a lawyer. I saw how my father was obsessed with it. I wanted to be immersed in nature, helping children. My Guru whispered to me often about it, how good it would be for me, how rewarding and grounding. After paying my absurd beer tab, Dick strongly recommended (a.k.a. threatened) that I renew my efforts to improve my grades if I wanted to get into law school. I whispered to myself that I deserved an Oscar for convincing him that I cared.

I enjoyed being SPE president. I changed a few rules about payment of membership dues and started enforcing fines for brothers who failed to pay their dues on time. That didn't make me popular with the brothers who were fined, but I focused on the payoff. The bank account of the fraternity began to swell. With the added funds, I recommended that the fraternity have more parties. That was met with a great hurrah, and surprise, surprise, my popularity began to grow.

One of the favorite fall parties was the Roman toga party. The drink served at the party was known as a "Purple Jesus" or "PJ." It was disgustingly mixed in a fifty-five-gallon Rubbermaid trash can with grain alcohol, fruit juices, Coca-Cola, Sprite, orange juice, sliced fruits, and grapes. In the basement of the fraternity house, brothers performed a candle-lit ritual to make the infamous drink the night before the party. The recipe was a trade secret of the SPE house, and only presidents and social chairmen knew its contents.

The party was a wild success. It was open to anyone who wore a toga, or at least a bedsheet. Prizes were handed out for best toga, best dancer, and best drunk. I borrowed some Bose speakers and set them up in the backyard. Around midnight, due to the wet conditions of the lawn, the brothers decided to have a mudslide.

Mudslides are great fun, with people running at full speed and jumping onto a downhill mud track and, in this case, sliding for forty yards and ending up at the bottom of the hill. A committee was formed to judge the slides, and cards were handed out numbered 1–10. There was no prize; the thrill of the slide was everyone's reward. The party broke up around 3:00 a.m. with many drunken bodies, in various stages of undress, passed out throughout the house and across the lawn. Properly made PJ has no taste of alcohol, and before people knew it, they had passed out.

I was called into the dean of students' office the next day. Dean Terry was a no-nonsense sort of person who did not like SPE because we would not submit to the open policy rule for fraternities. Dean Terry was looking for any excuse to have SPE lose its charter. Apparently, there had been some incidents with students causing trouble after returning from the toga party, including one student who had backed his car into a tree.

Dean Terry reprimanded me, as the president of the fraternity, and warned me that the school did not condone alcohol use by students under the legal drinking age of twenty-one. Any further incidents would be disciplined. I didn't bother arguing with Dean Terry; I knew that would be a wasted effort and probably bring more disciplinary action. I meekly said, "Yes, sir," and left. Of course, there was widespread use of alcohol and other substances on campus that was well known to the administration. Spies were everywhere.

My junior year, academically, was otherwise lackluster. I maintained my B average, much to the irritation of my father. I didn't date anyone and continued to nurse my heartache over JoAnn's ghost act. I kept calling UNCG, hoping to find some information about her. The administration either had no news or wouldn't share it. She remained a great mystery. My Warrior concluded what It had always witnessed—love hurts!—and vowed to steer me away from it in the future. From deep within, a great sigh escaped my Guru, and in its wake a delicate chime, one of the Guru's favorites, echoed three times and then faded away.

CHAPTER TWENTY-EIGHT

The Brain and Alcohol

As I have detailed earlier, I began my lifetime love-hate affair with alcohol in 1971. It was a crutch for my anxiety and depression, although it probably made them worse. Addiction is the malfunction of the pleasure centers of the brain that produce dopamine to reinforce positive behavior.

Several areas in the brain combine to regulate pleasure. These are the ventral tegmental area (VTA), the nucleus accumbens, the insula, the cingulate cortex, the orbitofrontal cortex, the amygdala, the hypothalamus, and the hippocampus. When we eat, meditate, have sex, and engage in pleasurable activities, these areas flood the brain with dopamine. In effect, the dopamine signals the brain to repeat the behavior to recreate the feeling of pleasure.[19]

Our brain responds to our environment in different ways, depending on whether the activity is culturally or physiologically beneficial or

---

19   Tarik Dahoun et al., "The Relationship Between Childhood Trauma, Dopamine Release and Dexamphetamine-induced Positive Psychotic Symptoms: A [11C]-(+)-PHNO PET Study," *Translational Psychiatry* 9, no. 1 (November 11, 2019), https://doi.org/10.1038/s41398-019-0627-y.

painful. Through trial and error, our brain figures out which behaviors are beneficial and which are dangerous. A good example would be the difference between masturbation and putting your hand on a hot stove. Both involve the use of our hand, but the pleasure centers are activated by masturbation, while the pain centers are activated by putting the hand on a hot stove.

The problems with alcohol and drugs are the result of the drugs' effect on our pleasure response. Due to the fact that we normally prefer pleasure to pain, our brains are hardwired to repeat behavior that causes pleasure. Alcohol and drugs produce much higher levels of dopamine than even healthy, pleasurable experiences, and, as a result, the brain focuses more on the drug experience than on more mundane, beneficial, and healthy behaviors that produce lower levels of dopamine. Thus, alcohol and drug use can render ordinarily pleasurable events seemingly boring, and we feel that these healthy experiences are lacking.

Substances that stimulate the dopamine-producing areas of the brain also create intense feelings of pleasure. Alcohol, opioids, nicotine, and other substances overstimulate these pleasure centers, which produce far more dopamine than is normally expected. As a result, the brain desires these substances more than any activity that would produce normal levels of dopamine. However, with chronic use of the substance, the brain's neuroplasticity adapts over time and becomes less sensitive to dopamine. Not only does the craving increase, but we build tolerance and need more and more of the substance to generate the level of high we crave. As a result, activities that would ordinarily create pleasure are no longer pleasurable.

The classic definition of addiction is any activity that includes adverse consequences that are ignored due to the compulsion to repeat the behavior. Alcoholism, for example, is the inability to control drinking alcohol, despite damage to the alcoholic's interpersonal relationships and physical health.

Alcoholics like to say that only the individual can decide if they are an alcoholic or not. To be more inclusive, the term "alcoholic" is no longer used; the friendlier term "substance use disorder" is now the term of art. Mental health professionals don't want the patient to feel bad about themselves. Individuals with a substance use disorder may have impaired thinking and behaviors beyond the effects of intoxication. These substances actually change the way the brain functions, especially in the areas of critical thinking, analysis, personality, and behavior. These people are usually aware of their problem, but may not be able to stop even if they want to and try to. The consequences of prolonged substance use disorder include the inability to control the amount consumed, adverse social problems, the absence of risk analysis, and, eventually, withdrawal symptoms. Addicts may resist getting help with their addictions because of the social stigma attached to admitting their problem. This is called denial. Society is lenient of substance use disorders until they cause adverse consequences affecting other people. Too many people have horrendous driving records with multiple driving while impaired (DWI) convictions. Many alcoholics or addicts may be highly functional despite their heavy alcohol or drug use. The tolerance effect leads them to use more and more, until it causes unacceptable adverse consequences.

Individuals suffering from trauma, depression, or anxiety may begin to use alcohol with other drugs to comfort themselves. Psychologists believe there is a connection between childhood trauma and substance use disorder, as well as obesity. That certainly is evidenced by my struggles with alcohol and being overweight. There is another connection between childhood trauma and substance use when substances were abused in the child's environment. The parents model substance abuse as a coping mechanism, which is copied by the child. This was my experience in a nutshell. The insecurity and negative self-image I formed as a child were a perfect excuse for drinking, especially since my parents were doing it.

There is a stronger likelihood for children exposed to ACEs to self-medicate than those who were not exposed to ACEs. Tragically, children or young adults who engage in substance abuse are more likely to experience more traumatic events, which become closed loops of abuse. I had been drinking during two of my NDEs, which likely caused these events to happen. Physical trauma causes pain, which often leads to self-medication and ultimately substance abuse.

The physical symptoms of addiction are remarkably similar to those of trauma.

Addiction Symptoms	Trauma Symptoms
Insomnia	Insomnia
Withdrawal	Fatigue
Poor digestion	Nervousness or fear
Withdrawal or cravings	Body aches and pains
Exhaustion	Tension
Sweating or trembling	Agitation
Appetite changes	Nightmares
Unpredictable behavior	Unpredictable behavior

The behavioral symptoms of addiction are also like those of trauma.

Addiction Behavior	Trauma Behavior
Losing interest in prior activities	Mood swings
Isolating	Isolating
Denial	Denial
Obsessing over substance use	Confusion
Financial and legal issues	Anger
Sacrificing relationships or career	Withdrawal
Adverse behavior patterns	Guilt, shame, or hopelessness

When trauma results in addiction, the consequences are often much more severe than a single diagnosis. In other words, the traumatic effects of addiction are amplified by underlying symptoms of physical, emotional, and mental trauma. The feelings of guilt, shame, anger, confusion, and other negative emotions are heightened and reinforced. Trauma-induced addiction is much more difficult to heal than simply trauma or addiction.

Alcohol affects every organ and tissue in the body. It can result in tissue injury and organ dysfunction. One of the most impactful effects of alcohol is how alcohol abuse disrupts the endocrine system. Almost every organ and cell of the body is regulated by the endocrine system. It controls metabolism and energy levels, electrolyte balances, growth, and development.[20]

The endocrine system is critical in the response to stress and injury. If the endocrine system is compromised, the autonomic nervous system may activate the Warrior unnecessarily and intensify its effects. Alcohol can multiply the intensity of stress, negative emotions, and depression, as well as suppress judgment, balance, and energy.

To put it bluntly, trying to manage stress and anxiety with substances or behavior designed to distract us from stress and anxiety carries an overwhelming risk of negative results. It is far more beneficial to focus on mastering our thoughts and emotions, rather than try to numb or distract ourselves from them.

---

20 Susanne Hiller-Sturmhöfel and Andrzej Bartke, "The Endocrine System: An Overview," 1998, https://pmc.ncbi.nlm.nih.gov/articles/PMC6761896/.

CHAPTER TWENTY-NINE

Summer Camp Comes to an End

In 1975, Bill Gates started Microsoft. The unemployment rate under Gerald Ford hit 9.2 percent, and the recession was recognized. King Faisal of Saudi Arabia was assassinated. Doctors went on strike for the first time in the US. Jimmy Hoffa disappeared. Patty Hearst became America's Most Wanted and was arrested for armed robbery. Motorola obtained a patent for the first mobile telephone. BIC introduced the first disposable razor. *Saturday Night Live* began on NBC, and *Jaws* and *One Flew Over the Cuckoo's Nest* were popular movies.

After my uneventful junior year, my senior year was exactly the opposite. I won a lottery of sorts and was able to get into the classiest dorm on campus, Duke Dormitory. I was in a suite with two other friends, right beside the gymnasium. It boasted a lot of amenities that the other dorms lacked, including rooftop sunning and two-room suites.

The Duke was usually reserved for elite athletes and honor students. Once again, I had slid under the radar and gotten a first-rate room. I had tired of the fraternity, and the politics and counterculture of being in an off-campus fraternity had worn thin. I wanted to get back into mainstream campus life, something that I had avoided as an SPE. I opted to move back on campus and lucked into Duke Dormitory.

My father was pushing me to apply to law school. Although I had no desire to go, I decided to at least check into the requirements to do so. In my junior year, I had realized the appeal of the Outward Bound program, and I secretly still wanted to become one of their counselors. I thought living outdoors and helping adolescents find their way would be a rewarding job. My Guru loved the idea and whispered to me often about it, how good it would be for me, how rewarding and grounding. I only mentioned it once to my parents, and their reaction was as volatile as it was predictable.

I hadn't heard my parents scream like that in several years. It even caught my Warrior off guard. I supposed that they thought if they said it loud enough, I would listen more. Nothing could have been further from the truth, but I wasn't committed to a career in counseling to the extent necessary to keep walking on that thin ice. When it came down to it, I simply wanted my parents to love me. Less important, but still true, I also still needed their financial support. If sacrificing my desires and living the life they wanted me to live offered that opportunity, I was willing to do that. Both my Guru and my Warrior cringed, but I ignored their dissent.

In the fall, I went to meet the pre-law advisor. Professor Minson was a philosophy professor who ran a tight ship in the pre-law department. He was very proud of his record of placing students in reputable law schools. He looked at me like something that had crawled out from behind the cabinet in his office.

When I informed him that I wanted to know what I needed to do to apply to law school, Minson laughed out loud. He was looking at my GPA on the computer in his office, and he thought I had about as much chance of being accepted into law school as I had of being accepted into the NASA space program. Minson was very critical of my record and told me it would be a waste of money for me to apply to law school.

My Warrior's chest instantly swelled. I loved nothing better than to prove people like Minson wrong. Even though I didn't yet fully want to go to law school, I vowed to get accepted to one and prove him wrong. Minson finally gave me the checklist of steps to take to apply to law school, and I immediately saw that I was about one year behind in the process.

The first thing I had to do was take the LSAT standardized test. Most students take the test in their junior year, so if the first score wasn't high enough, they could take it the following year. Luckily, I could take the test in the fall and in the spring. Minson continued to criticize me and recommend that I not waste the money, but I applied to take the fall test and see where it went.

My father was thrilled when I told him that I had signed up to take the LSAT. He told me not to worry about my GPA; he could get me accepted into any law school in North Carolina or Georgia. I doubted that, based on what Minson had told me, but I played along and promised to do better in my senior year. I took the LSAT and improved my grades slightly.

Surprisingly enough, I did quite well on the LSAT, scoring in the top 10 percent. It wasn't so much that I was that smart; the phenomenon was that I usually did quite well on standardized tests. I had an aptitude for multiple-choice questions that had nothing to do with knowing the correct answer. I would simply meditate on the answer, and the voices in my head would tell me which block to check. Even Minson was surprised at my score and begrudgingly admitted that I might have a chance to be accepted into law school.

I went home on fall break at Thanksgiving with better news than normal. Kitty had already been accepted into the Bowman Barclay School of Medicine early acceptance because she was a straight-A student at Berkeley University. She had continued her monk-like existence, studying both martial arts and pre-med with the same intensity. I pretty much steered clear of her; we both seemed to prefer it that way.

The one bright spot of the Thanksgiving fall break was that I decided to go with a group of hometown friends in Atlanta to see the George Harrison and Ravi Shankar concert at the Omni in Atlanta. I had never seen a Beatle or Indian musician perform. It was an amazing, epic concert, with hallucinogens and pot all around. I got so high that I had to be helped up the stairs and out into the car. I lost the use of my legs. I loved every minute of it.

For the rest of the school year, I experimented with psychedelics and hallucinogens. I couldn't get enough of them. Strangely, my grades didn't suffer. The greatest irony was when I retook the LSAT in the spring, I was on mescaline and high as a kite. I earned the second-highest grade that year. There was no explanation for it, other than that I just got into a zone with the voices in my head and got most of the questions right. My admission into law school was assured. My Guru and Warrior both were unsure how to feel as I put my dreams of guiding young people in the great outdoors to rest.

I was accepted into Wake Forest University Law School and Duke Law School. As Duke Law School was my father's alma mater, in his eyes I had redeemed myself and could do no wrong. As a formality, I was invited down to meet the dean of the Duke Law School, Dean Franklin Dye. I dressed in a suit and tie and wanted to impress. I hadn't decided which school to choose, but Franklin Dye would soon make up my mind for me.

Dean Dye did not beat around the bush. "I wanted to meet you in person, because you are not the type of student we normally accept here at Duke Law School," Dye stared at me intently. "We don't expect you to last more than one semester, but in honor of your father, we are going to give you the opportunity to come to school here."

I looked at him and thought, "Well this isn't going as expected."

Dean Dye asked me if I had anything to say.

I shrugged and said, "It looks like your opinion of me is already set in stone. I won't take any more of your time."

I went back home and informed my father that I wanted to go to Wake Forest University Law School. Law school was hard enough without the faculty already intent on flunking me out. My father reluctantly agreed, and my future was set. I would be going to Wake Forest University.

I graduated from Davidson College near the bottom of my class. The only notable item in my record was my admission to law school. My former fraternity brothers, as well as most of the rest of the class, were astonished that I was accepted. My Warrior's ego stung at the lack of belief in me. This fueled me to focus and prove everyone wrong in my new environment.

CHAPTER THIRTY

Impostor Syndrome

This was the beginning of a deep-seated feeling that I was a fake, a fraud, and an impostor. Impostor syndrome is a psychological phenomenon that reflects a subconscious or conscious belief that a person is inadequate and incompetent despite overwhelming evidence to the contrary. The individual may attribute their success to other people, luck, or circumstances beyond their control. In the same way that perfectionists constantly criticize their own performance, people with impostor syndrome are always berating their thoughts, words, and deeds as not being good enough.

People who suffer from this syndrome are constantly operating under the threat of being exposed as incompetent, ill-trained, or not good enough. They obsess over every word they speak, how they look, and what they do to avoid mistakes or failure. It doesn't matter how trained, educated, or talented they are. They are always in fear that people will discover that what they think of themselves is true: they don't know what they are doing.

People who come from families where they experienced abuse or high levels of conflict with rare displays of support are more prone to having these feelings of doubt and self-criticism. Parents who value achievement and heavily criticize what they consider underachievement often embed the impostor syndrome in their children. Likewise, parents who micromanage their children or are overprotective contribute to the development of impostor syndrome.

Whenever individuals change their environment or matriculate to more demanding jobs, they can experience impostor syndrome. The pressure to achieve and succeed, combined with a lack of experience, often creates feelings of inadequacy in new jobs or settings.

People who do not have a strong sense of self and belief in their ability to succeed in any situation often have impostor syndrome. Similarly, people who fear making mistakes or doubt their abilities often exhibit perfectionistic traits that interfere with confidence and self-esteem. This can cause people to fear asking for help and delay projects.

Impostor syndrome can also contribute to higher levels of anxiety, worry, insecurity, tension, and shame, as well as other negative emotions such as anger, shame, hurt, doubt, and confusion. People can also delude themselves that they are being unfairly judged or subjected to bias because they are doing that internally to themselves. When people feel like an outsider or like they don't belong, it could be impostor syndrome.

Other examples of the effects of impostor syndrome include:

- When you get a promotion or more responsibility, you feel unqualified, like you are a fraud. Rather than feeling excitement about the increased responsibility or compensation, you feel like it is only a matter of time before you are fired for incompetence. This activates the Warrior mode and prevents the logical thinking, intuition, and inspiration you need to rise to the occasion. Thus, the fears of being fired become real because of poor judgment and reactive behavior, which are the hallmarks of the Warrior mode.

- When you start a new position or a new business, you are reluctant to promote yourself and express your power because you compare yourself to others in similar roles and assume that everyone else knows what they are doing and doing it well. Because you don't have as much experience as they do, you doubt your ability to work or compete with them.

- If you win an award or certification, you feel like you don't deserve it because you aren't good enough. You are afraid that if people knew how afraid and stressed you are, they would take the award or certification away.

The problem with impostor syndrome is that no matter how well you perform or how good you are, the feeling that you are a fraud and an impostor will not go away. In fact, the more you accomplish, the more you feel like a fraud. It is like your brain is entirely shut off from acknowledging your successes. It also keeps your Warrior on constant alert that your perceived shortcomings will be discovered. I would feel this way for most of my adult life.

CHAPTER THIRTY-ONE

A Funny Thing Happened on the Way to Law School

It was 1976. It was the bicentennial year of American Independence, showcasing a series of observances, celebrations, and commemorations leading up to the two hundredth anniversary of the adoption of the Declaration of Independence on Sunday, July 4, 1976. Democratic candidate Jimmy Carter narrowly defeated incumbent Republican President Gerald Ford. Paul McCartney, Diana Ross, and the Bee Gees had hit after hit on the music charts. The Viking 1 spacecraft landed on Mars and sent back the first close-up color photos of the planet's surface. JVC introduced the VHS format in Japan, and *Rocky* was the highest-grossing film.

For once, my father didn't burden me with expectations of graduating first in my class. Although he did mention all too frequently that he graduated third in his class at Duke University and would have been first but for marrying my mother his last year in law school. He was secretly hoping I would do well, but given my academic performance at Davidson, he would have accepted graduation as enough.

The first day of class at Wake Forest, I went into a large auditorium with the rest of the first-year students for my first class with Dr. Robert

E. Lee. Dr. Lee was a fixture at Wake Forest, rumored to be older than dirt. He was a tyrant in the classroom, believing that putting students under pressure while standing was the best training they would have to be attorneys. He was also a holdover from antebellum Southern traditions, wearing a black suit and bow tie (even when having sex with his wife, some said). He was blind in one eye, which could have been a problem with the microphone he often butted his head into while glancing around the room.

I took an instant dislike to him because he promised that all the poets in the room would cease writing poetry when he was done. He promised to make them all think logically and legally and to put all romantic notions of creativity and poetry aside. "We'll see about that!" I said under my breath.

The biggest difference between law school and the education I had experienced before was that the only grade and the only test for the class semester was the final exam. No one would know where they stood until the grades for the final exams were posted after Christmas break.

Life quickly dulled into a routine. I would go to school early, returning to my apartment late at night. I enjoyed the atmosphere of the library, with all the dusty old books and other students staying late trying to keep up. I would usually return home around midnight. On the weekends, I stayed at home with my parents.

To everyone's surprise and delight, I excelled in my first semester, coming in eighth in my class. I found that I had a real talent for fitting into the law student role and mimicking the other, more serious students. In reality, I couldn't have cared less; perhaps that allowed me the ability to stand the stress.

I also had the additional perspective of my NDEs. I discovered I could tap into that feeling of peace and serenity whenever I remembered to do so. The fact that I was making As for the first time since kindergarten had everyone baffled.

My father was elated; he could not have hoped for that kind of success. Everyone backed off and let me do my thing. For the first time ever, I felt a tiny release from the expectation of my failing, both internally and externally. I blocked everything that didn't have to do with law school. I found that my focus was singular, almost compulsive. I was locked into a routine that felt safe. School, drinking, sex, and rugby were all I cared about.

Unfortunately, the second semester was not so grand. My substance abuse went into overdrive, and I focused on partying at the legal fraternity like I did in college. Old habits die hard. However, I did manage to stay in the top 10 percent of my class.

I also met Maggie Carswell, an undergraduate senior from Ohio. Maggie was cute, intelligent, and an accounting major. For a loner like me, to have a smart, attractive woman interested in me made me giddy. We were inseparable (as much as we could be), and I loved the notoriety of dating a sorority girl.

She was my first serious relationship since my freshman year with JoAnn. Maggie was graduating at the end of my first year of law school, and she got a job with a Big Eight accounting firm while studying for her CPA exam.

For the first time, I could see my life unfolding before me. I thought I loved her enough to marry her and fully let go of my great Outward Bound dreams. I could be a lawyer, like my father always wanted, and provide well for us. I just had to focus. My Warrior balked and tried to find something wrong with the plan.

With better grades came more drinking, which was becoming a daily routine. Classes, studying, and drinking became the new normal. I joined rugby for excitement, finding it to be rugged and counterculture enough to satisfy my omnipresent craving for thrills. My Warrior loved it.

It was a giddy experience for me, as I started enjoying a small bit of validation. Between good grades, partying every night, and playing rugby every weekend, from the outside it looked like I was balancing it all well. Yet I struggled with a nagging feeling that something was wrong, and my Guru was often seen wringing Its hands on the sidelines of my life. But the highs of alcohol and the elegant violence of rugby quieted my doubts.

I stayed in this routine for three years. The constant drinking didn't seem to be a problem for me. I had no adverse consequences beyond an occasional hangover. I graduated near the top of my class and passed the North Carolina bar exam, much to the delight of my parents. I decided to go back to Charlotte to practice law, also to the delight of my father. I finally felt like he was proud of me. My Guru and my Warrior both celebrated the small victory, although it still felt like a temporary fix.

At my graduation from Wake Forest University School of Law, I had another wake-up call. The dean read a list of awards that the students had won during their three years in law school. When the award was announced, the winner had to stand and be acknowledged.

I stood up sixteen times. The only other student to get that many awards was Gene Poussard, the valedictorian of our class. I was elated to receive as many awards as Gene, as he was a genius and would surely be an excellent lawyer. I fervently wished that my parents would be proud of me as well. As I walked out of the ceremony with them, my father's only comment was, "If only you had gotten one more award."

The familiar lonely feeling of failure, of never being good enough, enveloped me. I looked at my father, and my Guru crumbled to see that he had a look of authentic disappointment on his face. I asked myself, "What is it going to take to get his approval and love?"

My Warrior responded angrily, "Nothing! That will never happen. Stop seeking it!" On that sour note, I entered the practice of law.

Maggie and I got married that summer after I passed the North Carolina State Bar with flying colors. I got a job with the law firm my father founded before he was elected to the North Carolina Supreme Court. I am sure he pulled a few strings to get me hired. He told me that he was expecting great things from me and that I should make him proud. I nodded enthusiastically every time that he said it, while my Warrior sarcastically snarled, "Good thing there's no pressure."

CHAPTER THIRTY-TWO

Obsessive-Compulsive Personality Disorder

During my time in law school, I began experiencing an unusual inability to relax and be myself. It felt like I was on high alert most of the time. I developed rigid routines and could feel my Warrior operating at the forefront 90 percent of the time. I developed an overwhelming preoccupation with being organized, controlling my environment, and being perfect. I couldn't be flexible in my thoughts or behavior and found it difficult to compromise to navigate the challenges of life. I had difficulty with relationships because other people could not understand my need for control and organization. They would just tell me I was being unreasonable.

I began to suspect that I might have some kind of obsession or compulsive personality disorder, based on my pervasive preoccupation (obsession) with order, perfectionism, control, and specific ways of doing things. Other signs that I had obsessive-compulsive personality disorder (OCPD) included: preoccupation with and insisting on details, rules, lists, order, and organization; problems with completing tasks; neglecting my family; rigidity; fear of failure; inability to delegate tasks; difficulty with criticism; overly focusing on flaws in others; lack of intimacy and emotion; selfishness; and suspicion.

People with OCPD usually appear confident, organized, and high-achieving. Their exacting standards may even benefit them in certain jobs. However, their inability to compromise or change their behaviors usually negatively affects their relationships.

There are two causes of OCPD. The first is childhood trauma. The mind/brain adopts perfectionism and rigidity as survival mechanisms. By severely controlling their environment, teens and young adults feel safe. When they lose control or make mistakes, individuals with OCPD exhibit fear, anger, or panic because the deviation from their safety zone could be fatal. The second cause may be genetics. Scientists have identified a malfunctioning gene that may be a factor in OCPD. Researchers are also exploring genetic links to aggression, anxiety, and fear, which are traits that can play a role in personality disorders.[21]

People are also more likely to have OCPD if they have biological family members with personality disorders, anxiety, substance abuse, or depression. Left untreated, OCPD can result in poor relationships, work difficulties, isolation or impaired social functioning, anxiety, substance abuse, and depression. Individuals with OCPD obsess over looking for mistakes and paying attention to detail, which can prevent completion of projects.

I was overly dedicated to work and productivity, but my dedication was not motivated by financial necessity. As a result, I neglected leisure activities and relationships. I would take work with me so that I would not waste time. Time spent with friends, when it occurred, tended to be formally organized activities like sports. Hobbies and recreational activities were important tasks requiring organization and hard work to master; the goal was perfection.

---

21 Abid Rizvi and Tyler J. Torrico, "Obsessive-Compulsive Personality Disorder," StatPearls - NCBI Bookshelf, October 28, 2023, https://www.ncbi.nlm.nih.gov/books/NBK597372/.

A classic example of this was playing golf. I was a talented golfer, but I had to practice every day to achieve the level of performance I desired. I taught family members how to play so we could do something together. They did not have the same obsession I had with the game, so this resulted in me spending long hours every week away from them.

These symptoms became pronounced and continued for most of my legal career. I wasn't even aware of them until I started studying mental and personality disorders. That is one of the biggest problems with compulsive disorders: they aren't obvious to the subject. I just thought I was being focused and disciplined. Unfortunately, as I found out, it took its toll on my relationships and career.

CHAPTER THIRTY-THREE

Shit Hits the Fan

Baby boomers were known as the Me Generation, and I exemplified the phrase. The occasional disagreements with Maggie about my partying and social behavior were getting to be more than an annoyance, so we did what many couples do to force a change in their relationship: Maggie became pregnant. The winter of 1980 and spring of 1981 were centered on preparing for my son, who would be my parents' first grandchild. It didn't slow my drinking down substantially, but I was more careful about when and where it happened.

The year 1981 was as eventful in the world as it was in my life. The Iran hostages were released on Ronald Reagan's inauguration day, and later that year, Reagan was shot in the chest by John Hinckley. Lady Diana married Prince Charles. Sandra Day O'Connor became the first female justice on the United States Supreme Court. The first cases of AIDS were reported, and the movies *Raiders of the Lost Ark*, *Arthur*, *Stripes*, and *Chariots of Fire* were released. It was an exciting time.

Our son was born on April 21, 1981. We named him David Gray Johnson, and we decided to nickname him Digger. Being the firstborn grandchild, he would always be special to my parents. I was present at

Digger's birth; I was going to be sure that he was not put in a metal box for the beginning of his life.

The doctors had to perform an episiotomy on Maggie because Digger's head was so big. I would delight in telling him that repeatedly when he got older. I was overwhelmed with emotion when I first held him, after he was weighed by the operating room nurse. It felt like I was given a new opportunity and redemption. My Warrior roared at this new responsibility, while my Guru harbored high hopes for the changes a baby can bring. I wanted to be the best father in the history of mankind.

But alcohol would have something to say about that.

Maggie had retired when she became pregnant, so she was at home 100 percent of the time. Her need to control everything in her life began to take its toll on our relationship. She signed us up to teach Sunday school at the Lutheran church. That looked good on paper, but I found that my regular Sunday morning hangovers were interfering with my ability to enjoy teaching high school seniors about the Bible.

I continued to play rugby. There were several good teams in the city that were highly competitive. I was always showing up to work with stitches or a cast. My supervising partner, Dudley Lawford, was not impressed. He would comment from time to time that I needed to decide whether I wanted to practice law or play rugby. For me, playing rugby was much more gratifying than practicing law.

Maggie didn't like my rugby friends, or my out-of-town rugby trips when I came home late Saturday night, hammered. Weekly practices were also a topic of heated debate. I was constantly getting injured. Maggie wanted to start doing activities that would be supportive of my legal career. I felt like she was trying to make me into something I was not. My Warrior balked at the idea.

After Digger arrived, the pressure to change became unbearable. It seemed like Maggie criticized everything I did. My unhappiness and my Warrior's sense of being trapped grew stronger daily. Digger was a source of joy, but Maggie would even start criticizing how I held him and talked to him. My Warrior and I were about to explode.

On Memorial Day weekend, our relationship problems came to a head. I had started drinking heavily on Thursday night, as I had taken that Friday off. Maggie started nagging me about drinking so much, and something in me snapped. In an alcohol-induced haze, I had to escape. I called an old friend from Davidson who was living in Key Biscayne, Florida, and asked him if I could come visit. I got on a plane to Miami without telling Maggie and went to see my college friend.

I was far from thinking rationally. The conflict of doing something for a career that I didn't particularly like to please my parents, the substance abuse, and the constant disapproval of my wife and my boss at the law firm kept me at DEFCON 5. I felt like I would chew my own arm off, just to escape the intense shackles of expectation.

I stayed in an alcoholic blackout for several days. I don't remember much, only that I was having a very good time. The thought would cross my mind that I would have to return to reality at some point, but I would just open another beer and forget about it. Memorial Day weekend was a great party weekend on Key Biscayne, and I was single-handedly upholding the tradition.

Then my friend got a call from a police detective in Atlanta who was trying to locate me. Maggie had quite rightly become concerned about my whereabouts and was trying to find me. In my alcoholic stupor, I thought the world had ended, and the police were going to come and arrest me. That night, I left without any destination; I just wanted to run away. My Warrior and I took off into the darkness, my Guru's forehead etched in worry.

I hitchhiked out to the causeway and then caught a ride going south. I was picked up by a serviceman who was based at the US Coast Guard District 7 base and was going back to the base. I didn't care; I was really panicked, and all I wanted was to get away from the police. It didn't even dawn on me that the serviceman might have ulterior motives in taking me to his base. I wasn't thinking at all.

When the serviceman got me to the barracks, I stumbled into a bunk and passed out. At some point, I woke up with my hands tied to the bunk supports, a sock in my mouth, and three servicemen taking turns at anally raping me. I was still extremely drunk and started to struggle. One of the servicemen hit me with an elbow to the temple, and I left my body. Immediately, I was back in that place where I remembered floating in a place of pure joy. I felt detached from what was happening to me, which seemed like it was happening to someone else. The attack lasted over an hour, but I did not care. I wasn't even in my body for it. I was home.

Bob asked, *"So how are you enjoying your life so far? How much further into chaos do you have to go before you wake up?"*

I sighed. Even from my floating place, I couldn't deny the obvious truth. "Well, it seems that something needs to change, that is for sure."

Bob said, *"Are you sure that you want to be a lawyer?"*

I responded with an emphatic no.

Bob pushed further. *"Then why are you doing it? You are constantly doing things that you know are bad for you and have negative consequences. Why do you have to learn things the hard way?"*

I stammered my words, as they sounded disturbingly desperate, even to my own ears. "I am trying to get everyone to love me."

Bob snorted. *"Why?"*

I was surprised by the question. "I thought that was what everyone was supposed to do. And if people love me, maybe I can love myself."

Bob continued. *"All I can say is that you aren't getting anywhere with that plan. Perhaps you should do what you want to do instead of trying to manipulate others. Oh, and by the way, you have it backward. You must love yourself before anyone else will love you."*

I sighed deeply as the world turned darker than a raven, and I was left alone in the obsidian night.

The following morning, I woke up and my hands had been untied. The barracks were empty. I was quite sore and could hardly walk. Somehow, I managed to shuffle out of the barracks and limp out of the gate. I felt like I had to get back to Key Biscayne. If I could just get back there, everything would be alright. My Warrior, who had been fighting a losing fight since I left home, strode beside me, Its many injuries shining in the early morning light.

I hobbled along for most of the day, feeling sorry for myself, until I could get a ride back to Key Biscayne. My Warrior was roaring about revenge in my ear the whole way, but I did my best to shut him out. By the time I got to my friend's house, I started drinking to forget. My friend eventually arrived home to find me feeling much better about things. He asked me where I had gone the night before. I told him, leaving out the rape. Even without the gory details, his face went white.

He told me that the area that I had hitchhiked through the night before was known as Overtown, and it was the most dangerous place in Miami, if not the United States. He emphasized that I was lucky to have lived through it and must have a guardian angel looking over me. Blithely, I responded, "Well, all I can say is my guardian angel showed up late." When my friend asked me what I meant by that, I just winced as I shifted in my chair.

I returned home that Monday, Memorial Day, with renewed purpose. My mind had already gone to work repressing what had happened, but I knew that something had to change—and had changed. Once again, I stopped drinking for a while and stopped partying with my rugby friends. I wanted to give Digger a chance at a normal life with two respectable parents. Sometimes horrible things have unexpected consequences, and I was determined to make my experience in Florida have positive consequences. It was the only way both my Guru and my Warrior could reconcile the experience.

I expected some backlash from my disappearance, and I got it. Maggie was fit to be tied about my irresponsible behavior. All I could do was apologize and dial back my partying. I knew regaining her trust and forgiveness would be an uphill battle, but I wanted to stay in it for Digger.

Unsurprisingly, the constant criticism by Maggie did not let up. I was too early, too late, too fast, too slow, too loud, too quiet, and on and on. Nothing seemed to satisfy her. We began to have more and more conversations about separating and ending the marriage. Maggie had always had a "my way or the highway" kind of approach. The highway started looking better and better to me.

Finally, in 1982, we separated. I felt like a boil had been lanced, bringing bittersweet relief. Many couples try to stay together even though they are not compatible, and it deeply affects the children. I was certainly cognizant of the effect all those years of bickering between my parents had had on my well-being. I knew that my parents feared the social fallout of divorce more than they feared how their children would be affected by their constant dysfunctional discord. Fortunately, I didn't care so much about what society thought of me.

When the news broke, I was taken aback that no one was surprised by it. Most people knew that Maggie and I were wildly incompatible. I was too much of a free spirit, and she was too controlling. Most of my friends were relieved for me.

The separation was quick and painless. Both parties wanted out. I moved into a house rented by my rugby buddies, and Maggie stayed in the house. Digger was too young to realize what was going on; that would wait until later. My Guru hoped I could find more peace in a new environment, and of course my Warrior was armed and ready for anything.

CHAPTER THIRTY-FOUR

Adrenaline Junkies

Alcohol was **not the only** thing I had become addicted to. By that point I had also become a full-blown adrenaline junkie. Whenever the autonomic nervous system detects evidence of a threat, it automatically activates the Warrior and the sympathetic nervous system. This is done entirely by reflex, without thinking about it. Whenever the Warrior is activated, It signals various parts of the body to prepare for battle, otherwise known as the fight-or-flight response.

The first thing that happens is the amygdala signals the hypothalamus, which activates the sympathetic nervous system to trigger the adrenal glands to secrete adrenaline into the bloodstream. Adrenaline, also known as epinephrine, is a powerful chemical in our system.[22] It produces several responses, including:

- Increased blood pressure
- Increased heart rate
- Increased lung airways

---

22 Rajeev Dalal and Dejan Grujic, "Epinephrine," StatPearls - NCBI Bookshelf, November 23, 2024, https://www.ncbi.nlm.nih.gov/books/NBK482160/.

- Increased rate of breathing
- Dilated pupils
- Sweating
- Increased sensory perception
- Muscle exhortation
- Increased pain thresholds

In other words, the body prepares for battle. It is extremely thrilling and exciting. This may be more intense and pleasurable than normal pleasure responses and will lead the body to recreate this rush.

The Warrior is activated under several circumstances that do not involve combat, but are risky and could result in physical, financial, emotional, or mental harm. Extreme sports, first responder roles and other high-pressure careers, overworking, gambling, and antisocial behavior are examples of adrenaline-producing behavior.

Signs that behavior is being controlled by a craving for adrenaline include:

- Intense need for high-risk or high-pressure behavior
- Feelings of frustration and restlessness when not engaged in risky or high-pressure behavior
- Losing interest in mundane activities
- Repeating the behaviors despite repeated injury
- Feelings of addiction and compulsion, like the need to engage in risky behavior despite repeated adverse consequences

Mental health professionals won't go so far as to categorize adrenaline-producing behavior as addiction. However, many of the feelings and behaviors associated with the activation of the Warrior are very similar to the use of addictive substances. "Adrenaline junkies" continue to engage in risky behaviors or place themselves in high-pressure careers despite the toll it takes on their body.

Often adrenaline junkies will overcommit, overwork, or take on high amounts of responsibility to fuel their stress response. This is viewed as "advancement," "climbing up the ladder," or even "success." Too often, the "junkie" burns out and develops mental and emotional turmoil in their chase of adrenaline. Yet it is viewed as "normal" in a society where value is measured in achievement.

In my case, I started to recognize an addiction to chaos and excitement as a way to distract myself from the stress and anxiety of practicing law.

CHAPTER THIRTY-FIVE

Independence Day

The year 1982 started with record cold temperatures and blizzards in the Northeast and Midwest. Over 750,000 people attended a rally in Central Park in New York City protesting nuclear weapons. Michael Jackson released *Thriller*, still the most successful album of all time. A severe recession plagued the country, with unemployment reaching 10 percent, the highest since the Great Depression. The largest cash robbery in history occurred in New York when $9.8 million was stolen from an armored car. The world's largest oil rig (The Ocean Ranger) sank in the North Atlantic.

For me, the most significant change of the year was declaring my independence.

The nagging feeling that I was living a lie had become stronger and stronger. My law practice was interfering with my drinking and rugby playing. It was clear to me that the firm's law partners didn't want me there. They made a transparent statement by moving my office to the basement, away from the other lawyers. I picked up that message loud and clear.

My father was very concerned. He was in constant communication with the senior partners, and he was not getting good reports. Every time I went over to his house, I would get an earful about growing up and focusing on practicing law. I know he thought he was doing what he needed to do to sort me out, but to me, it was just more parental rejection. My Guru could be found curled up in the fetal position after these exchanges, so familiar since childhood.

I asked him one time why he felt he needed to be so critical all the time. His response was classic: "I am your father, not your friend." I often wondered what kind of hell he must have grown up in to adopt that attitude. Even a little friendship would have gone a long way for my self-esteem. With my failing law career, my divorce, and the constant criticism from my parents, depression became my constant companion, along with my Warrior's howls and my Guru's deep sighs.

Mike Gelding, one of my rugby friends, lived in the house I rented after my divorce from Maggie. Gelding had some experience managing a bar in Greenville, NC, and we started discussing opening a bar and restaurant.

I had never worked in a restaurant before, but that made no difference to me. A third friend, Jason Priestly, was the chef-owner of a restaurant in Charlotte, and the three of us made a loose plan to find a restaurant to own and manage together. We found a perfect place in Raleigh, North Carolina, across the street from the NC State campus, that could be divided into a bar on one side and a restaurant on the other. Given my contacts with the Raleigh Rugby Club, it seemed like a sure winner.

So, on July 4, 1982, I drove up to my parents' summer home in northwest North Carolina to break the news to my father that I was quitting. I hadn't seen my father in several weeks, and I was quite afraid of what was going to happen. But I had gone too far to be persuaded out of my decision. I finally fully believed that I was not cut from the cloth needed to succeed in a large law firm.

It was obvious that I was either going to have to make some fundamental lifestyle changes or quit. I had made my decision, but now I needed to tell my father that I was leaving. My Warrior was on high alert, and my Guru played with Its prayer beads just out of sight.

My father was much more emotional than I expected. Of course, I had anticipated some blowback anger from him, and true to form, he was first enraged. What I didn't see coming was witnessing his shoulders crumpling as despondency took over his body. He actually cried when he finally understood that I was sure of my decision and was leaving the firm. I wasn't surprised when he promised me that I would not be allowed back in their house and would be cut off from any more gifts. He had often used the carrot and the stick approach with me over the years, but this time I couldn't bring myself to care.

I often wondered why I seemed to attract people who had an all-or-nothing approach to life. My parents were either very proud or fully disgusted with me. Maggie was the same way. It would be many years before I would discover that that was how I treated myself.

My eyes involuntarily began glazing over during my father's standard "ungrateful bastard" lecture, but I had to laugh inside at the irony of him calling me a bastard. I couldn't resist (with a strong push from my Warrior) throwing it back at him. "Well, you should know." In the last of the series of unpleasant non-surprises, my next view was of the long, curved driveway after my father furiously threw me out of the house. I was later told by my mother that my father cried for several more hours, but all I could say to her was, "If he cared so much, why didn't he show it to me?"

I didn't understand then that he had a Guru and a Warrior inside of him too. I don't think he ever understood it either. What a tragedy it must have been for our Gurus to always miss connecting with each other, to watch our Warriors continuously drive us apart.

I headed off into the sunset towards Raleigh with high hopes to make a lot of money in the restaurant business. I purchased a condo with Gelding's father for us to live in together.

Reality did not take long to come knocking at the door. Eight days after the opening, Jason disappeared. Ironically, I had been oblivious to his drinking problem. We found empty liquor bottles hidden throughout the kitchen and the restaurant. The only thing I could do was jump in and take over the kitchen duties. It was quite fun for me, although it meant long hours. When the restaurant was loaded, it was even more exciting. My Warrior needed to be active, by any means possible.

Seeing my son Digger created a challenge, since I had to go back to Charlotte every other weekend. Gelding took over duties on those weekends. This proved to be problematic: while the books showed the restaurant was doing well, there was no money in the bank account.

The stress of managing and cooking was getting to me. I gained quite a bit of weight and was drinking heavily again. Me working in a bar was like a bee working in a garden. It's not going to be able to resist all that nectar. And I was no different.

The year before, I had met a beautiful woman named Mary who worked in the Mecklenburg County Tax Office. For me, it was love, and we were getting closer. Mary agreed to drive Digger up to Raleigh on my visitation weekends, and we started to act like a family. Many mornings my Guru woke up dancing.

Mary had a daughter named Nancy, and things started to feel like I had found the right family. Mary was very understanding and loving and appreciated my independence. She even started interviewing for jobs in the Raleigh area. It felt like I could start taking deep breaths soon.

I eventually began to suspect that money was disappearing from the cash register when I was away seeing Digger. I didn't know who was taking the money, but it was obvious that a significant amount of the weekend proceeds was not getting into the bank account. I was either going to have to put more money into the restaurant to keep it going or shut it down.

To make matters worse, one weekend I returned from Charlotte and found out that Gelding had unilaterally decided to move me out of our shared condo and put all my possessions into storage. Apparently, his girlfriend didn't get along with Mary and convinced Gelding that I had to go.

Being rejected like that absolutely gutted me. My Warrior stood screaming and spinning in a circle, swords in both hands. All my trust issues surfaced, and I dove deeply into the places where my trauma memories lived. My brain seemed to freeze, like it couldn't handle reality, and all the negative emotions that I had repressed over thirty-one years erupted. I clenched my fists, gritted my teeth, and had a complete meltdown. I had nowhere to go. I sat in my car outside of the condo for hours, trying to get my brain to work. I heard my Guru whispering to me and my Warrior screaming for some time before my mental systems went back online.

What Gelding didn't understand was that I owned the condo. Gelding's father had purchased the condo for Gelding, but for financing purposes, I had to be on the title. As a result, I forced his father to buy me out so I wouldn't sue Gelding for taking my possessions and throwing me out on the street. I got enough money out of the equity to quiet my Warrior and move back to Charlotte.

That was the final straw that broke the restaurant's back. I also felt like if I was going to work that hard, I wanted to make some money. I had kept my law license active over the two years I was in Raleigh, and I had occasionally represented some clients whom I acquired at the restaurant. I decided to move back to Charlotte to practice law again. I sold the restaurant and said a not very cordial goodbye to Gelding.

My attempt to escape my legal prison had only lasted two years. I yearned to be back in my parents' good graces and felt like coming home could be the first step. Despite my Guru's hopes and my Warrior's plans, it only opened the next chapter of a wild and crazy cowboy story.

CHAPTER THIRTY-SIX

Effect of Injury on the Mind

I was starting to wonder what, if any, effects all my serious injuries were having on my mind. Not only does physical injury damage the body, but it also has a detrimental effect on the mind. It was not a surprise to discover that the psychological response to injury can include negative moods (grief, shame, blame), depression, anger, anxiety, overeating or appetite loss, substance abuse, and PTSD.[23]

Other detrimental mental and emotional responses include low self-esteem, loss of identity, stress, loss of control, sadness, confusion, loss of motivation, apathy, frustration, fatigue, withdrawal, insomnia and other sleep disorders, fear, and restlessness.

In extreme cases, injuries can cause psychosis, schizophrenia, eating disorders, personality disorders, mood swings, and dissociation.

Many athletes identify with their physical prowess, and when they are injured, their self-image suffers. They get more stressed, which slows

---

[23] Center for Substance Abuse Treatment, "Understanding the Impact of Trauma," Trauma-Informed Care in Behavioral Health Services - NCBI Bookshelf, 2014, https://www.ncbi.nlm.nih.gov/books/NBK207191/.

the healing process and increases the likelihood of re-injury. Lowered self-esteem can also lead to riskier behavior to regain lost confidence.

Injury is a type of loss. Loss of self-image, loss of lifestyle, loss of confidence, loss of social status. As a result, injury can be followed by a predictable grief process, including denial, anger, blame, sadness, bargaining, depression, and finally release and acceptance. If we do not understand the grief process, we can get stuck in the negative emotions that naturally follow an injury.

The effects of bodily injury on mental health can vary depending on age. When we are young, the psychological impact may be more severe because the young have nothing to compare it with. If the ACE is unsupported and neglected by authority figures, younger children may display more despair and hopelessness. The neural pathways of the negative thoughts and emotions become hardened and ingrained, and the negative stress response becomes second nature.

As we get older, we have more experience and perspective to evaluate the effect the injury has on our lives. We understand that injury can be healed, and we have coping mechanisms for the discomfort and disruption of our routine. However, after middle age, injury can be more difficult to heal, as is the resulting depression. We are more aware of approaching death, and the prospect of resuming normal life is diminished. The leading cause of death in people over sixty-five is falling.

Repeated trauma makes the symptoms of the neurological changes and injury more severe. The more traumatic events occur, the higher the risk that more traumatic events will occur. We may repeat past trauma because we subconsciously want to find closure and fix an original traumatic event. Furthermore, we may recreate trauma because that is what we know. It is our "normal."

CHAPTER THIRTY-SEVEN

That's Going to Leave a Mark

When I turned thirty in 1983, I was flat broke. I had put all my meager savings into the restaurant, and I was facing not being able to pay my rent and child support. The payoff from the condo and the sale of the restaurant kept me going, but my financial situation was dire compared to what I had hoped for when I was in law school. I was determined to be successful, and so I went about finding a job as a lawyer once again.

I was also painfully aware of the fact that my sisters were doing very well. Kitty (now Kat) had become a physician with a specialty in internal medicine and infectious diseases. My younger sisters had both followed my path and become lawyers. All of them had been excellent students and were very successful in their careers. The discrepancy between my career path and theirs only heightened my shame and guilt.

In 1984, the world was rocking. The decade's emphasis on wealth and materialism was going strong. The world, however, was beginning to feel the pressure of such unrestrained spending, and signs began to emerge that all was not well. Indira Gandhi was assassinated, and hundreds died in Bhopal, India due to a toxic gas leak at the Union Carbide plant. Fifteen people died in Beirut when a terrorist bomb exploded outside the US Embassy. The USSR boycotted the Olympics in Los Angeles in retaliation for the US boycott of the Moscow Olympics four years earlier. Over seventy US banks failed due to mismanagement. The first Apple Macintosh computer went on sale. The first untethered spacewalk took place.

I was feeling quite untethered myself. While I was making the rounds interviewing at law firms, I thought I would get some exercise and went back to playing rugby. My old friends were still playing, and it was a perverse kind of support group that kept the party going. It also gave me a reason to get back in shape, and I started losing weight. Mary loved watching me play rugby and the people I played with.

Rugby is like American football without helmets or pads. The very last thing anyone wants to do is get hit in the head because it could prove fatal. When I had played rugby years before, I was very fit. Although I got injured all the time, nothing serious happened outside of some stitches or a broken bone or two. When I came back from Raleigh, I was not fit. I was overweight and as graceful as a gazebo.

On one fateful Sunday afternoon, I was picked to play in a game against my former Raleigh team. Towards the end of the game, the ball got loose, and I sprinted to pick it up. An opposing player was coming in the opposite direction. I got there first and picked up the ball on a dead run. Just as I looked up, the opposing player ran the top of his head directly into the bridge of my nose. If the angle of the blow had been any higher, I would have had my septum driven back into my frontal cortex, and that would have been the end of this story.

Instead, the septum was driven back into my sinus cavity with enough violence to shatter my septum. People on the field later reported that it sounded like a high-speed automobile collision. I was soon surrounded, but I was non-responsive. Once again, I had no pulse and wasn't breathing. There were enough EMTs present to begin CPR.

"Bob, is that you?" My own thought sounded like an echo.

"*Yes,*" said Bob.

"I am having one of those death experiences again, aren't I?" I asked.

"*You are,*" answered Bob solemnly. "*You haven't learned much about being kind to yourself over the years, have you?*"

"Am I going to get back to living?" I asked.

"*That depends on how you define living,*" replied Bob. "*Staying drunk all of the time and playing violent sports doesn't seem like much of a life.*"

"It is just a phase," I replied.

Bob pretended to check his nonexistent watch. "*It has been a long one. What are you afraid of?*"

I thought about that and said, "I guess I'm afraid I will always be a failure in my father's eyes. I thought I was a pretty good lawyer, but he was never impressed."

Bob snorted. "*Well why should he be? You never gave it your best effort.*"

I took that in. Then I got a bit mad at Bob. "Bullshit. I worked my ass off. The partner I worked for always took credit for what I did and blamed everything he screwed up on me. Why try in that sort of environment?"

Bob looked at me intently. "*Here's the deal: If you are trying to satisfy him, you will never get any respect. You must be the best whatever-you-want-to-be for your own sake.*

"*Trying to please your parents will never get you anywhere. Stop drinking and drugging, and especially quit blaming everything on other people. You are the creator of your reality, and you create everything that happens to you, either directly or indirectly. Quit judging everything and everyone as right or wrong or good or bad. Focus on what you are doing. If you can satisfy yourself that you are doing the best you can, then you will be a hell of a human.*

"*If you are always judging yourself through your parents' eyes, you will always be a failure. Take a deep breath, acknowledge what a good person you are, and be that.*

"When you stop judging yourself, you will see who you are. If you want to be happy, quit criticizing everyone, be honest, give up regretting your past, stop resenting your sisters, don't compare yourself to others, and embrace your fear."

"How the hell am I going to remember all of that?" I thought.

Suddenly, I felt a strong force pulling me away and back into my body. Someone was doing CPR on me as I came to consciousness in the tangible world. I was rushed to the emergency room, where they x-rayed my head. Amazingly enough, I only suffered a crushed septum that was lodged somewhere back in my sinus cavity. From the side, there was no nose. It would be the last game of rugby I ever played. My Warrior roared.

In the emergency room, since there was quite a bit of blood, there was a lot to do about very little. Lines were attached, blood drawn, X-rays taken. Since I had no insurance, I was very concerned about how much all of this was going to cost. They referred me to a specialist in facial reconstruction and discharged me. The final bill came to around $11,000 for thirty minutes in the emergency room. For 1984, that was quite a lot, and I was even more concerned about how much the surgery was going to cost, but it was one of those necessary evils. Obviously, I couldn't go through life with my nose missing.

The specialist's name was Ron Shirley, who was the older brother of one of my high school friends. He was known for his sense of humor and no-nonsense approach to surgery. I arrived at his office with the $11,000 X-rays and sat down on the examining chair. Ron came in and looked at me, shined a light up my nose, and simply said, "I am scheduling surgery for 9:00 a.m. the day after tomorrow."

I offered the X-rays to him and said, "Don't you want to look at the X-rays?"

Ron said, "No, I can see that your nose is broken."

"Great," I mumbled, "Nice way to waste $11,000."

Surgery was not such a big deal, at least to me. They wheeled me in half-sedated. As Ron was about to start, he looked down and said, "Just remember, I can't make a silk purse out of a sow's ear!"

Even in my compromised state, I didn't miss a beat and fired back, "Shirley, you jest."

Ron burst out laughing and motioned for the anesthesiologist to pass the gas. The next thing I knew, $25,000 later, I was in the recovery room with a huge headache.

Ron came in and explained that he had to reconstruct my septum and put a splint on either side of it to hold it in place. He asked me if I had broken my nose before, and I said, "Twice."

He frowned. "I strongly suggest you stop doing that. The septum very nearly missed your brain. Five millimeters one way or the other, you wouldn't be talking to me."

I agreed that not breaking my nose again was my plan too, although I knew my track record for things going according to plan was far from great.

I went to Mary's to recover and try to see where to go next. I hadn't seen my parents for quite some time. They didn't seem interested in seeing me, and I wasn't particularly interested in getting any more lectures. So, at odds we stayed. Also, Mary wasn't the "right kind" of girl, according to my parents, and I had no patience to hear any criticism about that.

I wondered whether I fell in love with girls that my parents didn't like because I was rebelling against my parents, or if I had some sort of inferiority complex and didn't like "society girls" as a result. I knew that it would take a special kind of woman to appreciate my independence and wild streak. I thought I had found that woman in Mary. We were living together now, and I had no plans to get married. That probably upset my parents as well, but I didn't let it bother me too much, as I knew I couldn't do anything right in their eyes anyway.

Unfortunately, I started having episodes of sleepwalking and sleep terrors again. I often found myself outside with no recollection of how I got there. When it happened growing up, my parents would find me wandering around in the house or outside. They would have to wake me up to get me back in bed. Occasionally, I would wake up while I was trying to find a doorway to get away in a nightmare I was having.

I continued having nightmares repeatedly, often waking up by screaming. These usually involved being in bed or a dark room, knowing that something was in the room with me and was there to hurt me. I couldn't move; I could only scream. This would wake Mary up every time, and she would have to calm me down and soothe me back to sleep while my Warrior quaked by my side. I felt like it had something to do with going back to practicing law, but nothing was going to stop me from getting back in my family's graces.

Interviewing for positions with law firms with two black eyes and a rebuilt face was perhaps one of my more surreal experiences to date. As I talked to the hiring attorneys, I couldn't help but wonder what in the world they were thinking about this broken-down war horse perched stiffly before them. It took all the courage I could muster to sit down in front of attorneys I knew from my prior stint with my father's firm and try to convince them that I was committed to redefining my practice of law—and that they should give me a chance to prove it.

A surprising break arrived when I was hired by some of my former law school colleagues. I was thrilled but also had a nagging thought that if they knew how screwed up I was, they would fire me immediately. That fear drove me to outperform their expectations. I worked hard and eventually made partner in just a few years.

It was a great day for me when they added my name to the firm name. Now there was a firm in Charlotte with the name Johnson, and I could hold my head up whenever I visited my parents. My visits were infrequent because my father would always find something to openly criticize, whether it was the clothes I wore, my size (by then I was about sixty pounds overweight), or my blended family.

It was a constant burden on my heart to have to continue to chase after my parents' love. My Warrior always stomped Its feet and gnashed Its teeth before we saw them and spent the time beforehand sharpening Its swords. My Guru would lie on Its back, humming a calming tune, always looking for any bright spot, even when they remained elusive. I, too, remained hungry for a compliment, which came few and far between. I didn't live where they wanted me to live, I didn't go to the right church, my children didn't behave properly, my wife didn't belong to the Junior League . . . it never stopped. There was constant tension between us, supported by the futility of it all. No matter what I did, I wasn't good enough. My depression persisted, and I began living in a fog. It felt like there was a levee between me and the world, and I had to stay as closed off as possible to prevent the powerful river of my feelings from flooding my life.

When I got hired, I bought a large antebellum house in the country with a seventeen-stall barn on the property and plenty of pasture for livestock and horses. The house was 125 years old and looked grand from the road. I thought even my parents would approve. We settled down into what I hoped might finally feel like some stability. My Warrior was already looking for the chinks in the armor.

CHAPTER THIRTY-EIGHT

Halley's Comet

The year 1986 felt full of combustion. The space shuttle Challenger exploded on takeoff, killing the seven astronauts aboard. The nuclear power plant in Chernobyl, Ukraine, melted down, and hundreds of thousands of people were evacuated. The nuclear fallout spread as far away as Eastern Europe and the Middle East. The *Oprah Winfrey Show* debuted nationally. Mad Cow Disease was first identified in cattle in Britain. Perhaps this was all due to the return of Halley's Comet after seventy-five years of wandering in space.

On July 21, 1986, my son Emory Richard Johnson came into the world. He had to be delivered by cesarean section because his head was too big to deliver naturally, and he didn't seem to want to come out. It seemed that I made big-headed boys, a detail that I found fascinating. After twenty-four hours of labor, the medical team determined he was in distress and, over Mary's objection, ordered the C-section.

Mary had delivered her first child in the backwoods of Tennessee by natural birth with a midwife, and she did not want surgery. However, Emory was struggling and not getting enough oxygen, so surgery was required. Was he destined to arrive with a Warrior as raring to go as mine had been, before I even had a hand in the matter?

When Emory came out, he was blue from lack of oxygen. He was quite large, as he came almost fourteen days late. He weighed almost three times more than I weighed at birth, over fourteen pounds. I was quite pleased. Emory turned out to be a large, healthy baby, and the stress he endured during birth was only temporary. My Guru breathed a sigh of relief.

In the summer of 1986, I thought it would be a great idea to take the family up to my parents' summer house to see Halley's Comet. Mary's parents and siblings came along as well. The air was thinner due to the elevation, and my parents had a large telescope to see the comet better.

I had been drinking on the way up to the mountain and was feeling no pain. When we got there, we discovered that there were almost no groceries, so I decided to go to the nearest town, ten miles away, to get breakfast supplies and mixers. (My parents had a fully stocked bar but had run out of mixers. If it could be helped, they never ran out of alcohol.)

As I was coming back, I drove past two highway patrol cars that were calibrating their radar detectors. When I got level to the troopers, one pulled out to follow me with his lights flashing. I knew I was in trouble. My Warrior and I briefly had thoughts of making a run for it, but I knew that the patrol car had too much power, and the Volvo station wagon I was driving was built for safety and not speed. I pulled over, planning to talk my way out of it.

The trooper was nice enough, but he was totally unimpressed with my assertion that I was a lawyer. It seemed to add fuel to the fire. He put me in his patrol car and took me back to the station. It was a small town, and the troopers were very familiar with my family. I took the breathalyzer test and blew a 0.17. At the time, 0.10 was legally intoxicated, so the charge was clear: Driving While Intoxicated.

Having a blood alcohol content of 0.17 would have most people at the point of passing out, but I barely felt buzzed. That should have told me something. I insisted that there was something wrong with the machine. It was no surprise that the troopers had heard that one before. I was then given a field sobriety test, which was a series of balancing tests that would have challenged a talented gymnast. Incredibly, I passed the test.

I had to call Mary to come pick me up. Everyone was upset with me, and I realized that the path of least resistance was to take responsibility and be appropriately contrite. My Warrior balked at the plan, but I did my best to keep my inner thoughts from escaping my tongue and buried behind blank expressions. The weekend party continued as planned. I wasn't going to let something as irritating as a DWI ruin a celebratory getaway. I thought I was going to get out of it, and I partied like nothing had happened.

I hired a lawyer named Frances Rosslyn to represent me. Rosslyn was a friend who had played football at Georgia Tech. He was an imposing figure, six feet, eight inches tall, who specialized in criminal law. When we met, Rosslyn looked at me and assured me that he could get the DWI reduced to a lesser offense. He said that between his popularity and my father's reputation, it was a sure thing.

My case came to trial in 1987, after repeated continuances requested by Rosslyn. I appeared with him in court, and after several hours of waiting in the courtroom, he informed me that there was nothing to do but plead guilty. I was shocked. After all the deals I had gotten for my clients, I couldn't believe that he was unable to get a reduced plea bargain. He shrugged and said that it would only be worse if we pled not guilty. The judge had stated that he was not going to give a lawyer any favors because it would look bad. I pled guilty and took my medicine.

I wondered if I needed help to control my drinking. My Guru uncharacteristically came forward and screamed, "You do!" The DWI was a serious business, and I knew that if I got another one, I would really be in trouble. Nah, I decided, I would just use self-control and limit my drinking to the weekends. My mother once had a DWI and went away to rehab in Florida for a month. She didn't stop drinking and continued driving after drinking. It was probably in my DNA to be able to handle heavy drinking. I wasn't that worried about it, although both my Guru and my Warrior thought differently.

CHAPTER THIRTY-NINE

Praise Jesus

In 1987, the US stock market crashed, losing 22.6 percent. Terry Waite, a special envoy for the Church of England and the Archbishop of Canterbury, was kidnapped in Lebanon. The world population hit five billion. Alan Greenspan became the chairman of the Federal Reserve Board. The drug AZT was approved to treat the rapidly increasing AIDS virus. Construction of the "Chunnel" between France and England began. Disposable contact lenses and Prozac were introduced to the public. The televangelist Jimmy Bakker scandal erupted. The iconic *Simpsons* TV show began as animated shorts on *The Tracy Ullman Show*.

As a part of my self-imposed penitence, I committed to going to church more often with Mary. She had started going to the First Baptist Church up the street. First Baptist was a member church of the Southern Baptist Convention. When I first started dating Mary, she loved to party just as much as I did, but after Emory's birth, she turned to religion in a big way. Without fail, she attended First Baptist every Wednesday night, Sunday morning, and Sunday night.

I had never been particularly religious. I leaned more towards a non-structured spiritual system that acknowledged the presence of God but concentrated more on moral behavior. I believed I got more from meditation than sitting in church. My Guru quietly agreed.

But to please Mary, I became immersed in the church. While I thought that the Southern Baptist approach to things was a bit over the top, what the hell. I jumped in like I did with most things, with both feet bare and little thought given to the eventual outcome. I gave generously to the church and showed up when the doors were open. To outsiders, we looked like a wealthy, God-fearing, happy family.

We were far from happy. For reasons she would not share with me, Mary had grown cold in the bedroom and would often ignore me when I tried to strike up a conversation with her. It was obvious that the honeymoon was over.

Needing excitement and enjoyment from some source (my Warrior was chomping at the bit), I returned to my love of horses. After all, I had a seventeen-stall barn in my backyard. I bought two horses and started to learn how to train them. One was a bay quarter horse named Troubles, and the other was a dappled gray quarter horse named Fancy. From the beginning, both my Guru and my Warrior loved them, for different reasons.

I had always wanted to be a cowboy. I could remember dressing up in my cowboy outfit when I was eight years old and running around playing the part like I was born for life on the range. Even though it had led to a beating over the accident with my younger sister, I never lost my love for the idea of being a cowboy. Owning my own horse was one of my fondest dreams, and it was finally coming true. To take my mind off my rocky marriage, I immersed myself in my horses.

I also became more and more involved in the church. A new preacher showed up, a charismatic fundamentalist named Teddy Small. Reverend Teddy was a tall, athletic, handsome man who was the heartthrob of most of the women in the church. I could see his appeal; he was emotional, dynamic, and dramatic.

Two other new things showed up in my life when Mary decided to have breast augmentation. She went from an A cup to a D cup with two unusually high beams. Sometimes when surgeons implant the inserts through the areolae, the nerve to the nipple is damaged, and the nipples become permanently erect. While Mary was quite proud of her new "girls," the church ladies were not so happy, especially when there was a young, handsome preacher around. Tongues would wag.

Rev. Teddy broke many unwritten rules by asking me to become a deacon. Traditionally, a deacon in the Southern Baptist Church is a lay preacher and serves as a buffer between the congregation and the preacher. Normally, deacons are of the highest moral standard without any blemish on their record. Since I had a DWI and was divorced, it was highly unusual that I would be selected for the role.

I suspected Rev. Teddy had an ulterior motive, perhaps more than one. Since I was one of the most successful members of the congregation and one of the most financially generous, it was both a reward and an encouragement for me to continue giving. The fact that I was a lawyer was also a plus; free legal advice was always worth something.

Thus, I became an ordained deacon of the Southern Baptist Church. I felt like a bit of a hypocrite, as I didn't buy into many of the Southern Baptist beliefs. Hoping that it would change the tone of my marriage, I accepted the position. I also agreed to be an adult Bible study leader.

At last, I had the image of a fine, upstanding figure of the community. Unfortunately, my relationship with Mary did not recover. I had stopped drinking entirely when I joined the Church and thought that things would start improving in my marriage. I couldn't understand why my wife continued to ignore me until I started hearing rumors that she was spending long hours with Rev. Teddy in the afternoons. The church tongue-waggers wanted to make something of that, but I chose to ignore it, although under the surface it did rankle my Warrior greatly.

Life went on, and I became more and more of a cowboy. I decided to take the family on a summer vacation to a cattle ranch in Montana. It had always been a dream of mine to work with cattle from horseback, just like the movie cowboys. I was given a brochure by my cousin Greta for a working guest ranch on the Crow Indian Reservation called the Double Spear Ranch, run by the Blackmore family.

When we got to the ranch, the reviews were mixed. I was focused on the lifestyle, getting to ride horses on the great High Plains on the Crow Indian Reservation, learning to rope, brand, and all those adventurous things. My sons were of the same mind; they were just as excited as I was to do all the country cowboy things.

The women were not so enthusiastic. The Ranch was financially holding on by its fingernails, and the accommodations were very rustic. Mary and Nancy hated it instantly. Mary especially hated the owner, Jim Bridger, who was the boss/owner of the outfit. Jim fancied himself as a John Wayne type, tall and full of stories. His language was very colorful, and he used terms that no respectable Southern Baptist woman would allow. Jim couldn't have cared less. In fact, when he noticed Mary's face redden, he doubled the use of these words, making her emotions boil hotter and hotter.

Nancy was a buffet for the local airborne biting insects. Within an hour of our arrival, she was covered head to foot with insect bites. Jim and his wife Dianne applied a local remedy of baking soda and hydrogen peroxide, which made her look like a big Alka-Seltzer. Unsurprisingly, this did not endear Nancy to the ranch.

She had assumed that this would be a luxury ranch like she had seen on TV, with swimming pools and staff waiting on her hand and foot. When she discovered that the pool was a watering trough, and the staff couldn't care less about her hands and feet, she formed a deep disdain for the whole affair.

Meanwhile, I instantly fell in love with the ranch. It was historic, scenic, and Jim was a very funny, charismatic fellow, almost a caricature of what I imagined a ranch owner to be. I learned the history of the reservation and the ranch's part in that history. Yellowstone National Park was fifty miles to the south, the Custer Battlefield was forty miles to the east, and the ranch sat at the foot of the Pryor Mountains. My Guru looked with pleasure in all directions, grounding into the earth of the ranch. I felt I had found my true home.

I started talking to Jim about buying more cattle and making the ranch profitable again. Done correctly, the cattle business could make quite a bit of profit, but the weather and market changes made the business risky. I thought that if I could teach Jim some basic business skills and oversee his impulsive spending nature, we could do quite well. Based on the numbers Jim gave me, it would be easy.

To Mary's horror, I decided to invest in the ranch and bought 250 pregnant beef cows at $1,000 each. I visited regularly to keep up on things. For the first several years, things were looking good. The cattle had high birth rates, and cattle prices were decent.

I became a fifty-fifty partner in both the cattle operation and the ranch. The bragging rights were worth the investment. I would own 50 percent for nearly twenty years and eventually ended up owning the ranch outright.

I also started training the horses we raised on the ranch. In addition to the seven horses I had back home, we had sixty-five more on the ranch. I loved training them, especially starting them to ride. The feeling of stepping into the saddle on a horse that had never been ridden was both terrifying and exhilarating. Over the years I started dozens of horses, and each time was like getting high. I got pretty good at it; people would bring their horses to me if they had behavior problems. I could easily see doing that for a living. My Warrior loved the excitement, and my Guru loved the relationships with the horses. Had I actually found a place where I could finally balance it all?

CHAPTER FORTY

The Blue Light Special

The world continued to ramp up its collective pace as it hit 1989. George H. W. Bush became president. The Exxon Valdez ran aground in Alaska and spilled eleven million gallons of crude oil into Alaska's Prince William Sound. Nintendo introduced the Game Boy video games and hijacked the minds of millions of adolescents and young adults. The Loma Prieta earthquake hit San Francisco and killed sixty-three people. Hurricane Hugo touched down on the coast of North and South Carolina and caused the costliest destruction to date. As a harbinger of bigger things to come, the US government spent $150 billion to bail out 25 percent of the savings and loans in the country that had failed due to risky real estate mortgages and regulatory irregularities.

I was living like I needed some kind of bailout too. My drinking resumed and was getting worse. Somehow, I continued to succeed on the professional level and was ranked "AV" (the highest rating possible) by my peers, holding a coveted rating as one of the best lawyers in my area. Yet I still drank like a fish every weekend. Even I was surprised that I could drink two six-packs of beer a day. But in 1989 it all came to a screeching halt.

I loaded up my pickup truck with my son Digger and my 150-pound Rottweiler to go pay a bill for the restoration of a 1968 Delta 88 convertible I had bought. I'd already been drinking all morning, but didn't feel overly intoxicated. The Georgia Highway Patrol stopped me for speeding 75 mph in a 55-mph zone.

As Mary was out of town, I had to find someone to come get my son, Digger, and the dog. After waiting an hour for me to try to find someone, the trooper decided to put Digger in the back of the patrol car and leave the dog in the truck. It was fairly safe, since not many people would want to steal a 150-pound Rottweiler that they don't know. We went to the courthouse in Atlanta, where I worked every day, for processing.

I didn't have a shirt, so the patrolman paraded me through the courthouse with my hands shackled behind my back and Digger in tow. My Warrior roared and, inside me, tried to break the chains. Numerous attorneys I knew saw the scene, and to say I was humiliated would be an understatement. The district attorney would later tell me that he thought that I had been arrested for child abuse or molestation. While I was being charged and processed, my cousin who worked in the DA's office came downstairs and offered to take Digger home. I would be forever grateful to her for that.

Once again, I registered a 0.17 on the blood alcohol breathalyzer, double the legal limit. It was clear I had a problem. At that moment, I decided to go into treatment. Most attorneys resist inpatient treatment because it means leaving their law practice for twenty-eight days. However, I felt like if I stayed in my environment as an outpatient, I would be too tempted to fail. For strategic reasons, I also decided to go to treatment because days in inpatient treatment are credited against jail time. Although I did not expect any mercy from the local judges, I wanted to have that count for me.

I went to a treatment facility in Southern Pines, North Carolina, far away enough that I was unlikely to get visitors I didn't want. I completed the treatment and got sober. I hoped that my wife would start loving me again, and my parents would show me some respect. My Guru always maintained a vigil of hope, but my Warrior hated both the time locked up and the idea of going home to the same battles.

There is a saying in addiction recovery programs, "If you sober up a horse thief, you still have a horse thief." Even though I was newly sober, I still had all my emotional baggage. No matter how hard I worked or how much money I made, I continued getting the cold shoulder from my wife and criticism from my parents. I felt like I would never be good enough, but I knew I couldn't drink, because that would only make it worse.

There is another saying, "Don't drink and keep coming to meetings." I was white knuckling my sobriety but kept going to meetings. Sometimes I would go to two meetings a day. One of the benefits of attending them was that, at some point, it started feeling like a safe harbor. My Guru began enjoying the community, the support I was hard-pressed to find elsewhere. My life continued to be a storm with the pressures of practicing law, bending over backwards to please my unpleasable wife and parents, living in a stressful household, and trying to figure out how to live a happy life. In some ways, it seemed closer than it had at other times, but in other ways it remained like a mirage. From a distance, it looked good, but when you got close, it had almost no substance at all.

CHAPTER FORTY-ONE

Self-Sabotage

For most of my adult life, it felt like I was getting in my own way. No matter my motive, many of my decisions were not appreciated by my family and certainly not by my parents. I did not appreciate my victories (which were expected), and I was overwhelmed by my failures (which I felt were my destiny). I wouldn't allow myself to enjoy my life, and I felt like I was my own worst enemy.

Attachment theory is a psychological theory that a person's ability to cope and succeed depends upon the relationships they form with authority figures as an infant.[24] When these bonds fail to form, it can lead to a host of problems in dealing with day-to-day life. Children who are raised in a dysfunctional family can fail to form healthy

---

24   Jude Cassidy, Jason D. Jones, and Phillip R. Shaver, "Contributions of Attachment Theory and Research: A Framework for Future Research, Translation, and Policy," *Development and Psychopathology* 25, no. 4pt2 (November 1, 2013): 1415–34, https://doi.org/10.1017/s0954579413000692. Jude Cassidy, Jason D. Jones, and Phillip R. Shaver, "Contributions of Attachment Theory and Research: A Framework for Future Research, Translation, and Policy," *Development and Psychopathology* 25, no. 4pt2 (November 1, 2013): 1415–34, https://doi.org/10.1017/s0954579413000692.

attachments to their parents, which leads to problems later in life, especially self-sabotage.

When one or more of the parents behaves in a frightening way, the child may form a style of attachment that is called "fearful avoidant attachment." I experienced many frightening episodes with my father, who was prone to attacks of rage, shouting, and abusive criticism. I expect that this was the source of my PTSD diagnosis later in life. Studies have discovered that people with fearful avoidant attachment styles often experience low self-esteem, self-criticism, and depression.[25]

These experiences can cause self-sabotage, mainly because these people fear the things that they crave, especially intimacy, responsibility, and success. When my parents repeatedly told me that I would not be successful without their help, I believed them. Whenever I would start to be successful, I often unconsciously behaved in ways that scuttled that success because I had conflicting beliefs that I wanted success but couldn't achieve it without my parents telling me what to do. This is called cognitive dissonance, and it caused me to reject the things in life that I truly desired.

There are many signs of self-sabotage, including: negative self-talk, seeking distractions, lack of boundaries, blaming the past, comparing oneself negatively to others, a need to control, perfectionism, promiscuity, and fear of failure.

Self-sabotage includes procrastination, overeating, self-medicating, and fear of success. I certainly experienced all these symptoms repeatedly throughout my adult life. Other examples of self-sabotage I engaged in were people-pleasing, putting others' needs ahead of my own, and creating chaos to relieve boredom. I can't count the number of metaphorical hand grenades I threw into situations to "liven things up."

---

25   Paula Dagnino et al., "Depression and Attachment: How Do Personality Styles and Social Support Influence This Relation?," *Research in Psychotherapy Psychopathology Process and Outcome* 20, no. 1 (April 13, 2017), https://doi.org/10.4081/ripppo.2017.237.

Children who experience dysfunctional families often develop avoidance coping skills that make adult life more difficult. We avoid talking about difficult subjects, we delay dealing with problems, or we avoid stressful situations. All these self-destructive tendencies only serve to create more anxiety, stress, and negativity. In my case, I tended to say yes to whatever burdens were placed on me, even though on some level I knew these burdens would only increase my anxiety and depression.

Learning how to stop self-sabotage is possible. For me, it involved recognizing my behavior and taking responsibility for my self-sabotage. After all, whatever we resist becomes more ingrained in our neural pathways. It took me a long time to gather the confidence to start engaging in difficult conversations that were needed to resolve conflict. Being aware of my motivation was the most important step in any path to growth and recovery. Why I did things, why I had those thoughts, and why I felt the way I felt were the most important questions I could ask myself.

Self-awareness and healing self-sabotage require more of a change of lifestyle than a change of mind. I had to start asking myself these questions before I engaged in any potentially self-destructive behaviors. I had to trust my instinct and emotions, and if something felt wrong, I had to commit to saying no. I had to stop criticizing myself and start being kind to myself. I had to commit to staying away from drama and negativity. I had to let go of trying to control people and focus solely on myself. Above all, I had to master my thoughts and emotions to begin to create what I wanted.

CHAPTER FORTY-TWO

The Definition of Insanity

In 1989, the world was experiencing huge changes. Communism began to crumble in the Eastern bloc, and the Berlin Wall was taken down. The Tiananmen Square uprising was cruelly suppressed by the Chinese Communist Party. Brazil held its first presidential election in twenty-nine years. South Africa began dismantling its apartheid policies. The first commercial internet providers started operating. Emperor Hirohito died. The Lexus and Infiniti automobiles were introduced in the US. George H. W. Bush was sworn in as the president of the United States.

I was doing everything that I thought I should be doing, and I was miserable. I loved the ranch and my horses but hated practicing law. I knew if I quit practicing law and moved to Montana, two things were likely to happen: One, my wife would not move, and two, I would not have enough money to live the lifestyle I wanted. Therefore, I did what I learned in recovery: If you don't know what to do, don't do anything.

A large hole lay gaping and untended in my heart. I couldn't accept that I wasn't getting the love and support of my parents that I needed. It seemed that every comment I got from my father was a criticism wrapped passive-aggressively within a backhanded compliment. If I ever spoke of needing support, the response was, "Grow up." My inner child and my Warrior, sworn to protect it, were ready for war at the comment.

Then, in a huge turn of events, my father and sister decided to leave their respective positions and form their own boutique firm of litigators. My father had tired of being a Supreme Court justice and knew he could make a fortune if he went into private practice.

My sister, Lisette, knew that she would get rich with my father, so she jumped at the chance. In an unexpected plot twist, they asked me to join them. I was thrilled and determined to make this partnership work. I had the tools of sobriety, and despite my misgivings about practicing law with my father every day, I jumped at the chance of reuniting with him. I forgot the definition of insanity, which is "repeating the same behavior and expecting different results."

My wife was not so thrilled. She never felt accepted by my parents, for good reason. Whenever we went to visit, my parents would constantly criticize my children's behavior and my wife's refusal to join the Charlotte Junior League society. She often repeated a joke about Junior Leaguers, "Did you hear about the two women who got kicked out of the Junior League? One got a job, and the other had an orgasm."

She was especially upset that my parents favored my son Digger over all the other grandchildren and didn't show Nancy or Emory the same attention or affection. I was between a rock and a hard place; I craved my parents' approval, but it seemed it came at the cost of Mary's. The horns of my dilemma were sharp, and it seemed impossible that everyone would remain unscathed.

Life became a routine of working long hours and coming home to a silent bed. My soul hardened to the reality that my emotions had to be sacrificed on the altar of having a successful career and seeking the love of a dysfunctional family. My Guru and my Warrior both lamented my resolution.

It seemed that my parents' dysfunction infected my relationship with my wife and children. I masked that pain by working long hours and making a lot of money. My one source of joy was the ranch.

Mary was always complaining about my parents, my love of the ranch and horses, and my never being home. It seemed to me that if she wanted me around more, she had a misguided way of showing it. I most often came home to cold silence and isolation.

She started asking me if I was seeing someone else, cheating on her. I was floored. It was ironic to the extreme that with all the rumors flying around the church about her and Rev. Teddy, she would accuse me of infidelity.

It seemed Mary was keeping the children away from me, planning outings that she knew I was not interested in, usually involving the Church. Life dulled into a routine that lacked any joy or satisfaction. No matter how hard I worked or how many successes I amassed at work, my life was a mess. I couldn't do anything right or satisfy anyone I loved. My Guru wept, and my Warrior thundered that I was allowing my life to be reduced to anxiety and despair.

CHAPTER FORTY-THREE

Perfectionism

It seemed that I could do nothing right or good enough. I had excelled in law school and was a successful attorney. Nevertheless, I was stressed and depressed, and I felt like everything I did could have been done better. I was like many professionals and entrepreneurs who have high expectations and standards. This can be a positive motivator for success and achievement, but it also can be a source of great anxiety and stress. Perfectionism is an overemphasis on performing perfectly without mistakes. Rather than take a healthy approach to mistakes as a learning opportunity, perfectionists view mistakes or unintended results as failure.

Perfectionism emphasizes the avoidance of mistakes rather than great achievement. It is linked to anxiety, obsessive-compulsive disorder, and depression. According to mental health professionals, perfectionism is an inborn trait that can be hardwired into our personalities early in life.[26] It influences how people perceive their world.

---

26 Carmen Iranzo-Tatay et al., "Genetic and environmental contributions to perfectionism and its common factors," *Psychiatry Research* 230, no. 3 (n.d.): 932–39, https://doi.org/10.1016/j.psychres.2015.11.020.

Perfectionists believe that they are born with natural talents and abilities that they must prove daily. They set high standards that must be met or exceeded. Anything less is failure, which reflects on their self-worth. This is known as a "fixed mindset." Healthy psyches believe in their ability to overcome and grow. Resilience is easily achieved, and less-than-stellar or underachievement results are accepted and analyzed for growth. Failure is not connected to their self-worth. This is a "growth mindset."[27]

Several warning signs signal perfectionist tendencies:

- Obsession with superior results
- Obsession with order and neatness
- Devastation after mistakes
- Inability to accept criticism
- Out of control inner critic
- Inability to see the opportunity for growth

Perfectionism can absolutely engage the Warrior mode. Perfectionists only value performance and achievement, and when their performance falls short of their expectations, it triggers their compulsive fear of failure, engaging the sympathetic nervous system. Their brain does not accept anything less than extraordinary performance as worthwhile and can't accept ordinary or less than average whatsoever. Consequently, when things go wrong, perfectionists tend to obsess over their perceived shortcomings, thus feeding their anxiety.

In an environment where people are not in complete control of their achievements and they must rely on others to contribute to their success, perfectionists inappropriately take the blame for other people's mistakes. They feel like failures because of other people's mistakes.

---

27   "Growth Mindset Vs. Fixed Mindset: What's the Difference?," Business Insights Blog, March 10, 2022, https://online.hbs.edu/blog/post/growth-mindset-vs-fixed-mindset.

This has been called playing God. They can be extremely codependent and allow other people's negativity to destroy their joy.

Perfectionists probably learned this mindset from birth. Parents often insist on high achievements from their children and encourage high performance. Oftentimes the parents can get upset if their children don't receive perfect grades or excel in all their endeavors. When parents criticize their children for less-than-perfect performance, it sends a signal to the child that love depends on their performance.

This mindset drives children to excel, not for the experience, but to avoid losing their parents' love. They may be superior students and achieve impressive scholarship, but there is always the sword of Damocles hanging over their heads; they could lose their self-worth and their parents' love if they don't measure up. That fear drives intense anxiety and could result in performance anxiety.

Many lawyers suffer from both impostor syndrome and perfectionism. This is what happens when they have unreasonable expectations of excellence, coupled with very small margins of error. Some typos could be meaningless, but some could determine the outcome of their case. Surgeons, who have zero tolerance for mistakes, often suffer from similar pathologies. It would take a massive shift in my consciousness to find a solution.

CHAPTER FORTY-FOUR

Strike Two

The year 1999 was tumultuous and not nearly as good as the singer and recording artist Prince's song had forecast. The Y2K panic gripped the nation. One of the first major school shootings occurred, the Columbine High School massacre. President Bill Clinton's impeachment trial concluded. Bill Gates became the richest man in the world. Napster, the internet music service, began, and the Melissa virus attacked the internet. Both Scotland and Wales elected a parliament and a prime minister while the Kosovo War raged on. *Star Wars: Episode I - The Phantom Menace*, the first in the Star Wars series, was released and became one of the highest-grossing films to that date in history. Most notable for me: I declared my independence.

In January 1999, I decided to compete in a bodybuilding contest. I was tired of being overweight and pushed myself to hire a trainer. That required me to get up at 5:00 a.m. and drive to the gym to work out for an hour. I was eating a restricted diet of chicken and minimal carbs and working out two to three times a day. By March, I had dropped forty pounds and was the most fit I had ever been in my life. I had already run several marathons, but this was the best shape I had ever been in. I was sober and fit for the first time in years. It almost felt like I was in a new body, and both my Guru and my Warrior loved it.

I filmed a continuing legal education film for the North Carolina State Bar with Mary. It was a great experience, but she was still depressed about the thought of me cheating on her. No number of protests would do any good; she had already charged, tried, and convicted me in her heart. For my own sanity, I quit trying to convince her that I was and had always been faithful to her. I started studying new age spiritualism, reading everything I could find on new ways to understand God. When I read Neal Donald Walsh's *Conversations with God*, I was so impressed that I gave a copy of it to Mary for her birthday.[28]

Two days later, she gave the book back to me and told me to stop worshiping the devil. I had no clue what she was talking about. She claimed that the new preacher at the church told her the book was the work of the devil. Rev. Teddy had left because of rumors of his interactions with several women in the congregation. The word from the tongue-waggers was that he quit preaching and became a car salesman. I was glad to see him go. The new preacher was more fundamentalist, a fire-and-brimstone kind of preacher. In his eyes, we all were going to hell, and Mary hung on his every word. The divide between us grew wider.

In April 1999, I was training a stallion I had brought back from the ranch. The horse was named Tybalt after the character in Romeo and Juliet. Like all stallions, he was a handful. One Saturday morning, I decided it was time for Tybalt's first ride. After all, I had started dozens of horses on the ranch. I felt like I knew what I was doing.

I saddled him up and got on and off several times. Everything was going well. I got on and urged Tybalt to go forward. He took a few steps, and everything felt fine. Then Tybalt did a crow hop, twisted and bucked, and I found myself ten feet in the air with nothing but hard North Carolina red clay beneath me. I was completely inverted, my

---

28 Neale Donald Walsch. 1996. *Conversations with God: An Uncommon Dialogue. Book 1.* Penguin Publishing.

body pointing upside down at the hard red clay. Knowing I was going to land on my head, I put my hand out to cushion the blow, unfortunately with disastrous results for my arm and my head.

When I landed, the shock of the blow destroyed my wrist, pushing my carpal bone four inches into my forearm. It shattered both forearm bones, severed five ligaments, and did untold damage to my tendons. The blow to my head knocked me out cold. I experienced another out-of-body experience and looked down at my unconscious body and the horse standing over me. Over my Warrior's screams, I thought to myself, "This is not good," even though I felt completely at ease, with no pain.

Bob said to me, *"Welcome back. It has been a while."*

I struggled to reply. "Oh, crap. I can't die. I have too much to accomplish! I'm not ready to go."

Bob laughed and said, *"No, it's not your time yet, but you act like you want to die. Your risky behavior, pushing people away, hating yourself. It certainly seems like you want to die. What are you trying to prove?"*

I answered slowly, feeling the weight of my words. "I just want to feel loved. It seems like whatever I do, it upsets someone. I am doing what everybody wants me to do, and I still can't make anyone happy. I hate my life."

Bob sighed, and I wondered if I frustrated him too. *"You have it all wrong. You are creating all of this. All you must do is change your mind. That will change your reality. You got on that horse. That is your responsibility. You are unhappy; that is your responsibility. You hate yourself. That is your responsibility. You overwork. That is your responsibility. If you don't like your life, change it. That is your responsibility."*

This wasn't the response I wanted. "So, how do I change?"

Bob replied in an unexpectedly comforting tone. *"Don't worry. If you become willing, I will show you how. Now get back in your body."*

I couldn't let him leave that soon. "Wait a minute, I have so many questions."

"Just ask your intuition. When you meditate, go within, and I will be there. You meditate, but you don't ask any questions, and you don't listen when we talk to you."

Frustrated, I said, "I don't understand what you're saying. I thought I was supposed to focus on silencing my mind."

"That is just the first step. Once your ego stops talking, you must start listening."

"How will I know you are the one talking instead of my ego?"

Bob said, "Oh, you'll know. Don't listen with your head. Listen with your heart."

"How do I listen with my heart?"

Bob grew serious. "Focus your attention on your feelings. What they tell you will show you the way."

My expression transparently showed that I still didn't understand.

Bob said, "You will. Every time you leave your body, you get closer to your soul. It is your ego that is blocking your connection to your soul. All the time you have spent with me has connected you more and more deeply to your true self. This has given you the ability to know everything you need to know. When you truly connect with your true self, you can do anything. Now, back you go!"

I woke up in great pain. My head hurt, and I couldn't move my right hand or arm. I got up and mounted Tybalt again, one-handed, to show him who was boss. After riding for a few minutes, I got off, unsaddled the horse, and put him in his stable. I went inside and told Mary that I had to go to the hospital, then fainted. I woke up to her shaking me violently while she hysterically cried over my rigid body.

I had her drive me to the local emergency care clinic, where I was x-rayed. When the attending doctor came out, his face was drained of color, which I took as a bad sign. He urged us to go immediately to the emergency room at a hospital; my injuries were too bad for him to treat. My Warrior's screams reverberated off every corner of the car on the excruciating ride there, and although I knew she couldn't, the tension on Mary's face looked like she could hear it too.

Mary took me to the emergency room of Bowman Barclay Hospital, the hospital where I had been treated so many times before. They informed me that the bad news was my wrist would require immediate surgery, but the good news was that one of the best hand and arm surgeons in the world had just returned from one of his trips abroad and was available to perform it.

I asked them about my head injuries. They indicated my head was fine, but I probably had a concussion. I concluded that I must have an extremely hard head. Next came the reconstruction of my wrist. The doctor was as good as advertised; he put everything back in place with the help of five pins and an external fixator. Due to the nature of the injury, he didn't want any movement in the wrist while it was mending. An external fixator is a bridge that spans the fracture with screws coming out of the arm, anchoring the ends with an adjustable bridge attached to them. It looked just like a luggage handle sticking out of my forearm and was totally gross.

Between the fracture and the surgery, I tried three domestic hearings, winning all of them. It was phenomenal that I could work at all, as the pain was excruciating. I hardly remembered the hearings. One of my law partners, a former Green Beret, thought it was the craziest thing he had ever heard of, saying, "You aren't human!" I just thought I had a high pain threshold.

One week in May 1999, I was reviewing that week's Bible study lesson. The Southern Baptist Church disseminated lesson plans for its Bible study classes, which followed Southern Baptist doctrine. The lesson stated that babies go to hell because they have not been saved. In the Southern Baptist Church, people must profess their sin, ask God and Jesus to save them, and commit to the Southern Baptist Church. Once you have done that, you can go to heaven. If not, you go to hell. I thought it was the most abject doctrine I could imagine, and I refused to teach it. My Guru and my Warrior also found it extremist and supported my choice to not put it in young, impressionable minds.

The following week, I was called into the preacher's office and asked to explain why I didn't teach the lesson plan. The new preacher was an old-school fundamentalist, the same one who had told Mary that *Conversations with God* was the work of the devil and preached that Harry Potter was the devil. The preacher made it clear that he expected the Sunday school teachers, especially the adult Bible study teachers, to follow the lesson plan. If they didn't, they should resign. I resigned on the spot. I went home and informed Mary that I would not be going back to First Baptist.

We went to some neighborhood churches, but I realized that I was done with organized religion. Near the end of May, Mary came to me and demanded that I go back to church with her. I refused, telling her, "I won't. God is not inside a building. He is in our hearts, and I plan to find him there."

Mary looked at me with disgust, her words dripping with malice. "You know that you're a sinner, and you are going to hell. Do you want to drag us into hell too?"

I couldn't take the battle any longer. "Of course not. If that is how you feel about it, I can leave."

Mary's face hardened as she straightened her back and said, with no hesitation, "Please do."

As the saying goes, I didn't let the door hit me in the ass. My Warrior cheered, and even my Guru let a tiny smile slip, although It was already thinking of the children. I moved in with a friend down the street. The worst part was that Emory took it very hard. I reassured him that I was just down the street, and we could see each other anytime he wanted. I was at the house every day, anyway, maintaining the grounds and taking care of the horses.

In one last attempt to find a solution, I asked Mary to go to marriage counseling with a counselor she chose. After six sessions, the counselor pulled me aside and told me that counseling was not helping. He said I should decide to either accept her as she was or leave; she would not compromise or change. The counselor continued, "In twenty years of counseling, I have never encountered anyone like that. I don't know how you stood it as long as you did." I just shrugged. The counselor suggested that Mary get psychiatric counseling, which she refused. So that was that. Mary never spoke to me again.

Mary Chimes In

Before it went all the way south, Gray and I grew more distant every day.

Sometimes it felt like we were once part of the same land mass but somehow became surrounded by a cold ocean and broke off into two icebergs, still trying to bob near each other in the frigid sea. I know that he'd tell the story of me being a control freak, a Jesus freak, an unforgiving homebody . . . And God knows what else.

I'm sure he'd also love to share those inferences about me and the reverend.

Really, I'm sure he's telling you, impressionable reader, all my failings and insecurities in his eyes.

But I have a side of the story too.

My Warrior has been screaming at me and prompting me to make poor choices for as long as I can remember. The expectations for a Southern woman can be so rigid, and my police chief father drove home points that made my Warrior battle every day:

1. *Don't speak unless spoken to.*
2. *Prepare only to be a dutiful wife and mother.*
3. *Keep your legs and mind closed.*
4. *Don't share any family secrets. Ever.*

I equated love with fear and sex with aggression, for reasons I don't feel like getting into.

When I met Gray, I thought he'd be different. I thought that we'd be different from the loveless and volatile marriage I witnessed growing up. Gray had a soft side to him, one he hid from many people, but when we first met, he did occasionally let down his guard and show me what seemed to be a very soft underbelly. I knew that his father and his job rode him like a tired old racing horse and often treated him like a whipping boy, which is why I thought he found comfort in my arms. I knew that Gray would never be violent, with me or the children I had hoped we'd have. I liked that he'd been married once already. I felt like, since he made the mistakes with her, now he'd know better with me. We had such fun together at first. I thought I'd finally outrun my Warrior's constant cries.

But even during our vows, my Warrior hovered nearby. Gray's family made it clear that they thought I was beneath him, so even during our wedding dance, my insecurities plagued me. I'd never danced formally before and had two left feet. Only Kitty was kind enough to pull me aside and give me a quick hug, welcoming me to the family. The rest of them didn't even acknowledge my presence, which was hard to do, as I was the bride! When I was pregnant with Emory, I thought for sure my Guru would be by my side. I had wanted a second baby for so long and truly believed that it would change everything for the better. But my Warrior stayed ever vigilant, whispering in my ear all the potential dangers for a new life in this world. By the time Emory arrived, I was scared of almost everything! That's why I ran headlong into the church. Gray started drinking more and more heavily, and the chasm between us constantly grew wider. Every time I thought of crossing it, I would look, and he would seem even further away than before. Church was the only place that I could hear my Guru or feel Its presence at all.

And did I cross a boundary with the reverend? That's between me and my God. I know that I'm made of flesh and bones, and I'm fallible, and I needed to find some spark of joy somewhere. People also wanted to make a big fuss about me wanting to change my body. Some tongues will wag no matter what, and I just did my best to ignore them and go on about my Christian life.

And as I started with, what about all that I suffered? What about his family, who tried to make me feel inferior every chance they got? What about that awful ranch and the quarter of a million dollars he spent on cows without even consulting me? What about his endless accidents, his DWIs, and the fact that he was never home? When he had to go into that treatment facility, all my feelings felt justified. I thought the validation might bring me a bit of solace, an acknowledgment that I couldn't make it work if I tried.

But my Guru rarely sits with me. I almost never feel at peace. And I fear that I'm infecting my beloved Emory and Nancy with all of my fears, all of my inner chaos.

So for now I'll keep devoting myself to the church. I may not be able to fully hear my Guru there, but sometimes I do think that I feel it near me.

Without that, I feel like I'm drowning. Drowning in failed expectations. Drowning in the alcohol Gray chooses daily instead of me. Drowning in the ways I feel I'm failing Emory and Nancy as a mother.

And anything feels better than drowning, that place just under the surface where I can see my world through a blur and my Warrior's screams echo and reverberate so loudly, even underwater.

CHAPTER FORTY-FIVE

Dysfunction: The Gift That Keeps on Giving

Addiction is a common denominator between generations of dysfunction. Addictive ancestors create an atmosphere of unhealthy relationships as "love" and perpetuate this curse generation after generation.

For years, I felt like my relationships with my parents and sisters had affected my relationships with my ex-wives and my sons. I didn't fully understand what was wrong with the way I was raised, but I knew something was terribly destructive. It seemed like I was living a generational curse that infected all my relationships and my life. Everyone told me that I was lucky to have my parents and my sisters. I just couldn't understand why I didn't feel that way.

A dysfunctional family is like a chameleon. It changes to adapt to the environment it lives in, but it is an illusion. Oftentimes, from the outside, it looks like a happy, healthy family unit, but it is a lie. A dysfunctional family is characterized by conflict, abuse, and inappropriate behavior that is hidden from public view.

The primary concern of a dysfunctional family is how other people view it. No matter how abusive, conflicted, or destructive the family is to each other, the façade that is portrayed to the public is loving and compassionate. Interpersonal relationships between family members are tense and filled with yelling, violence, or neglect. The children are trained to accept negative attention as love. Due to neglect, dysfunctional children grow up believing that negative attention is better than no attention at all.

Dysfunctional families set themselves up for failure and anger by insisting that children get it right all the time, a standard even the parents know they can't meet. The parents attempt to make their children live the life they weren't allowed to live and deny their children the life that the children want. Children who are living with the knowledge that they will never be good enough for their family's unrealistic expectations can experience long-term damage to their emotional health.

Dysfunctional families normalize abusive behavior. When children are trained that they deserve the abuse, it will be repeated generation after generation. Most do not have the courage to question the abuse; they are afraid that, if they do so, they will be rejected and abandoned.

The basic problem is that trust is impossible in a dysfunctional family. When children are living with constant uncertainty and fear, they are constantly in Warrior mode. If you never know how your parents will respond, you are on high alert for more conflict. Children are not allowed to express themselves honestly. They just wait for the constant criticism. Vacations and holidays are dreaded events.

Dysfunctional families grow up with conditional love. Family members are manipulative with affection, only expressing love when they want something. When family members learn to withhold their love, they crave love so much that they will do anything to please each other.

It is impossible to relax and be yourself in that environment. In short, dysfunctional families reject any emotional state that allows growth and expansion. Parents make decisions for the children and ignore their wants and needs. They are bullies, actively discouraging children from asserting themselves or speaking up.

Parents do not allow children to personify and explore what they want. No one has any space; parents micromanage every detail of their children's lives. No one respects each other as an individual; it is every boy or girl for him or herself.

Dysfunctional families aren't close. There is no honest emotional support. The only people whose emotions count are the authority figures. Relationships are superficial, rather than emotionally available. It is hard for children to be close with anyone. There is always tension, and the children don't feel safe expressing themselves. Parents don't respect anyone's time or preferences.

The insidious aspect of dysfunctional families is that the children grow up thinking the gaslighting, manipulating, and conditional love is normal. Traditional notions of support and open-mindedness are nonexistent. If one of the members of the family attempts to leave or assert their independence, the others attack them with threats of mental or emotional ostracization if it might embarrass the image of the family.

Any attempts to seek help or outside support are viewed as a betrayal by other family members. They usually make the pain and suffering of the one seeking help solely the fault of the helpless member. Any attack on the sanctity of the dysfunctional family is also viewed as betrayal, and the dysfunctional members band together to pile blame and guilt on the person seeking help.

The constant overreacting of dysfunctional parents permanently damages the psyche of their children. Children feel unworthy and undeserving. They feel isolated and rejected, oftentimes becoming anxious and depressed. In adulthood, the abused child criticizes themselves, second-guesses their choices, and hesitates to decide. It is hard to heal these symptoms because the adult tells them they aren't as good as others, and they don't have emotional or mental support to teach them otherwise.

Some toxic traits of dysfunctional families are as follows:

- They lie or deny
- Criticism is often cruel
- Abuse is normal
- Negative attention is better than no attention
- Disagreements often escalate into cruel behavior
- Silent treatment is often used as a weapon
- Right and wrong are black and white
- Family members pick fights with each other
- Blame and shame are used to control other members
- Guilt trips are constantly used to smother a disagreement
- The past is often used as a weapon

One of the most insidious methods of control used by dysfunctional families is called gaslighting. Gaslighting occurs when the abuser attempts to manipulate someone by creating self-doubt and confusion. Gaslighters seek to gain control of the other person by insisting that the other is wrong, confused, or lying despite evidence to the contrary.

Gaslighters often shift the blame to the other person to avoid responsibility. Typically, gaslighters seek to gain power and control over others by persuading them to doubt their own judgment. Here are some examples of gaslighting:

- Insisting that your memory is incorrect
- Changing the subject or refusing to listen when accused of inappropriate behavior
- Telling you that you're overreacting
- Excusing their behavior by claiming you are the cause of that behavior

- Claiming your version of events is irrational or untrue
- Minimizing their behaviors
- Insisting that their false version of events is the truth

The ultimate price that dysfunctional families must pay is that, until someone has the courage to speak up, the behavior can be passed on from generation to generation. When someone speaks up, it often comes at the cost of being vilified. When someone establishes healthy boundaries and frees themselves of the toxic effects of dysfunction, they are branded a traitor and troublemaker. This is exactly what happened to me and how I felt.

CHAPTER FORTY-SIX

The End of the Beginning

The next five years of my life played out like a bad dream, one you struggle in but cannot wake from. At best, I was able to tread proverbial water, and at worst, I was swimming upstream with a fifty-pound lead weight tied to one foot. No matter what I did, tried, or changed, the result was the same. My world was slowly but surely closing in on me, as I became more and more exhausted and depressed. Both my Guru and my Warrior felt worse for wear, too, although both remained relentlessly protective.

The years 2000–2004 saw Y2K come and go. The bombing of the World Trade Center on September 11, 2001, rocked the world, especially US citizens. Wikipedia launched. The first international space crew arrived at the International Space Station. George W. Bush defeated Al Gore for president and gave his "Axis of Evil" speech. The Space Shuttle Columbia suffered a breach on its ascent and broke up during its reentry, killing all seven crew members. The DC snipers killed ten people, spreading panic and fear. The Human Genome Project was completed.

I felt like I had done everything I was supposed to do. Except for halfhearted attempts to escape my prison of family expectations, I had done what my parents wanted, even if it meant sacrificing my dreams, my own family, and my sanity.

I was the third senior partner in the law firm, but I was well down the food chain. Even though I was in the top five highest fee producers, I was paid a much lower salary than my younger partners who generated less, including my younger sister, Lisette.

When I spoke to my father about that, he would always tell me that he was trying to feed a lot of mouths, and he would make it up to me in other ways. He never did.

I repeatedly won awards from the local and state bar associations, which were routinely ignored by my partners. The trophies that I won were taken off the lobby table that I put them on and put in a closet. I was being ghosted and marginalized in transparently passive-aggressive ways. I watched my poorly rooted self-esteem evaporate like the morning mist, while my Warrior stayed in a livid, overwrought state.

It was made perfectly clear to me in many unspoken ways that my partners did not like the fact that I was going through my second divorce, and that I spent a lot of time on my cattle ranch in Montana. I didn't fit the "corporate" mold they wanted to convey to the public. I certainly did not kiss enough ass like my younger partners. It was becoming more and more stressful to show up to work every day.

Ironically, the staff and the rest of the lawyers in my county loved me. The judges admired my individuality and creative thinking. They were impressed with my preparation and litigation talents, and I was often complimented by the judges and the court staff. They seemed to believe that I made their lives more interesting. Similarly, the law firm staff supported me, appreciating how authentic and accessible I was.

Whenever something was bothering them, they would come to me for advice. The very things that seemed to bother my partners about me, others seemed to enjoy. But my Warrior focused only on what was going wrong, not what was going right, and work continued to be a source of great stress.

My divorce case with Mary was dragging on and on. I made repeated, generous offers to settle our property division, but all offers were refused without any counteroffers. Neither Mary nor Nancy would speak to me, which hurt, but I wouldn't have known what to say anyway. It was clear there would be no amicable resolution, which further made me feel like a failure.

In the spring of 2004, I won a huge verdict in a case that I had to manage single-handedly. All the support staff were committed to other cases and had no time for mine. In a rarity for our firm, I tried the case with no other firm lawyers or support staff and won a $1 million+ verdict for my client, for which I got a 33 percent contingency fee. At the time, that was a huge fee to bring in all by myself. It would have put me in the top three income generators for the year.

It was like a ghost town when I returned to the office. When I announced my victory, it was to a room of silence, perhaps the loudest a room has ever felt. Lisette quietly congratulated me, but few others even acknowledged it. My sight shrank to tunnel vision so that I could make it to my office without betraying the nearly overwhelming loneliness overtaking me. This world, the one I hadn't even wanted to be a part of but had still excelled in against all odds, this world was breaking apart, cracking at the seams.

When I won, it was ignored. When I lost, I was ignored. It didn't really matter what I did; all reactions pointed to "UnworthinessVille" and "NotGoodEnough City." These were my lifelong stomping grounds. My partner's share was shrinking while my revenues were increasing. My Warrior was boiling just under the surface while my Guru cloaked Itself beside the tiny remaining ember of the celebration fire from the big win. It was obvious to me that working with my father was a dead end.

During the Easter weekend of 2004, I had a talk with Lisette, who at work felt like a stranger, a far cry from the little sister I had known, scared to death of spiders. She came into my office, unannounced, and sat down. She started off kindly. "I have something to say, but I first want to tell you that I love you." That threw me off guard, as I could count on one hand how many times my sisters had said they loved me. All my defense mechanisms went on high alert, my Warrior barely able to be held back.

She continued, "But I don't understand why you're being such an ass to our father. He's done everything for you and hired you when you weren't even employable."

My first thought was what kind of drugs she was on. When we started the firm, I was one of the few people who were bringing in fees. She didn't start making money until our father started hand-feeding her paying clients. My Guru helped me hold back from pointing all this out, and I asked her, "How am I being an ass?"

She said, "Your whole lifestyle is embarrassing to the family. We haven't said anything to you, but your divorces, the way you dress, your social life, all of it! It's just a huge embarrassment."

I could feel my blood pressure rising. The last thing I needed was her sanctimonious diatribe on what I should or should not do with my life. My Warrior was ready to burst through my skin and take her down in one swoop. I swallowed my scorn and managed, "Thank you for your concern."

Clearly ruffled that she hadn't gotten to me, she left my office, slamming the door behind her. It took my Warrior hours to stop battling with the cold air she left in her wake.

Soon thereafter, Memorial Day weekend dawned on a Friday in 2004. I woke up and could not get out of bed. All I could do was lie there, head in my hands, dreading going into work. The Warrior sat on my chest, holding every weapon It had in Its arsenal, and their combined weight rendered me helpless and unable to move a muscle. Totally depressed and both emotionally and physically exhausted (spiritually too, but I didn't know that yet), all I could do was call my sister and tell her that I could not come to work, that I was done. I couldn't practice law anymore.

At the time, there was no such thing as burnout. No one used that term. The only thing I could say was that I was having a nervous breakdown; I needed to get away. I couldn't fight the fight anymore. When I finally got the strength to go into the office, I was immediately summoned to my father's office, where I was cross-examined harshly about my actions and intentions.

It went as badly as I feared. My father was outraged. He felt like I had betrayed him yet again. Loyalty was a big thing with my father, and he had built his life around that principle. He would not let me give him my carefully considered reasons for leaving, and only became more and more livid when I would not reconsider. My Warrior was getting equally incensed by his complete lack of respect for my decision.

When he asked me what I was going to do, I responded, "I am going to be a healer." In hindsight, that was not the best answer at that moment. Energy healing was totally foreign to my father, and he reacted like I had lost my mind. I was also thinking that perhaps I had lost my mind, if all my best efforts had led to this. I didn't have the tools to deal with the events from the last year of my life, and I needed to change. Changing careers is a big step, but I felt like if I didn't, I would drown in the cold and unforgiving water that my father and the law firm swam in.

As I was leaving, I turned back to my father and said, "You've always ridiculed me for being too nice to be a lawyer. Well, you were right. I don't have the killer instinct you do, and I've hated living my life this way."

He scoffed. "I hope you realize that you'll never get anything from me again." I had expected that response; my father's carrot-and-stick approach had always been about money.

His words may have been predictable, but he was taken aback by mine: "Dad, whatever you do with your money is totally up to you. I never wanted your money; I wanted your love."

My father's face flushed bright red, and he ushered me angrily to the door. As one parting shot, he added, "And you can forget about your share of that million-dollar verdict you just won. Thank you very much."

From somewhere deep within me, an authentic smile burst across my face, eager to deliver words he never saw coming. "My freedom is worth way more than any fee. Besides, you have been promising me that you would be fair with my compensation, but you never have. Keep your money, I don't want it."

It was no surprise when he doubled down, looking me squarely in the eyes and snarling, "I wasted all of that money to give you a legal education."

I had to laugh as I shot back, "I think if you look at all of the fees I brought in, you were repaid many times."

My hands and voice were shaking, and I was close to tears, but I was determined not to cry. To do so would have been weak in his eyes, and what was left of my self-esteem would not allow that. All I could do was walk out of his office, my head held high while my heart was plummeting into the hole it always returned to. My Warrior's fierce clamor nearly succeeded in completely drowning out the sound of my Guru's calming incantations.

One thought kept going through my mind as I went through this gauntlet: "Whose life is this anyway?" After fifty years, most of which I had tried to live the life my parents wanted for me, I was obviously being pulled in another direction, one which had yet to be revealed. Up until now, I only had two paths, my parents' path or the fuck you/fuck up/rebel path. Neither one was working.

I supposed that the dysfunctional theory of the universe was true. Families are like solar systems, and everyone must behave in a certain way for the solar system to function properly. When one planet leaves or changes its orbit, the solar system falls apart. On a deeper level, I knew that my actions forced everyone to examine their own life choices.

When I stood up to my father and decided to live my life the way I wanted to live it, it made my sisters question all the times when they had just given in rather than challenge our father. When I left Mary, there had been a similar judgmental reaction against me because I "embarrassed the family." My sisters made sure I knew how big a mistake they thought I was making. Through email, the coldest form of communication, they assailed me with their thoughts and criticisms. I have yet to get an invitation to go to their houses.

It would take several weeks before I could leave. When you quit a law practice, you don't just immediately disappear. I had to find replacement lawyers for my clients, and I had to explain to my colleagues what was going on in each case. I had dozens of active cases; it was not an easy task. I also had to get court permission to exit most of the cases, so it was about two months before I was done. I finally left the office for good on my fifty-first birthday. It was the greatest birthday I could remember. My Guru and Warrior cautiously celebrated in the empty streets of The Unknown.

CHAPTER FORTY-SEVEN

Emotional Maturity

For many years, I felt like my emotions were out of control. I was depressed when I thought I should be happy, and I would experience repeated panic attacks over nothing. As my law partners would say, I was "pole-vaulting over mouse turds." Despite logically knowing that I could gain more control, I wrestled with self-regulation until I did the work to learn new ways of processing my experiences.

Emotions are a part of our existence and change the way we perceive the world. We can have over three hundred emotions that affect how we feel. We usually label these emotions either positive (pleasure/comfort) or negative (pain/discomfort). We can have a positive mindset or a negative mindset, which we can change at any time with the brain's neuroplasticity.

When we live with people who have a negative mindset, we often mimic their behavior if they are in positions of authority and power. When our parents are negative, we are trained to assume that is normal, and our brains make the neural pathways of negativity.

The brain does not make the distinction between negative and positive. Negative and positive are functions of how our thoughts make us feel. Although it may be oversimplifying things, when we are in Warrior mode, we are often negative, while in the Guru mode we can be positive. The brain only recognizes patterns and repetition. If we are constantly thinking thoughts that are negative, the neuroplasticity of the brain will create neural pathways that continue those patterns.[29]

The good news is that new thoughts and ways of thinking can be embedded into our brains with repetition. That is all that it takes, repetition. Repetition establishes new pathways that will become our default way of thinking.

By definition, emotional maturity is being an adult and taking responsibility for your emotions, including being aware of and mastering your emotions. A person who understands and masters their emotions has a choice of how to respond, rather than react, to situations that might be difficult or overwhelming. Emotional maturity helps us problem-solve and stay in control. People who are emotionally mature exhibit various traits that mirror the level of maturity they have reached. These include flexibility, responsibility, acceptance, looking for the positive lessons and opportunities for growth, appreciating other viewpoints and seeking other points of view, calmness, optimism, and humor.

The higher the level of maturity, the more these traits are integrated into our thoughts, behavior, and experience. Not only do these traits help us be successful, but we also experience a much more pleasant quality of life.

People with a high level of emotional maturity don't try to suppress or deny their emotions. After all, emotions are what make life so interesting. The key is not to be attached to an emotion or get stuck in the emotion, especially if the emotion is negative. Cherish the emotions and let them pass through like clouds in the sky. Being aware of emotions in the moment and letting them pass is the hallmark of an emotionally mature person. Emotional maturity means mastering

---

29   Matt Puderbaugh and Prabhu D. Emmady, "Neuroplasticity," StatPearls - NCBI Bookshelf, May 1, 2023, https://www.ncbi.nlm.nih.gov/books/NBK557811/.

your emotions and not being controlled by them. There are four stages of emotional growth:

1. **Fear**: This is the Warrior mode, where everything is ruled by fear and engaged in fighting or running away. Fear is the predominant emotion, and life is exhausting. Negative emotions (anger, guilt, shame) take the stage, while positive emotions (peace, love, relaxation) are nonexistent. We are victims with little or no choice in life.

2. **Risk avoidance**: This is still Warrior mode, and everything is limited by avoiding risk. We live in a bubble where we feel safe and avoid responsibilities. Life is lived according to the rules given to us by our social group. Our self-image is based on what we believe other people think about us. This is conflict avoidance and a refusal to step outside our comfort zone.

3. **Achievement**: This is Warrior mode, but taking more responsibility for thoughts, beliefs, and actions. We have discipline and are goal-oriented and focused. We base our self-esteem on performance, which causes us to live with a chronic anxiety about failure and uneasiness about not being quite good enough. Life is still stressful. We attempt to control our emotions, but rather than let go of emotions, we bury them.

4. **Peace**: The Guru appears, and life is calm and relaxed. We allow our emotions to flow quickly and easily and then release them. We are aware of our emotions and can observe them, rather than be overwhelmed by them. We recognize that emotions are our body's way of dealing with our environment. We take responsibility for our emotions and recognize that we are not our thoughts or emotions. We recognize that what we do is not who we are. Life is fulfilling, and achievement is a by-product of our journey.

In effect, emotional maturity is the mastery of our emotions. Negative thoughts and emotions can be stopped in their tracks by shifting from Warrior to Guru mode and focusing on the positive aspects of our experience. The only difference between fear and excitement is the decision to feel excited rather than afraid. Our quality of life is much higher when we master our emotions.

CHAPTER FORTY-EIGHT

Elvis Has Left the Building

In 2004, Facebook was launched by Mark Zuckerberg. The Summer Olympics were held in Athens, Greece. The Boston Red Sox won the World Series for the first time since 1918. Multiple suicide bombings occurred around the world. George Bush was reelected as president of the United States. Nintendo launched the Nintendo DS, its first handheld game console with a touchscreen.

My whole life felt broken, my heart shattered into shards of glass that even I was frightened to touch. Full of guilt and shame, I started going to a psychologist who was from Lima, Peru. Her name was Cora. To my surprise (and delight), not only was she a psychologist, but she was also a spiritual shaman and a follower of Neem Karoli Baba, a very famous Indian guru. Her therapy didn't consist of couch analysis; it was spiritually based. I began learning about spirituality, meditation on a higher level, tarot cards, mantras, and energy transmissions.

Cora took me further under her skilled wings, and I started traveling with her, meeting people who were deeply involved in spirituality and Eastern philosophy. I met Krishna Das and Ram Dass in Taos, New Mexico. Ram Dass had written *Be Here Now*, a groundbreaking book extolling the benefits of living in the present.[30] I loved it and was soaking up these new ideas and teachings. My Guru's songs were much louder these days, and Its strength was growing as my peace increased.

I was sitting on the porch of an ashram (place of worship), looking out at a field where various campers had pitched their tents. In the past, these people would have been called hippies. I remembered my dreams of being an Outward Bound counselor, and my face must have reflected some of my long-buried disappointment about not following that path.

Suddenly Cora appeared and asked me, "Why are you so sad, Mr. Robinson?"

My words spilled out, my regrets of not being one of the tent people out in the field.

She looked thoughtfully at those I was in envy of. "Mr. Robinson, where are you right now?"

I stated the obvious, "On this porch."

And she continued, "Where are those tent people right now?"

I responded, "In that field."

Cora chewed on her lower lip for a moment, breathing slowly, deliberately. "Would you say that you all are in the same place right now?"

I was beginning to follow her thinking. "Yes."

"So, could you say that you all ended up at the same place?" Cora asked with a wry smile.

My eyes widened as the light bulb came on for me. We all travel along paths that intersect at certain points, and we always have a chance to change our paths.

I saw that even though I had chosen not to follow the path of being an outdoor counselor years ago, I had been brought back to the same place I could have been if I had. We all get to where we are supposed to be, regardless of what decisions we make. I began to understand the concept of destiny a little bit better.

---

30   Ram Dass and Lama Foundation, *Be Here Now, Remember* (San Cristobal, NM: Lama Foundation, 1971).

Later that day, I met with Ram Dass and Krishna Das. They were describing their experiences with Neem Karoli Baba. Ram Dass had recently had a stroke and wasn't saying much, but Krishna Das was telling story after story of this well-known Indian guru. I was mesmerized.

I had been searching for someone to help me make sense of my life. Unfortunately, Baba had passed on several years ago. I asked Cora if there were any other gurus with whom I might study.

Cora told me about a guru in India named Sathya Sai Baba. This man was worshiped by millions all around the world and had built ashrams, hospitals, water systems, orphanages, and many other facilities to help poor communities. I was amazed that I had never heard of this man. Cora had been to see him and told me of the many miracles attributed to him.

The thing that Cora recommended I do right away was to resume meditating. I hadn't meditated in several years and had not had any conversations with Bob in quite some time either. I had entirely forgotten about finding him there. When I started meditating again, it gave me some peace about my circumstances. I also started hearing whispers from Bob—not too loud, but when I meditated, I was aware that Bob was watching, observing me.

Cora took me on several trips to Peru to experience the ancient energies of Machu Picchu and other sacred sites. We met with native shamans who showed us how to perform ancient spiritual ceremonies that called upon their ancestors to give guidance, inspiration, and healing.

Sitting and watching these ceremonies, I felt a level of connectedness I had never known, as if I were born for this training. I was honored beyond words that I was allowed to witness these ancient traditions and teachings. My Guru added it to the growing list of proof of my self-worth. With Cora's connections, we were taken to several secret sacred sites used by the Incas over a thousand years ago. The energy was palpable, and I felt myself begin to move beyond my westernized thoughts. Memories, ones that seemed to belong to my ancestors, now moved like a lazy river growing in speed inside of me. I started to understand that I was not just a failed lawyer from North Carolina; there was so much more involved.

I realized that I didn't have to be imprisoned in my law career. There was so much of the world that I didn't know and could learn about. My desire to be an energy healer was filling every cell of my body and began spilling out in tangible ways. I had lost my desire to be a lawyer (if I truly had ever even had one), and my soul expanded, knowing that I had found something I could be passionate about. Impostor thoughts tried briefly to intrude on my burgeoning mindset, but both my Guru and my Warrior chased them away, and soon they stopped coming. I let go of my guilt and shame and felt better about my decision to become a healer.

Although Cora taught me many things about spirituality, she didn't believe I should be a healer. I had to find a different teacher to guide me on how to heal. My first step was to attend a healing clinic in Dallas, Texas, held by an internationally known healer named Estrella.

Estrella was a well-known psychic and healer and helped clients around the world. She was academically brilliant (she had been inducted into the Mensa society at an early age) and remarkably attuned to other realms. She taught people how to heal others and devised a system called Light Language, which taught people how to talk to God in colors and three-dimensional geometric shapes.

Her healing system was called Divine Intervention. She taught several of the classes in the workshop herself, and during them became impressed with my abilities. In a move I didn't see coming, she invited me to live with her. My Guru, after dancing for what seemed like hours straight, wept with joy. Even my Warrior seemed pleased with the decision. I moved to Navasota, Texas, to be her apprentice. I would stay for two years.

If I could imagine a version of heaven, my new life looked like it. I became a walking encyclopedia of metaphysics. Estrella taught me all kinds of magic courses from the old school. She was a walking encyclopedia of motivation and linguistics and introduced me to the power and intricacies of words. I didn't know it then, but it was an early form of neurolinguistics. I did know that my Guru and I both loved it, and my Warrior was quieter than It had been in years.

Estrella used to say, "What comes out of your mouth is much more important than what goes in it." Neurolinguistics is a pseudoscience that psychoanalyzes language to determine what lies underneath the conscious mind. We use words and sentences all the time that can indicate the emotional and mental landscape of our subconscious mind. She was a master at analyzing her clients based on a few minutes of conversation. I soaked it all up like a sea sponge.

I dreamed of using the ranch as a retreat center. It was ideal—remote, quiet, and beautiful on the picturesque Crow Reservation. I imagined people there, learning modalities on authentic Native American land, creating healing, and giving honor to native traditions. I talked it over with Jim and held my first workshop on the Ranch.

It was a nightmare! Jim acted like the participants were beneath contempt. I was horrified by his behavior. Jim fired the cook the week before the retreat and said he would do the cooking. The first morning, he came downstairs in his underwear and began slamming around the kitchen and grumbling as he did.

The participants looked at me with a "WTF?" look. One of them loudly expressed what were probably the thoughts of many. "There isn't anything that man could cook that I would eat!"

Jim looked at her coldly and shot back, "It looks like you could lose a few pounds anyway."

At that point, I strode to stand right in front of him, to deliver a message I had not fully thought through. "Go upstairs and put on your clothes! I'll do the cooking from now on."

I not only had to teach the healing class and entertain the guests, but now I also had to cook for everyone. When preparing food, it is important to pay attention to your thoughts because they go into the food and can improve or spoil the taste. I could tell when someone was angry when they cooked, as usually the food tasted bitter or burned in some way. When food is prepared with love and attention to detail, it tastes wonderful. Throughout their stay, the guests understood this more and more and could see why they (even the most serene in the group) had been so resistant to Jim's cooking.

Jim did serve a purpose, though. Most teachers want their students to lose their tempers early in a workshop so the students and teachers can work on the issues that are revealed under duress. Jim triggered almost everyone in the group in different ways, and as a result, the guests worked through a lot of the issues that had limited their success throughout their lives.

Once people can identify the issues that commonly trigger them, they can heal and no longer be controlled by them. In many cases, thanks to Jim, there was a lot of healing during that workshop. On one occasion, one of the guests fell and jammed her hip. In sports terminology, she had a hip pointer, which is extremely painful. To demonstrate the power of healing, I did a simple healing technique on her hip, and the pain went away immediately. My Guru stood by my side, beaming and clapping Its hands in a rain of applause. Even my Warrior looked impressed.

I had similar success with the animals at the ranch. That spring, Jim had acquired a champion paint stallion to breed with the mares on the ranch. The stallion was put into a pasture by the house so Jim could keep an eye on it. In typical Jim fashion, he didn't check the pasture for dangerous objects, and there was some loose wire lying on the ground.

One night, I went out to check on the animals and saw the stallion standing in the snow, surrounded by bloody tracks that stood out starkly against the landscape of winter white. I went into the pasture and saw that the stallion had wrapped the loose wire around his front hooves, and it had sliced through his legs just above the hooves. It was a bloody mess. My Warrior roared like It hadn't in some time, while my Guru tried to comfort the stallion in hushed tones. Both sounds carried across the winter night winds, and it seemed like all the animals raised their heads to hear them.

The farrier (horse specialist) was called, and he said there was nothing to be done; the tendons had been severed. The tendon right above the hoof is highly dynamic and, when severed, will not heal. The horse would have to be put down. I couldn't let that happen and said that I would work with him.

The farrier thought it was cruel to let the horse suffer for no reason, but I insisted. I wrapped the hooves with antibiotic cream and gauze and did healing on the hooves three times a day. When the farrier came back in a week, the cuts were completely healed, and the horse fully recovered. Again my Warrior and my Guru cheered in unison, and secretly my pride swelled that I had been able to save the horse's life.

The farrier could not believe his eyes. He wanted to know what I had done. I just said, "I prayed." Trying to explain the healing process would go beyond the farrier's understanding of the world. Whenever I was asked what I did to heal something, I would just say, "I prayed." People accepted that answer without question or scrutiny, as a matter of faith.

Thankfully, my animal healing didn't end there. The ranch manager had a horse that she really liked and kept as her own. One day, the horse was down on its side and wouldn't get up. The manager and I got the horse up with the front-end loader, and it was obvious something had hurt its front left leg. We got it in a trailer and set off to the vet, who was an hour's drive away. I stood in the back with the horse and did healing on its leg. By the time we arrived at the vet, it was clear the horse was walking much better.

X-rays discovered that although the horse had broken a leg, it was already healed. The X-rays clearly showed that the break was recently healed. The ranch manager looked at me appreciatively, but also like I had three eyes, and grilled me as we returned to the ranch. Again, I attributed it to active prayer. Her horse also made a full recovery.

I began to heal animals and people, and it seemed to come naturally to me. Perhaps I could have done it way back when I met that first horse I connected with as a child, but I had ignored it for my whole life. This thought made my Guru uncomfortable and my Warrior retroactively angry, so I tried to stay away from it. People would come to see me for migraines, broken bones, and diseases. Some healed, some didn't. At first, I couldn't predict who would heal and who wouldn't. But soon I started to understand that I could not heal people unless they wanted to be healed. If they chose to heal, they did. Animals didn't have that subconscious resistance; they could heal instantly.

Watching people stand in the way of their own healing was troubling, but I began to understand that the subconscious mind often plays the primary role in healing. This means that healing may just be a placebo effect. Modern medicine is well aware of the power of the placebo effect, and I learned to make peace with those who didn't understand how to harness it.

After the fiasco with the workshop, the relationship between Jim and me deteriorated. I discovered that he was spending money on nonessential equipment while the property taxes hadn't been paid for several years. As I was now a 50 percent owner in the ranch, I confronted him, my Warrior raging, and Jim and I had a huge fight. I was done. Although I was hugely disappointed, I knew that I could no longer partner with Jim. I demanded that he buy me out of the ranch. A contract was signed, and I took my horses and left.

I decided to take the horses to a friend who had a riding stable in Tobermory, Ontario, Canada. On the way, I ran out of gas in Minnesota, which apparently didn't have many exits on the interstate.

I was sitting by the road contemplating what to do with my truck and a trailer full of horses. It was at least ten miles to the next exit. I started locking everything up and preparing to hitchhike. Then it struck me, why hitchhike when I can ride?

I brought out my most dependable horse, a Belgian/Fjord mix named Prince, and saddled him up. It was quite a ride down the median on the interstate. Cars stopped and took our photograph. The only time that was a bit dicey was when I had to cross a bridge over a river.

Horses don't like crossing bridges, as the echo off the bridge tends to make them afraid. Prince took it like the royalty he was named after, and we made it into town. I bought a can of diesel fuel, strapped it on my saddle, and rode back to my truck. Once again, cars were stopping to take my photograph, this time with a can of gas strapped on my saddle. My Guru chuckled much of the way.

When I got back to the truck, two highway patrol cars were bracketing my truck and trailer. I rode up and dismounted and was immediately surrounded by troopers. They thought I was poaching on someone's ranch, but when they saw the diesel can, they smiled and realized what the situation was. The troopers were very helpful and helped me get Prince back into the trailer and my truck down the road.

I got to Tobermory and dropped the horses off. I then returned to Texas and Estrella to continue my magical apprenticeship. I started to notice that whenever problems arose in my life, the solution would present itself almost instantly. The universe was manifesting solutions almost as fast as I was manifesting the problems. My Warrior mode was deactivated, and my Guru mode was taking over.

CHAPTER FORTY-NINE

The Search for Enlightenment

As I began trudging the path of happy destiny, I started taking a closer look at a term I heard often from spiritual people: enlightenment. Enlightenment is one of those words that means far different things to different people. There are two completely different concepts of the word in Eastern and Western civilizations. In the East, enlightenment is a state of consciousness. In the West, it is a movement that brought us out of the Dark Ages into the Renaissance.

In the West, the Enlightenment was the age of science and reason that blossomed from an escape from the dogma of the Catholic Church and the horrors of the Inquisition. It grew from the writings of René Descartes, who in 1637 declared, "I think, therefore I am."

The concept of enlightenment shifted dogma to analysis, faith to proof and the importance of reason. Anything that could not be explained was rejected, especially religious orthodoxy. Reason and knowledge became the new gods.

The term enlightenment changed in the West in the 1800s through the writings of Max Muller. It changed from rationality to the sudden insight of transcendental truth or reality. Enlightenment became aligned with self-realization of the true self, rather than the thinking of self, based on layers of social conditioning. It is liberation through the recognition of the illusion of the world and detachment from identification with the mind and body.

In the East, enlightenment is synonymous with the term "awakening." In Sanskrit (the ancient Indo-European language of India), the term is "bodhi," which has the same root word as "Buddha." We are all buddhas in varying stages of awakening. It encompasses the concepts of insight, knowledge, and the release of negative beliefs, emotions, and cravings.

Enlightenment became popularized in the West through the teachings of Maharishi Mahesh Yogi, who mentored numerous celebrities in the 1960s and 1970s, such as the Beatles and the Beach Boys. He created TM as a form of meditation that became popular in the 1970s in the US, with over five million practitioners. He advocated that enlightenment could only be achieved through meditation, which should be practiced at least twice a day.

The term enlightenment is still debated because of the numerous sources of understanding. Signs or symptoms of enlightenment include:

1. **Observation**: Many people go through life without much attention to what they are doing. They live their life based on what they were taught or copied from others. The journey to enlightenment requires self-analysis and questioning why we do what we do. This includes the observation of thoughts, emotions, and beliefs, and the realization that our awareness is not attached to our thoughts, emotions, or beliefs.

2. **Detachment**: When we become aware of our thoughts, we can realize that we are not our thoughts or beliefs. Many people form beliefs about who or what they are based on what they have been told, rather than separating themselves from those thoughts and discovering their true nature on their own. This allows us to separate from the past and the future, which are illusions. The

past is an illusion because we filter our memories through our emotions and biases, while the future does not exist. When we detach from our emotions, we stop being controlled by them. Fear, anger, guilt, and shame no longer manipulate our behavior.

3. **Non-judgment**: Enlightenment requires the release of judgment. Terms such as good/bad, right/wrong, ugly/beautiful, and like/dislike no longer occupy our minds. When we release judgment, we can begin to see the world as it really is. Our subconscious mind is filled with beliefs and biases that change our perception of the world. To truly understand the world, we must release those beliefs and biases.

4. **Acceptance**: Enlightenment allows us to drop our expectations and stop resisting life. Stress is the result of resisting life as it occurs and wishing it were different. When we can accept life as it is, we are more open to different possibilities and can use that to our advantage. Instead of struggling with life, we learn to dance with it. We accept, then learn, then grow. We also allow other people to have their experience with the knowledge that we are all one. We stop trying to change other people, and we focus on changing ourselves.

5. **Immortality**: With enlightenment, we do not fear death. There is only one fear at the base of our psyche: the fear of death. When we release our fear of death, we can live more fully and expansively. Most enlightened philosophies and all religions recognize that death is not the end. Eastern philosophies consider death as merely a change of form and as a natural part of eternal divinity, which we are.

6. **Connection to the Divine**: Enlightenment is the realization that we are part of something much bigger and universal. While we are individual and unique, we are something much bigger, which is defined by our existence. We recognize that we are

connected energetically to a larger energetic field known as universal consciousness.

These concepts gave me a measure of peace and serenity. I was free from the misconceptions that kept me imprisoned in my mind, and I was starting to understand the bigger picture of life and the role my mind played in it. I would continue to learn more and more about the mind, the brain, and my body, but at least I was focusing on matters that were important to me.

CHAPTER FIFTY

High Magic

In 2005, Hurricane Katrina hit the Louisiana Delta, and over 1,800 people died. New Orleans was decimated, and it would take years for it to recover. George Bush started his second term as president, and many would argue that his presidency was just as traumatic as Katrina. YouTube started, and a cultural phenomenon began as millions of people posted videos for the world to see. Information was becoming available at a scale never seen before in human history. England implemented the Civil Partnership Act, allowing same-sex civil partnerships. Disneyland turned fifty. Star Wars and Harry Potter continued to crank out their franchise movies with *Star Wars: Episode III* and *Harry Potter and the Goblet of Fire*, and *Brokeback Mountain* garnered critical acclaim. I moved in with Estrella and began formally learning the art of healing.

Estrella was an icon and frontrunner in many alternative medicine techniques. Not only had she developed her Divine Intervention and Light Language healing modalities, but she also continued the study of magic. This was not sleight of hand; it was magic wands, candles, cloaks, ceremonies, and ritual. I loved it.

At last, I was learning what I always wanted to learn, and that was how to be a wizard. From the start, I was very good at it; I understood the details and rhythms of creating magical results. I could feel the hand of my Guru guiding me and voicing appreciation for the new ways I could communicate with It. Not only did I hone my healing abilities, but I also learned the techniques of transmutation, translocation, bilocation, astral travel, youthing (becoming younger), and other esoteric magical practices. Even Estrella was impressed with how quickly I learned the various techniques and excelled in classes.

I lived with Estrella and her husband in their compound in Navasota, Texas, which was a rambling complex of buildings in the middle of nowhere somewhere near College Station, Texas. I spent almost all my time at Estrella's compound, as there was no real reason to go into town except to get groceries.

Estrella had a system for everything and was extremely disciplined in her lifestyle. She was obsessive about cleanliness and organization; she believed that the condition of one's environment affected the flow of energy in and around its inhabitants.

A very powerful motivator, she understood the power of words and neurolinguistic programming. I learned to pay attention to what was coming out of my mouth. She continued to show me that what comes out of our mouth is more important than what goes in it.

In the fall of 2005, Estrella and her husband bought a geodesic dome church in Hot Springs, Arkansas, and we moved from Navasota, Texas, into the church. It was a beautiful building in need of some maintenance. There was a large open kitchen and cafeteria, and a sanctuary that seated nearly one thousand people.

I loved the sleeping arrangements, as I was allowed to sleep on the altar. Surrounding it were numerous huge quartz crystals excavated from the local crystal mine. Being near such gigantic crystals made my dreams of the angels even more vivid, and my Guru and I were in high spirits to go to sleep every night. It was a good time for me, and I continued to absorb everything I could learn about magical practices and healing. I finally felt like I was following the path my soul intended. My Guru barely left my side.

Estrella taught that there are two kinds of teachings, taught teachings and caught teachings. Taught teachings are lessons we learn through verbal communication and through watching. Caught teachings are teachings we acquire subliminally through proximity and our subconscious minds.

Estrella advised her students to sleep with their texts under their pillows to get caught up on teachings energetically as they slept. I asked her husband once if he slept with the texts under his pillow. He replied, "No, I don't have to, I sleep with the teacher!" My Guru and I laughed and laughed at this unconventional drop of wisdom.

The last workshop that Estrella and I did together was a month-long retreat in Vieques, Puerto Rico, in August 2006. She had rented a house on Dead Horse Cove with a beautiful view of the ocean. This was Estrella's signature monthly retreat. She taught techniques on walking on water, teleportation, astral projection, bilocation, and other mystical techniques. I discovered that I could do these things, although perhaps only briefly. More importantly, I had a chance to do some healings while we were there, including instantly healing a very deep cut the chef inflicted on herself, and healing the migraines her husband had suffered for years.

Even Estrella was a bit surprised by the results. I wrote most of the content for the workshop and created a very impressive workbook. I discovered I had a talent for creating content for workshops. Most importantly, I formed relationships with several other students from Europe, Hong Kong, and the Middle East; I would be able to facilitate workshops around the world with them for many years.

Estrella had taught me all she knew, and she told me it was time to move on. She perceptively told me I had been associating with women for most of my time with her, and it was time for me to experience more male energy to balance out my training. She recommended that I go train with a guru in Ireland, Derek O'Neill. My Guru and my

Warrior were both looking forward to what was next, my Warrior's trepidation at its lowest point ever, and my Guru's face beaming with the light of all that was to come.

CHAPTER FIFTY-ONE

Freedom from Our Mind

During this time, I began to study the mind and how it affects our experiences. In the United States, we consider ourselves lucky for all the freedoms that we have. The irony is that even though we have freedoms unequaled in any other country in the world, many people are still imprisoned by their own minds.

In spiritual terms, the mind is a tool that was formed to help us to survive on this planet and hopefully move from survival mode to relaxation and happiness. In other words, to escape from our Warrior prison and live with the freedom of the Guru.

Unfortunately, many of us are stuck in Warrior mode and spend most of the day scheming and thinking about what we lack and how to get it, or about all the injustice being done to us and others. This is the biggest prison in the world, and to some extent, we all spend time there sometimes. Many people don't just visit; they live there.

One of the fastest-growing industries on the planet involves setting ourselves free from this prison. Religious leaders, spiritual leaders, monks, and housewives are all writing books and teaching seminars on how to free ourselves from anxiety and stress and achieve whatever it is we want. Unfortunately, most of this does not create any sustainable change. After all, "We cannot solve a problem with the same mind that created it," which is a sentiment often attributed to Einstein.

The only way to escape our individual (and collective) mental prisons is to realize that it is our thinking that is keeping us prisoner. Our minds have been trained since birth to keep us imprisoned in a jail so that we can be controlled and herded like sheep to buy, consume, desire, compete, and compare ourselves. It is an intentional design that is ruining our quality of life. We are destroying the rainforests to clear pastures for substandard beef to make into hamburgers that we eat to become obese and unhealthy.

And many of us don't care.

But I believe you do. And I know that the Guru in all of us cares, and our Warriors do too. We must first realize that we are in a prison, and then, armed with our new self-awareness, take action to change. There is a story about Sathya Sai Baba, who told a man who was having trouble sleeping to go to a yoga master for help. The man returned to thank Baba because the yoga master helped the man start getting restful sleep. Baba replied: "Good. When you want to wake up, come to me."

What keeps us imprisoned in our suffering is our unwillingness to take responsibility for our lives. We blame others, and the state of the world, and believe that we are victims. When we do that, we take on the consciousness of lack. And our Warriors are vigilant; for many of us, they have been running our emotional show for as long as we can remember. We are all too familiar with the hot-running emotions and responses of our Warriors, and our neural pathways that these run down are deeply grooved. This is why it is incredibly easy to fall back into the same old prison, and why it is so important to become aware and take control of our thoughts. What we must realize is that we are creating everything, including our thoughts, for our own enlightenment.

The path to enlightenment must include the realization that we are divine.

Whether we believe that we are hopeless and helpless or wealthy beyond imagination, we are all divine. The only way to be free of all this illusion and insanity is to accept the fact that we created our reality, and we can change it by simply applying this one teaching.

We are not helpless and hopeless; we do not need wealth beyond belief. All of that is an illusion of the ego. We are simply individual capsules of consciousness having experiences.

When we start to wake up to the fact that we are creating what we need to be enlightened, we will start to behave in different ways. We will have compassion for each other, shift judgment to understanding, and start to share what we have with others. We will learn to practice the way of non-violence towards ourselves and others, which will eliminate the need for wars and politics. We will understand there is no longer "them." There is only "us."

We do not have to change the planet; we only must take responsibility for ourselves. We do not need to change the world, only our minds. When we start understanding that we are creating our reality, we have no more excuses—we are powerful beyond belief. When we believe in how powerful we are, everything changes. Our reality changes. Our relationships change. Our opinion of ourselves changes. Our grasp expands to match our reach. Our fortunes change. We come to see the world as it really is. We learn to bloom wherever we are planted. And we can uproot ourselves and go anywhere we choose, even if in the present moment that is only in our minds.

CHAPTER FIFTY-TWO

The Leprechauns

In 2006, I moved to New York City. In that year, Twitter launched. Pluto was downgraded from planet to "dwarf planet." Google purchased YouTube for $1.65 billion. Saddam Hussein was executed. Sony released the PlayStation 3. "Crowdfunding" and "crowdsourcing" were designated as words. The Great American Boycott took place to protest for immigration rights. Shakira's hips didn't lie, and *Borat* hit the theaters, much to the chagrin of some people and the delight of others.

I was starting to teach workshops around the world. I often went to Israel, Europe, Hong Kong, and South America. There seemed to be a lot of people who were interested in learning about magic and mysticism. I was also holding healing clinics that were quite successful. I watched all sorts of diseases and medical problems heal instantly. Sometimes I was more surprised by the results than the client. After all, they knew whether they expected to heal, while I never knew what they were truly believing about their recovery.

The friendships that I had made in Vieques were fruiting wonderful opportunities. The workshops in Tel Aviv and Jerusalem were hugely popular, as were those in Hong Kong, Europe, and South America. I held weekly healing clinics and workshops in Manhattan and was enjoying being the new "flavor of the week." I knew that it was a fleeting role, as whenever a successful healer or teacher with new modalities comes to New York City, they have instant cachet. However, after a few months or years, the newness wears off, and the practitioner must be authentically committed to expanding their healing practices.

I started training with Derek O'Neill. I originally met him at his workshop in Coeur d'Alene, Idaho, in June of 2006. It was a two-day workshop, six hours per day. I had never experienced anything like it before, and my Guru and Warrior both were blown away. Derek combined psychotherapy, martial arts, chiropractic adjustments, visualization, mysticism, meditation, and music into the greatest show on earth.

Since he liked to play music during his workshops, Estrella referred to him as "the spiritual DJ." Derek chose songs and tones, intentionally orchestrated to generate a wide range of emotional responses in the participants. I'd sit, mesmerized, and watch people around me experience a gamut of reactions from falling out of their seats in ecstasy to fits of sobbing in the fetal position.

Derek would ask for questions, and people would raise their hands. If someone raised their hand, Derek would ask them to walk to a microphone in the middle of the floor, and he would have a conversation with the participant. Sometimes he would simply give the participant an answer, sometimes a chiropractic adjustment, and sometimes he would wave his hands around the participant, who would usually drop to the floor. It reminded me of some of the tent revivals I had gone to during my Southern Baptist years.

I thought I would give it a go and ask about my attraction to toxic women. I raised my hand and was called to the microphone. As briefly as I could, I described my childhood and dysfunctional relationship with my parents, then asked why I couldn't find a woman who loved me as much as I loved them. When I stopped, Derek just looked at me and yelled, "GET OVER IT!"

That was not the kind of response I was looking for. I wanted hand-waving, spiritual chiropractic adjustments, and golden chariots coming from the ceiling in a star-studded vortex. I felt that I had been cheated of a chance for a great healing and returned to my seat, my Warrior rising, always ready to resume Its fighting stance. I was not impressed. I noted an underlying theme of hero worship from the participants, and I wasn't impressed with that either.

In addition to his weekend workshops, Derek offered two week-long workshops in Dublin, Ireland, in June and October. I decided to give Derek another chance and went to the October 2006 workshop. You know how you look back at your life and can see where there were big forks in the road, and you made a decision that changed things forever? This change in direction, this following my instincts to give it another chance, swooped me onto a path I didn't see coming.

Derek talked a lot about Sathya Sai Baba, the Indian guru to whom Cora had introduced me years before. Apparently, Derek was also a student of Sai Baba (as he was more commonly called) and echoed many of his teachings about the five human values: truth, right conduct, peace, love, and non-violence. In contrast to our first meeting, I totally resonated with the teachings Derek gave that week.

Derek again spent a great deal of time interacting with individuals at the microphone, but this time it clicked, and I understood that their issues were my issues, and their healing was my healing. There were several dozen of Estrella's students there as well, so I developed a greater connection to the group than before. My Guru felt at ease, and I started going to more and more of Derek's workshops.

I had learned my lesson and did not go up to the microphone. For some reason, my desire for attention had abated, and I was content to watch, my Guru humming on my shoulder. I discovered that when I quit looking for things to heal, my anxiety and stress were greatly reduced. I knew that just being in the retreat center was healing in and of itself.

Derek would spend time with each student, which was extremely beneficial. He had an intuitive grasp of my issues in a way that felt uncanny. It was like he could see my mind and my heart and tell what was broken. He was much kinder one-on-one and talked to me about forgiveness and grace. It still didn't quite sink in, but eventually I would understand what he was saying.

My mother had been seriously ill for years. She had lung cancer, osteoporosis, a host of complications from alcoholism, and the iron constitution of a steel magnolia. Even though she had been bedridden for over a year, she managed to hang on, even though every day she was weaker and weaker. I regretted living so far away but went to see her occasionally to see how she was doing and let her know how grateful I was for all she did for me. My Guru helped me to find the words. Then, in November 2007, I was in Israel teaching a seminar when I got a message that she had slipped into a coma and was not expected to last the night.

I called my parents' house and spoke to the hospice nurse. She confirmed that she was unconscious, and the rest of the family was there. My heart sank, knowing how far I was from the room where she lay dying, and I asked the nurse to put the telephone up to my mother's ear. When she did so, I spoke some Aramaic words that Jesus said to the lame man who picked up his bed and walked. Through muffled tears, I said goodbye, and that her loved ones were waiting for her to come to the other side, and she had nothing to worry about.

The next morning, I called to see if my mother had lasted the night. The nurse's breathlessly excited answer surged through our connection. "I don't know what you said to her last night, but about thirty minutes after you hung up, she regained consciousness, and she is doing better every hour!"

I was not that surprised. I had seen some miraculous things in the few short years I had been doing healings. I got to talk to my mother, who couldn't remember anything about what I said to her. I told her how much I loved her and that I would come to see her when I returned from Israel.

Unfortunately, I didn't get that chance. I talked to her every morning, and she seemed to be gaining strength. Three days after she woke up, she told everyone to leave the room; she wanted some time to herself. The nurse later told me that when everyone was out of the room, she got quiet, looked straight up, and sighed, "Oh," and peacefully fell into the sleep that lasts forever. I didn't get a chance to see her again, but I counted every minute of those three more days to say goodbye as an extended blessing.

I returned to study with Derek. He had started teaching a healing technique called the Rising Star. There was a precise process, as was the custom in other healing techniques I had learned. My Guru beamed as I mastered the Rising Star technique, my fourteenth certification in healing modalities. All this from a guy who used to be ruled by his Warrior.

I was also certified to teach practitioners, so I started traveling, teaching this new healing system around the globe. It was especially popular in Israel and Hong Kong. For the next several years, I taught on four continents, guiding people to be able to heal themselves and others. There didn't seem to be anything these techniques failed to repair if the client was truly ready.

One case that stands out in my mind was when I was in Hong Kong. I received a call from a woman I didn't know who had terminal brain cancer and had been given the dire prognosis of only a few days to live. I went over to the hospital at her request and spent some time working with her.

When I got back to the healing clinic, the client called to say they had taken her for an MRI, and all the tumors had disappeared. I asked her what the doctors said and smiled broadly when she told me the doctors said they must have made a mistaken diagnosis. I knew that some doctors just can't accept the fact that people have the power to heal themselves.

In the spring of 2007, Derek and his wife Linda opened a wellness and healing center in New Ross, Ireland, named Creacon Lodge Wellness Centre. I went there repeatedly over the next several years. My Guru and I liked to go there for solitude and inspiration, and my Warrior found it to be a place where It could unclench Its mighty jaws.

I wrote four books there: *The Secret to Healing, How Big Is Your But?, What Is Love?,* and *Living to Die, Dying to Live.* I was elated when *How Big Is Your But?* and *What Is Love?* received numerous domestic and international awards.

In a bit of ironic humor, Derek asked me to be his bodyguard. When Derek did events, he was often deluged by followers who tried to sneak in the back and disrupt his solitude. It was my job to keep people away from him behind and on stage. I relished the role; I wore a black suit and looked the part. I often pretended to be talking into my wristwatch, and people thought I was an arrogant ass. I was unphased, my Warrior barely aroused. I took to heart the admonition "What other people think of me is none of my business."

I also ghostwrote several books for other spiritual teachers, which did well. I decided to leave New York; I was only home for six weeks out of the year. I put all my belongings into storage and fully embraced life as a nomad. When I wasn't on the road teaching, I would bounce around visiting friends or my sons, and I even lived with a friend in Atlanta for one year. My chief focus was to be able to teach and travel and continue to expand my skills and my own mind. In the following five years, I made these goals come true in Brazil, Argentina, Peru, Canada, Scotland, England, Germany, Israel, Egypt, Saudi Arabia, Australia, and all over the US. It was an amazing period in my life, one when I had become so familiar with my own Guru and Warrior and was over the moon to be able to teach so many others about theirs.

In October 2008, I attended one of Derek O'Neill's workshops in Liffey Valley near Dublin, Ireland. The workshop was going well enough, but midway through the week was October 31, Halloween. While Halloween was a relatively peaceful holiday in the US, in Dublin,

Ireland, it was another matter. The ancient Druid ceremonies still occurred in Dublin, with huge bonfires lit all around County Dublin. The park beside the workshop venue was no exception, and as I looked out of the hotel, I saw dozens of huge bonfires burning all around it. Derek had issued a warning to all the people at the workshop to not even consider venturing out. Apparently, crime and violence spiked during the Halloween workshop, and no one was safe outside of the hotel. I never got the message.

I went out to investigate the bonfires. Since they were burning in a public park, I didn't know of the potential risk I was taking by going outside. Each bonfire was built and maintained by a local gang, and outsiders were not welcome. I unknowingly walked into an ambush. As I was walking by some bushes growing beside the public path through the park, I heard someone say, "Where are you from?" I didn't answer. Presumably taking it as disrespect, heaped on top of the audacity to disregard all street rules around territories, a young man leapt forward and began beating me in the back of the head with a baseball bat. Within seconds, I was unconscious.

"Bob, is that you?" I asked.

"*Yes.*"

I sighed deeply. "What am I doing? I thought I was getting better about this pain and suffering approach to life."

Bob said, "*You are, you are a lot better. But you should know that you have some big lessons coming up.*"

I groaned, "It seems that I have been suffering all my life. What difference does it make now?"

Bob's words uncharacteristically dripped judgment. "*Self-pity doesn't look good on you.*"

I bristled. "You know, I suffered through my childhood with parents who wanted me to be who they wanted me to be. They had no interest in what I wanted to do. I really wanted to be an Outward Bound counselor. I wanted a life of meaning. Now I am finally following my passion for healing, and here I am again, walking the line between life and death. I feel like if I wake up again, I really don't know what the fuck I am doing."

Bob was quiet for a while and then said, *"You seem so oblivious to how important you are, how smart you are, how handsome you are, and how much you can help people. You just need to be you and quit trying to impress people with what you can do. You could still slow down a little on the drinking as well. Here's the deal: You care too much about how people see you. The only thing that is important is what you think about yourself. Your newest passion for healing other people is powerful and holds the meaning that you seek, but you must heal this hole in your heart that you want to fill with your father's love. He is never going to behave the way you want him to behave, so quit wishing he was different. The cause of all suffering is wishing that your life were different."*

He paused, then continued. *"Let me ask you something."*

"What?"

"What if you didn't ever heal anyone and you never proved that you were worthy of your father's love?"

My face wrinkled in critical thought. "I don't think that was God's purpose in leading me down this path."

Bob said, *"Then get up off your ass, fully release old expectations, and be the most impactful James Gray Robinson you can be. You have a lot of good work ahead of you. Be brave. Embrace your destiny. You have spent all your life trying to please others. Now follow your heart, your passions. Heal thyself first, then others."*

I woke up with blood pouring from my head down my face. I stood up and faced my attackers. Most thought I was dead, so it caught them off guard when I rose like a bloody Phoenix. The one with the bat took another swing at me, and all my years of karate took over, supported by the wild swings of my Warrior. I took the bat from him and had both attackers on the ground. I seized my opportunity and took off running back to the hotel.

When I got back, limping and wheezing, I walked in the front door looking like something that had risen from the grave in a B-horror movie. My face and sweatshirt were covered with blood. People from the workshop who were in the lobby began pouring in, their hysteria rising. I just asked for some help to get back to my room.

I felt okay, and miraculously, the blows from the bat didn't do any permanent damage. I got back to my room and got the bleeding to stop. I had cleaned up and changed into some clean clothes by the time Derek came to see what had happened. All the blood had come from some superficial wounds that healed almost instantly.

I declined an invitation to go to the hospital; I was a superglue and duct tape kind of guy anyway. Derek was amazed that I healed so quickly, but I knew that my prior experiences had given me the ability to heal almost instantly. I had gotten used to NDEs. At that point, I almost felt renewed afterwards, given yet another chance to do my life right. All Derek said was, "You must have something very important to accomplish in this world, to survive all of these brushes with death."

I simply smiled. I kept to myself that the beings on the other side of the veil had said the same thing. The one thing that was very clear to me was that these experiences were connecting me deeper and deeper with universal intelligence and the divine. My Guru swelled, Its light filling my chest cavity and finally, finally beginning to spill out of me.

CHAPTER FIFTY-THREE

The Illusion of Desire

I had to learn a lot of new concepts to heal all the programming I received in my childhood and past. One of the most important things I had to learn was the illusion of desire. Buddha taught that desire and ignorance are the root of all suffering. The craving for pleasure (addiction), material possessions (appearances), and immortality (the fear of death) can never be satisfied and therefore causes all suffering. The root of all desire is the need for peace and safety. At the core of Buddhist philosophy are what are called the Four Noble Truths: (1) life is suffering, (2) attachment to desire is suffering, (3) detachment from desire ends suffering, and (4) the Eightfold Path is the journey of liberation from suffering.

There are four kinds of desire: Physical desire (hunger/thirst); intellectual desire (curiosity); sexual desire (lust); and economic desire (material possessions/money). The Eightfold Path to achieve liberation from these desires consists of:

1. Right understanding
2. Right thought

3. Right speech
4. Right action
5. Right livelihood
6. Right effort
7. Right mindfulness
8. Right concentration

These components have been consolidated into three central principles: ethical conduct, mental discipline, and wisdom. Ethical conduct consists of right speech, right action, and right livelihood. Honesty, compassion, integrity of thought, word, and deed, and do no harm are central to ethical conduct.

Mental discipline consists of right effort, right mindfulness, and right concentration. Preventing evil, awareness of self, and focus are the keys to mental discipline. Wisdom consists of right thought and right understanding. Love, non-violence, detachment, and release of negativity are critical to wisdom.

These principles are echoed throughout all religions and spiritual practices. They apply to neurobiology through neuroplasticity. What we think creates neural pathways, which reinforce the thinking pattern. When we focus on lack and the desire to accumulate wealth, this forms neural pathways that become embedded in our psyches. When we focus on gratitude and forgiveness, we change the neural pathways from the habitual thinking of what we don't have to thoughts of what we do have. This is the only way to achieve peace within our own minds. This is the practical difference between the Warrior and the Guru.

The gap between achievement and fulfillment bears this out. Here in the United States, we are consumed with the pursuit of happiness, not the state of happiness. This is the illusion that causes all suffering. Happiness is fulfillment, which is a decision, not a journey. The survival mechanism of the Warrior (the ego) focuses on lack to help us survive. It is always concerned with survival; that is Its only purpose.

If the Warrior had Its way, we would never be happy, never be fulfilled.

Desire is a symptom of being in Warrior mode. It gives the ego something to do. It is always calculating, measuring, comparing, judging, and suffering. This is not real. It is just a mindset. When we deactivate the Warrior and activate the Guru, thoughts of lack evaporate, and we can enjoy life. We certainly can be more fulfilled and happier, but this comes from a place of fulfillment and happiness. It cannot come from a place of lack.

There is an old saying, "Success is getting what you want; happiness is wanting what you get." The Warrior is obsessed with getting what we want, the Guru is fulfilled with what we have. The illusion built into the Warrior mode of thinking is that we never get what we want, and we are never completely successful. To feel safe, the Warrior always wants the next victory, the next achievement. The bar is always raised just out of reach.

A 2020 post-COVID survey found that only 14 percent of the United States felt happy most of the time.[31] That is a clear indication that most of us are stuck in Warrior mode. The fear of lack and the desire for more activate the Warrior and keep us suffering, stressed, and worried. We must focus on what we have versus what we want. When we are in Guru mode, we can appreciate how far we have come and be grateful, versus focusing on what we don't have and suffering.

---

31 NORC, "Historic Shift in Americans' Happiness Amid Pandemic," 2020, https://www.norc.org/content/dam/norc-org/pdfs/Historic%20Shift%20in%20 Americans%20Happiness%20Amid%20Pandemic.pdf.

CHAPTER FIFTY-FOUR

The Greatest Lesson

In 2012, I was bored. Even though I was traveling around the world teaching and having successful healing clinics, I felt there was something missing in my life. I didn't realize it was self-love, and that I had one more lesson to learn. The events of 2012 were giving signs of what was to come.

Hurricane Sandy devastated the East Coast, killing three hundred people and causing $50 billion of damage. A gunman in Aurora, Colorado, killed and injured dozens of people at the screening of *The Dark Knight Rises*. President Barack Obama was reelected. A young man opened fire at the Sandy Hook Elementary School in one of the deadliest school shootings in US history. The ballyhooed end of the Mayan Calendar proved, like Y2K, to be a non-event. I joined a cult.

In August of 2012, near my fifty-ninth birthday, I was teaching workshops and doing healings in Calgary, Alberta, Canada. My promoter had just returned from California to see an Alabama mystic named Sadji who claimed to have the power to change matter and crops with his "transmissions" and connect people closer to God. The promoter went on and on about how powerful the man was and recommended that I get a "blessing." Curious, I went online and signed up for a remote blessing. At the appointed time, I lay down on my bed and closed my eyes.

I could see a road stretching out before me and a fork dividing the road into two directions. One branch went down into a valley where there were small, quaint villages and wide-open fields. The other branch went up into the mountains and disappeared into the crags and cliffs jutting high up in the dark clouds. I felt Bob come up behind me.

"*Where are you?*" asked Bob.

I pondered before answering, "It looks like a proverbial crossroads. I can keep doing what I am doing and live a very peaceful and contented life, which is symbolized by the road going down into the villages and fields. On the other hand, if I want to raise my consciousness and grow spiritually by quantum leaps and bounds, I will have to choose the road going up into the mountains. The path may feel difficult and fraught with peril, but in the end, I will gain enlightenment and total consciousness."

Bob said, "*What if you get enlightenment but lose everything?*"

I couldn't help making a wry face. "Well, that wouldn't be much fun."

Bob turned to leave but cried over his shoulder, "*Just remember that the spiritual journey is oftentimes painful. Remember your experiences.*"

I skidded back into my body and woke up.

After the session was over, I felt that it had been a clear sign that I should go find out more about Sadji. I was intrigued by the power of that session; I had never had such a clear vision during meditation. I understood that the universe was obviously telling me that I was going to make big changes in my life. What I could not yet know was how devastating those changes would be.

I started going to workshops offered by Sadji. Every time I went, I would feel energy shooting through my body, infusing me with calm and contentment. It felt like Sadji had a true gift of being able to transmit energy into others. He claimed that scientific experiments had proven that he could make crops grow bigger and faster without chemicals. I was hooked. I had been looking for someone who had a "magic wand," and I felt like this Alabama mystic had the magical powers that I had been seeking since I was a child reading books about Merlin and magical beings.

Sadji's real name was Robert Slovnik, and he was humbly born to farming parents in southeastern Alabama. He went to India to study mysticism, and while there, claimed to have had a blessing from an Indian holy man, which transformed him from a Southern farm boy to a holy man blessed by God. I enjoyed talking to Sadji about his experience, primarily because I was hoping for a similar transformation for myself. Sadji oozed confidence, poise, and charisma. He wore expensive suits made for Hollywood stars, and he rubbed elbows with the rich and famous. I idolized him to the point that I willingly handed over my own sense of power in support of his.

I started following Sadji around the country, as I had been able to do with my other teachers, and after about a year, I became part of the inner circle. I was given responsibilities for organizing and staffing the events he was producing.

Sadji seemed to be very happy with me. He was giving me extra blessings and started telling me that I would be the first person that he would empower to bestow transmissions to others. I started doing my own experiments and discovered that I could make crops grow faster and bigger just like Sadji.

Sadji continued to be impressed with my abilities and began inviting me up on stage with him during his events. I loved getting up in front of the thousands of people at these events, sharing my experiences with Sadji and getting the attention and admiration of many of the participants.

As I got deeper and deeper into Sadji's organization, several things started to bother me, and that again awoke my Warrior from Its occasional brief dormant state. Sadji was often abusive to his employees and was sued repeatedly for inappropriate behavior. Sadji explained that it was all rooted in jealousy, all baseless lies. Yet I observed that his healing clinics were chaotic and unstructured. After I was put in charge of organization and operations and made suggestions, he refused to make even the simplest changes to make the client's experience better.

Sadji was constantly trying to get me to go into business with him, selling products he reportedly blessed, such as blessed food (pork skins), blessed iced tea, blessed T-shirts, and blessed headscarves. Despite Sadji's claims that he was "chosen by God," in my opinion, these endeavors were not reflective of what a deity would choose to offer on Earth.

Slightly changing his tactic, he began to approach me about new investments. The first was an energy drink company called Elixir. Sadji assured me that it was founded by celebrity investors, with his spiritual consultation. He emphasized what a sure thing it was, and how lucky I was that he could get me in on the ground floor. Believing that the product would be an unequivocal success, I invested $1 million in the company.

Sadji continued to fill my head with promises of huge profits, saying that I would reap funds many times greater than my investment. After all, Sadji was chosen by God. That struck a chord with me. As always, I was seeking my father's approval and wanted to prove to my father that I could be a successful businessman. I felt that if my investment became as successful as promised, my father would have to acknowledge me.

Next, Sadji convinced me to start a beef company called Blessed Beef. I had no interest in investing in beef. My earlier experiences with the beef business taught me that it was very risky, and I knew that I didn't have the expertise to run a cattle company.

Sadji told me that if I didn't invest in the company, he would cut all ties with me. Even though this was a red flag and should have made me leave (my Warrior was also in a frenzy), I realized that I was completely disempowering myself to Sadji. Fearing the loss of the chance to be acknowledged as a miracle worker (in my delusion, I forgot I had already performed hundreds of miracles), I reluctantly agreed to invest in the company. Sadji promised to invest $1 million and match my $1 million. Given that he was willing to put his own money into the company, I felt a little more comfortable about the risk. I had completely swallowed the Kool-Aid and drank it down while my Warrior roared and tried to hold my lips closed.

Finally, Sadji approached me with a third investment in a company located in Waycross, GA, which manufactured a protective coating for exterior surfaces that was unique in that it was extremely hard and came in thousands of colors. The company had once been very successful but had fallen on hard times.

Sadji told me that he would use his powers to make it profitable. Once again, I had no interest in that sort of investment, especially since it would wipe out my liquidity and make me totally dependent on the success of the three businesses Sadji had promised to make successful. Sadji told me that if I made the investment, I would be the next Sadji "master," and he would announce that I could do the blessings. He knew that was the exact carrot to dangle to keep me on the hook.

In 2013, I approached Sadji and told him that the cattle business needed the $1 million that he had agreed to invest. Instead of making the investment he had committed to, he said that he was no longer interested in the cattle business. Mincing no words, he told me that it was all mine. I was dumbfounded. I couldn't believe that he would just breach the agreement like that. It would be an indicator of even worse to come, yet Sadji was still reassuring me that I was to be the next master.

Soon after, Sadji announced that his sixteen-year-old bride was the next master. Once again, I felt betrayed. He had been telling me repeatedly that I was going to be the next master, and I had invested millions of dollars in Sadji's businesses. He kept telling me not to worry, I would be the next master soon.

Sadji decided to take a select group of his faithful to India. He appointed me to oversee logistics, including getting everyone passports. I felt honored to be given so much responsibility, but it was like herding cats. Sadji gave me dozens of designer suits to wear, claiming that as his next master, I needed to dress the part. I was feeling better about my relationship with him.

It turned out to be a very stressful trip. The participants constantly complained and refused to follow directions. Sadji would publicly criticize me for not having control of the group. He demanded to know why I did not control the group, and I responded, "You picked them. They don't care what I tell them; they do as they please." I felt that I was between a rock and a hard place. My Guru had harbored such high hopes for the trip, but my Warrior was beginning to rear Its head again, taking angry note of all the things that seemed amiss.

During the trip, several things started to bother me. In many of the religious sites that we visited, Sadji was unfamiliar with the ceremonies that were being performed. He asked me to explain to the group the purpose of the ceremony and what was being done. It seemed rather odd that he was asking me to explain these rituals.

I also started hearing other people comment that they were going to be the next master. I hoped that was wishful thinking, but Sadji was telling people that he would announce the next master soon. His decision would be up to God.

I thought it was a great marketing ploy, to raise people's hopes up and encourage them to spend as much money as possible on his products with the unspoken promise that it may lead to something special. I started to feel very strange about what was going on. I felt like I had fallen into quicksand. I was really scared about my investments. The only thing I could do was to let the drama unfold.

In the fall of 2013, I was encouraged to some extent because Sadji instructed me to go to India to visit one of his Indian masters. The man had been a devotee of Sadji for some time. Sadji said the pupil would prepare me for being the next master. I went to India and spent three days with the pupil. Sadji's website also started referring to me as a Sadji Master. I was feeling much better about my chances of being formally named the next master.

Two things bothered me about the trip. The first was the man who was my guide and interpreter. The man was supposed to translate for me with the pupil, and it was clear that he was not translating what the pupil was saying. I asked several questions about being the next master and what life would be like, and the pupil would give lengthy answers.

The translator would only give a one-sentence translation, and my internal lie detector was going off. I knew that something was wrong. I later found out that Sadji had been telling the translator that the translator would be the next master. I then found out that Sadji had promised numerous people that they would be the next master. I was now truly scared.

In the fall of 2013, Sadji announced that God would choose the next master on November 9, 2013. It was going to be on his weekly broadcast. I had been hosting this broadcast for almost a year. I went to Sadji and asked him whether I was going to be the next master. I told him that if not, he needed to know so that he could be professional on the broadcast.

Sadji told me that I had nothing to worry about. That fateful day arrived, and Sadji gave me a new suit to wear for the broadcast. I was starting to feel more at ease with the situation, because why in the world would he give me a new suit if he was going to name someone else the new master? On the other hand, I still had a nagging suspicion that I was being set up for a huge betrayal. I could not shake the feeling that Sadji was lying to me.

On that fateful day, Sadji got to the studio, took me outside, and informed me that God had told him to name another woman as the new master. I would not be the next master. He also told me to get on stage and announce that the new master was his mistress. I was dumbfounded. The woman had never expressed any interest in being a master.

I was totally in shock, and I felt betrayed and deceived. Somehow, I got through the broadcast and went home. That night, another employee called to tell me that Sadji wanted me to clean out my office and not come to the office anymore. I felt like the world was crashing down on me. I had invested millions of dollars in the promises of this man who had just betrayed me and lied to me. I suddenly had the responsibility for these three companies dumped on my shoulders, as Sadji had broken all his promises.

Two months later, Sadji met with me and revealed that the concrete company that manufactured a protective coating for exterior surfaces was a total failure and was bankrupt. He told me that he was abandoning the project and that I could have it. I told him that he had made a lot of promises to a lot of people who had invested money in the company and that he needed to stay and fulfill the promises he had made to those people, including me.

Sadji told me that I could have it or he would shut the doors, and everyone would lose their money. Again, I couldn't believe what I was hearing. Sadji had not only persuaded me to invest, but he had also gotten other people to invest their life's savings in the company. I felt that Sadji was the most immoral, corrupt, fraudulent, and predatory person I had ever had the misfortune to be involved with. Not only had Sadji misled me about being named a master, but I also felt he had obviously lied about his powers and abilities.

I spent the next five years keeping everything running. The beef company eventually became a success. The energy drink company filed for bankruptcy. I kept the concrete business running for as long as I could, then eventually liquidated it.

I learned a lot from my experience with Sadji. First, I learned never to disempower myself to anyone again. I realized that I was just as powerful as any guru, and I did not need to ignore my inner guidance ever again. I would never give up my own power again.

My family helped me through the winding up of the business affairs. I had to borrow money from my father to help keep the doors open, and he was very gracious and kind to support me. My sisters supported me and recommended to my father that he help me. I was gratefully surprised by their support. I believe that it helped mend some fences that had been broken when I stopped practicing law. My

Guru, with my Warrior still reeling from the recent events, took the helm of my mind again.

CHAPTER FIFTY-FIVE

Healing Myself

I desperately needed a way to understand what these experiences were trying to teach me. Obviously, I needed to stop disempowering myself to "gurus." The only guru I needed was inside me. I had learned that my mind creates my reality, but I wasn't sure how to change my mind from negativity to positivity. I learned how to do this through Ho'oponopono.

Believed to be an ancient Hawaiian practice, Ho'oponopono burst onto the international scene by virtue of the book *Zero Limits* by Dr. Joe Vitale and Dr. Ihaleakala Hew Len.[32] Dr. Hew Len tells the story that by using Ho'oponopono, he helped heal an entire psychiatric ward for the criminally insane in the Hawaii State Hospital without meeting any of the patients. Even though these claims have been contested, thousands of people have embraced the practice to heal their emotional and mental challenges.

The practice is based upon the concept of "total responsibility." Also known as "all perception is projection," the belief proposes that

---

32 Dr. Joe Vitale and Dr. Ihaleakala Hew Len, *Zero Limits: The Secret Hawaiian System for Wealth, Health, Peace, and More* (Wiley 2008).

everything that we perceive not only exists outside of us but exists inside of us as well. If we perceive something in our outer world that is a problem, it is caused (or created) by a problem within us in our inner world. Happily, if we perceive something in our outer world that is positive, that is caused by something positive inside of us as well.

Hoʻoponopono means "correction" or "to make right." It recognizes that all illnesses or problems in the world are caused by transgressions of others or the person who is suffering. For the illness or problem to be resolved, all parties must undergo a ceremonial cleansing and forgiveness.

I was originally introduced to this practice by a kahuna from Hawaii whom I met while I was with Estrella. She conducted a ceremony that was very dramatic and entertaining, but totally unnecessary to the application of the technique.

The practice is simple enough. It involves the use of four statements (mantras) that are to be repeated as many times as possible by the practitioner. The order of the statements is determined by the practitioner; whatever feels correct is perfect. The object is to say this mantra over and over until it creates new neural pathways and becomes second nature. As Drs. Hew Len and Vitale would say, "You become the prayer."

It is important to make these statements with positive intention. It is not some dry recitation without feeling. The quality of the emotion used will increase the effect of the practice. The four parts of the mantra are as follows:

1. **I love you.** The "you" here refers to both the participant and the perceived problem. You can only love someone as much as you love yourself. This is not only quantitative; it is qualitative. If you don't love yourself, or your definition of love is flawed, it is likely that your perception is skewed, creating the problem. You must feel love, affection, and compassion for yourself and the problem. As the famous poem by Kent Keith says, "Love them anyway."

2. **I'm sorry.** This does not mean blame, guilt, and shame. Victimhood is not allowed. This means that we take ownership and responsibility for what we perceive. We also take ownership and responsibility for whatever needs to heal inside of us. The first step in any conflict resolution is to admit that there is a problem. It is the acknowledgment of the problem that allows our compassion to liberate our hearts and psyche to heal. When we accept responsibility, we are empowered to heal. If we say, "This is someone else's fault," we disempower ourselves.

3. **Please forgive me.** Self-forgiveness is the great cleanser. It allows us to let go of our burdens and struggles. For lawyers burdened with guilt or regret, self-forgiveness is oftentimes the healing that they need. The request is to whomever we seek guidance from or pray to, either internally or externally. Ultimately, we are the source of our pain and suffering, and we are the only ones who can heal that pain and suffering. We must have the grace to forgive. This does not mean that we forget the lessons we have learned from our experiences. Even with forgiveness, we grow.

4. **Thank you.** Gratitude is one of the magic emotions that overrides all other emotions. When we practice gratitude, we can heal any internal suffering. To be thankful for all that we experience is one of the most powerful prayers in any religion. We are given life to learn and grow emotionally, mentally, and spiritually. When we are truly grateful for our experiences, not only do we grow, but we also heal any misunderstandings or misconceptions.

This practice is both meditative and healing. Practitioners report relief from negative thoughts, emotions, and behaviors. By focusing on these four principles of love, compassion, forgiveness, and gratitude, we can create new neural pathways and thought patterns that transform our experience from negative to positive. If this practice helps any problem in our exterior lives, that is an added benefit, for its primary purpose is to heal the practitioner.

Everyone can certainly use this in several applications in their professional and personal lives. Remember that when a problem arises, you are made aware of it in order to heal some aspect of yourself. The aspect is usually subconscious; you are not aware of it. The problem can be a difficult client, finances, opposing counsel, adverse rulings, disagreements with colleagues, or problem family members. Simply acknowledge the problem and say the four phrases with the intention that you will heal. Say the phrases one at a time, slowly. The more you can feel the associated emotion (love, compassion, grace, and gratitude) as you say each phrase, the more quickly it will heal.

Ho'oponopono has been recognized as a legitimate alternative form of conflict resolution in Hawaii. All parties to a conflict (civil or criminal) agree to a mediated process involving all parties taking responsibility and offering forgiveness. It is described as "cutting the cord." In 2000, the Hawaii State Legislature recognized the effectiveness of Ho'oponopono for alternative dispute resolution in family law courts.

I became a certified advanced Ho'oponopono teacher and practitioner. The reason that I became interested in this somewhat unknown spiritual practice is that I wanted to learn an easy way to manage stress, anxiety, and worry. It is also a great way to increase emotional maturity, manage emotions, achieve mental clarity, and feel positive. I started using it repeatedly throughout my day, and it has brought great relief to my consciousness.

CHAPTER FIFTY-SIX

Goodbye, Dad

In 2015, Greece experienced financial default on its major obligations, and its creditors took control. The US and Cuba reestablished diplomatic relations. Microsoft released Windows 10. Queen Elizabeth II became the longest-reigning British monarch. Volkswagen was accused of rigging auto emission tests. My father died.

During my experience with Sadji, my father's health began to fade. He suffered several strokes and suffered from Alzheimer's disease. He also had advanced coronary problems and was often bruised and in pain. It is a very cathartic experience to watch a parent go through these struggles. There were times when he could remember long-term memory events, but his short-term memory was totally absent. He would get very confused and angry when he couldn't remember who someone was or what was happening around him. He had moved from his palatial home into an assisted living community. From 2014 onward, he had a companion staying with him who could help him if he fell or lost his bearings.

I would get updates from my sisters, and they often weren't optimistic. There were repeated episodes where my father would fall and be rushed to the hospital. When he arrived, he would be disoriented and try to defend himself against the medical staff. He would try to escape and would be verbally abusive to the staff when they insisted that he stay. I was grateful that my sisters were there to help him in his decline.

My father finally graduated from Earth School in July 2015 at the age of ninety. He had lived a long and prolific life, and there were almost a thousand people at his funeral to pay their respects. He received a twenty-one-gun salute from the military, and his West Point ring was melted down to be recast for a future graduate. His ashes were placed in his trial briefcase, which was buried beside my mother in the family plot in God's Acre in Charlotte.

My father was an icon in the community and left a legacy for future generations. For me, I was relieved. Anyone whose parents have suffered through the issues of old age, pain, suffering, and dementia would understand how difficult it is to watch your parent go through such suffering. At least my father was no longer in pain.

The loss of my father seemed to galvanize something in me. Sigmund Freud, in the preface to his second edition of *The Interpretation of Dreams*, writes that, "a father's death is the most important event, the most heartbreaking and poignant loss in a man's life."[33] In *Totem and Taboo*, he writes, "at bottom, God is nothing other than an exalted father."[34] When my father left, I had nothing more to push against. My whole life had been a conflict with my father. I had defined myself in relationship to him, and now that he was gone, I had to discover myself again.

Even though my life had been one of what felt like great loss—loss of wealth, loss of identity, loss of heart, loss of parents, loss of self—it was in this vacuum that I finally learned to love myself. Loving myself was something I had never learned to do all those years. I always

---

33 Sigmund Freud, *The Interpretation of Dreams*, 2nd ed., trans. A.A. Brill (Franz Deuticke, 1909).

34 Sigmund Freud, *Totem and Taboo*, trans. A.A. Brill (Beacon Press, 1913).

looked for validation in others and success in the material world, using those as markers of success. This was the legacy of the world that spawned the baby boomer generation. When the last connection to that world died, I was free to become who I wanted to be without having to explain to anyone. When my father left this world, it seemed that there was finally enough room for me to exist as my true self.

I stopped worrying about the future and simply started living day to day. I enjoyed the little things in life: waking up, food, celebrating with friends, nutrition, exercise, supporting others, and seeking how to serve others. It was this change in mindset, in attitude, that seemed to create opportunities that had not presented themselves before. Again, but sustainably this time, I had activated my Guru.

I felt empowered for the first time in my life. I no longer needed an authority figure to tell me what to do; there was no longer any reason to disempower myself to others. I felt that I could speak my mind and not apologize. Ironically, most of the conflicts I had with my family disappeared. We started communicating again.

I had to admit that my life was good. I had a bed, clean water, friends, and work to keep me fulfilled. I realized that when I have all of that, there is no reason to complain. I had read that all questions are created by the ego, and when you let the ego go, there are no questions. I was starting to understand that philosophy. I stopped asking why or when or how. I instinctively knew that the more I reached out and connected to people, the "who" would answer the "how."

I began to concentrate on the enjoyable things in my life, with my Guru cheering me on, and my life became enjoyable. I started to understand that happiness was not getting what I wanted; it was wanting what I had. Life became less stressful, and opportunities began to appear.

After a few failed romances, I vowed never to seek love again. I dismissed the idea of needing a romantic partner and focused on myself. In the most perfect example of what happens when you release desire and need, I met the love of my life on LinkedIn, a business social media platform. Neither one of us was looking for romance, only friendship. We have celebrated our seventh wedding anniversary as I finish this book. She is the partner I looked for all along, and when I stopped being so needy in my search, poof! She appeared. And I realized that it wasn't magic; it was readiness. I was finally ready to let love in.

CHAPTER FIFTY-SEVEN

All Perception Is Projection

As I learned more and more about the brain and my mind, I became aware of an important aspect that had influenced what I had experienced in my life. This aspect explained a lot of the misconceptions I had suffered during my life and how I had created the beliefs that impacted all my choices.

Many spiritual people say the mantra "All perception is projection," without really understanding why that is true. Perception is much more than simple observing. As discussed at the beginning of the book, our perception is determined by which autonomic nervous system (Warrior/Guru) is activated. It is also determined by our cognitive biases and beliefs. Events that conflict with our beliefs are judged to be bad; events that are in alignment with our beliefs are considered good.

Projection is how we look at the world. Cognitive biases are the conclusions we form about the world based on our experiences. Our brain tends to seek evidence to prove our biases are right. If we have a belief that we are a failure, we will scan our environment for evidence that we are right. Subconsciously, we create scenarios that prove our biases are correct. As Henry Ford once said, "Whether you think you can, or you think you can't, you're right."

We are constantly being bombarded by information through our senses. Science proposes that we receive up to sixty million bits of data a second. What we choose to notice is up to our subconscious mind and memory. We pick and choose which bytes of data we notice to support our beliefs and biases. Every person is a mixture of good and evil. What we notice is largely what we are looking for. According to the Law of Attraction, we manifest what resonates with our thoughts and beliefs.

Another important aspect of this concept is the difference between our inner and outer environments. Our outer landscape mirrors our inner landscape. This includes our conscious beliefs, biases, judgments, and prejudices as well as our unconscious beliefs, biases, judgments, and prejudices.

I can state with a high degree of certainty that what we perceive is a mirror of what we believe about ourselves. If we have an inner conflict, we will notice conflict in our outer world. If we don't love ourselves, we will not find love outside of ourselves. If we feel incomplete and seek completeness outside of ourselves, it will be a fruitless search. We cannot find outside of ourselves that which we don't have inside of us.

This is why I struggled so hard for most of my life. I did not have the inner peace and tranquility I needed to manifest a peaceful and tranquil world. I was stuck in Warrior mode, and I kept looking for fights to confirm what I felt inside. After my father died, I finally learned that I didn't have to go to every fight that I was invited to.

We are hardwired to seek evidence that confirms our beliefs. All we must do is observe what is going on around us to discover what is going on inside of us. This is not a criticism; it is a truth that spiritualists have known for thousands of years. So within, so without; so above, so below.

What we think is just as important as what we do or say. Negative emotions lead to negative thoughts, which lead to negative behavior, which leads to negative outcomes. It is a painful cycle that will keep repeating itself until we deactivate the Warrior and activate the Guru. What we think becomes our reality.

That is why affirmations and mantras are so important. As we have discussed, our brains tend to hardwire habitual thinking. When we repetitively think negative thoughts, we create neural pathways that compel more negative thoughts. When we repetitively think positive thoughts, we create neural pathways that compel more positive thoughts.

Here are some affirmations that are very helpful to create positive neural pathways:

- I can achieve greatness.
- Something wonderful is going to happen today.
- Everything is in my own best interest.
- I am brimming with energy and overflowing with joy.
- I love and accept myself for who I am.
- Every day, I am becoming better and better in every way.
- My body is healthy. My mind is brilliant. My soul is at peace.
- I am curious.
- I can do anything.
- I forgive myself and everyone who has harmed me, so I can be free of the past.
- My potential for success is limitless.
- I am happy and grateful to be alive.
- I am filled with hope, courage, faith, and confidence.
- I deserve all of the love, joy, and abundance the universe has to offer—and more.
- Thank you.
- May I, and all the beings of the world, be happy.

- I am manifesting my dreams, and no dream is too big.
- I am more than this physical body.
- My thoughts create my life.
- I can always control my thoughts.
- I am responsible for the way I see things.
- I am entitled to miracles.
- I have the strength to feel and release my feelings.
- There is power in vulnerability.
- Fear is a prayer to God for love.
- I have a purpose.
- I constantly expand and try new things.
- I choose to be excited.
- I deserve to feel loved.
- Everyone I meet reflects me.
- I am always a teacher to someone.
- I trust everything is helping me be better.
- I am worthy and valuable.
- I define my success.
- I am enough.
- I give what I want to receive.
- Rejection is only fear.
- I can do anything.
- Let (inhale) go (exhale).
- I loosen my grip on everything.
- Love is who I am.
- I deserve the best.

- Wow.
- Yum. (This reconnects you to your heart when you are in your head.)
- I am kind.
- I am full of peace.
- I am love.
- Just for today, I will feel happy.
- I decide how I feel.
- Fear is only ignorance.
- All perception is a reflection of me.
- The only love I need is my own.
- I am getting better every day.
- I am excited about the future.
- I am God in action.
- Fear is an illusion.
- Everything that I feel is a programmed reaction to what I see.
- My experiences make me strong.
- My experiences make me unique.
- The only difference between pleasure and pain is perception.
- Happiness is an inside job.
- The only difference between a miracle and a disaster is time.
- I am an angel in disguise.
- I can heal anything with a smile.
- Everything happens for a reason.
- I am a miracle.
- I am here to help.

CHAPTER FIFTY-EIGHT

Redemption

After healing people for over seventeen years, I discovered that there was only one reason that people didn't heal. Despite their statements to the contrary, they did not want to heal. They did not want to heal for a variety of reasons:

- Secondary gain
- Negative beliefs about themselves
- Limiting decisions
- Addiction to suffering
- Fear of the future
- Normalization of suffering

I decided to train in neurolinguistics, hypnosis, cognitive behavior therapy, timeline therapy, and coaching so I could help my clients release their negative blocks. With these tools (and the help of Genius Unlocked Coaching), I have greatly increased the efficiency and efficacy of my healing programs.

I also decided to focus on helping lawyers with stress and burnout, the place where my healing journey began. In 2016, the ABA and the Hazelden Betty Ford Foundation did a study of thousands of lawyers and found that a disproportionate number of practicing lawyers were suffering from stress, anxiety, and burnout, as well as alcoholism.[35]

In 2023, after COVID, the Massachusetts State Bar did a wellness survey of 4,500 attorneys and discovered that 72 percent were burned out and considering quitting their careers.[36] Lawyers were stressed, burned out, and spiraling out of control. This is the result of the uncontrolled Warrior mode.

As a result, I have spoken frequently to local bar associations, state bar associations, and the American Bar Association about the causes of stress and burnout and how to heal them. It is important to me to use my training and experience to help not only lawyers, but all businessmen, professionals, and entrepreneurs heal their stress and anxiety.

I have healed my demons and learned how to heal yours. My mission is to bring everyone back into homeostasis and activate their Guru mode. Not only have I healed my relationship with myself, but I have also healed my relationships with my family and countless friends.

Even better, my business and professional relationships have taken on a depth and connection far beyond anything I have experienced in the past. I am constantly making new, close, and profitable business friendships. Gone are the days when I could not trust myself or my business partners. This is the power of this work. There is no limit to what you can accomplish while you are in Guru mode. I know that your life will drastically change when you activate your true state of being.

---

35 Krill, Patrick R., Ryan Johnson, and Linda Albert. 2016. "The Prevalence of Substance Use and Other Mental Health Concerns among American Attorneys." *Journal of Addiction Medicine* 10 (1): 46–52. https://doi.org/10.1097/adm.0000000000000182.

36 Jenna Sirkin, PhD Jared Sawyer, MPH Samantha Augenbraun, MPH Rebecca Rasky Maysoun Freij, PhD. *Lawyer Well-Being in Massachusetts.* https://www.worcestercountybar.org/wp-content/uploads/2023/02/Lawyer-Well-Being-Report.pdf : NORC at the University of Chicago, 2022.

CHAPTER FIFTY-NINE

Activate the Guru

One of the most important things I have learned about the brain during my journey is that there are simple physical techniques we can use to instantaneously turn off the Warrior and turn on the Guru. Neurobiologists have found that activating the vagus nerve will disengage the Warrior and automatically turn on the Guru mode, which is what we want. The vagus nerve connects our autonomic nervous system to our internal organs and is the information highway that controls the mind-body connection.[37]

The good news is that some simple physical action can accomplish this switch from Warrior to Guru. I have found that when we manipulate muscles, nerves, and organs that are connected to the vagus nerve, this sends electrical impulses that activate the Guru. For example, facial nerves are connected to the cranial nerve, which is connected to the vagus nerve. Smiling and rubbing our face and forehead sends impulses to the vagus nerve. Eye movements will stimulate the orbital

---

37 TEDx Talks, "Control the Warrior and Activate Your Guru | Sir Jame Gray Robinson, Esq. | TEDxMellen Street," March 12, 2024, https://www.youtube.com/watch?v=rTueqWePVyI.

muscles around our eyes and stimulate the same nerves, which activates the Guru. In a similar fashion, the nerves that control our larynx are connected to the vagus nerve. So singing, breathing (pranayama yoga), or humming will make us relax and feel better. That is why spiritual people say "OM" all the time; it is activating their vagus nerve. The nerves that control the lungs are connected to the vagus nerve, so deep breathing will activate our lungs and chest cavity, which will stimulate the vagus nerve and make us relax.

Cold water has been shown to be highly effective in stimulating the vagus nerve. Taking a cold shower or bath, or splashing cold water on our face, neck, or hands, will activate the vagus nerve and send us instantly into the Guru mode. Exercise will also activate the vagus nerve and put us in a relaxed state.

We must be in Guru mode to be socially connected, foster healthy relationships, be happy, have fun, and be intimate. The secret to a successful, mentally and emotionally healthy life is the ability to feel safe.

A Final Word from Our Invisible Guides, the Guru and the Warrior

It's actually just me, your Guru. I created a distraction for your Warrior so that I could have one last word alone with you.

You may have read this book because you barely know me at all. You may have read it because you have at some time experienced the feeling of letting me run the show, and you want more of those good feelings. You may have read this book because even if you know about me, you're so used to calling on your Warrior (you've probably had a lifetime of practice) that you forget to look for me until it's too late.

But get to know me. Spend time with me. As we tried to tell the Warriors at the Great Meeting in the sky, I can solve many of your problems before they get bigger. Invite me when you're going down a neural pathway (which correlates with the choices we make) that doesn't feel good—and doesn't end well—and I'll guide you back to paths to calmer waters, bluer mental skies.

I hope that now that you know about me, you'll think of me often. We can work together.

I hear the thunder of the Warrior's steps approaching. Don't forget about me!

Love,

Your G

Epilogue

As this book goes to publishing, I am going through the process of being knighted into the Royal Order of Constantine the Great and Saint Helen. I laugh, because that is where we started this story, the fantasies of knights and wizards. We never know how prophetic young minds can be. The dreams and fantasies of childhood can become our heart's wildest dreams. It is said that the longest distance is the divide between the heart and mind. Never give up on your dreams; the Guru can get you there. I have also received the Presidential Lifetime Achievement Award from President Joe Biden. I have received an International Man of the Year Award from Men with Hearts Foundation, a global humanitarian organization. When you connect with your Guru, your possibilities become limitless.

It is critically important to listen to those soft whispers from your Guru, your inspiration. Even though our practical minds will say "Yes, but" to our dreams, it is our dreams that will bring us the greatest fulfillment and happiness. That is why parents must support their children's dreams and not bend them to parental will.

Though your Warrior is loud and insistent, your Guru speaks with quiet wisdom. Listen to that soft voice to realize your fullest potential. Focus on what brings you joy, excitement, freedom, and fulfillment, for that is where your Guru thrives—and where your true power lives. Civilizations were built by Gurus and defended by Warriors, but the Warrior has dominated for too long, with some highly detrimental results. Both are necessary to survive, but it's in listening to your Guru that you'll find your deepest happiness and strength. Remind yourself as often as needed: "Hack your brain so your Guru can reign." The outcomes that you can create may well exceed anything that you've experienced in your life so far, and your nervous system will reward you as you give it the balance it so desperately craves.

Off you go . . .

www.ingramcontent.com/pod-product-compliance
Lightning Source LLC
Chambersburg PA
CBHW070735170426
43200CB00007B/531